Meyerhold speaks
Meyerhold rehearses

Russian Theatre Archive

A series of books edited by John Freedman (Moscow), Leon Gitelman
(St Petersburg) and Anatoly Smeliansky (Moscow)

Meyerhold speaks
Meyerhold rehearses

by Aleksandr Gladkov

translated, edited and with an introduction by
Alma Law

Routledge
Taylor & Francis Group

LONDON AND NEW YORK

Copyright © 1997
Harwood Academic Publishers.

Reprinted 2004
By Routledge
2 Park Square, Milton Park, Abingdon, Oxon, OX14 4RN

Transferred to Digital Printing 2004

Routledge is an imprint of the Taylor & Francis Group

British Library Cataloguing in Publication Data

Gladkov, Aleksandr
  Meyerhold speaks/Meyerhold rehearses. – (Russian theatre
archive; V. 11)
  1. Meierkhold, V. E. Vsevolod Emilevich), 1874–1940 –
Criticism and interpretation   2. Theatrical producers and directors – Russia –
Moscow   3. Theater – production and direction – Russia – Moscow
I. Title   II. Law, Alma
792'.0233'092

  ISBN 90-5702-044-0 (HB)
        90-5702-045-9 (PB)

Cover illustration: Meyerhold at a rehearsal of Bezymensky's *The Shot* (1929).

For Eric and Keith

CONTENTS

INTRODUCTION TO THE SERIES

The Russian Theatre Archive makes available in English the best avant-garde plays from the pre-Revolutionary period to the present day. It features monographs on major playwrights and theatre directors, introductions to previously unknown works, and studies of the main artistic groups and periods.

Plays are presented in performing edition translations, including (where appropriate) musical scores, and instructions for music and dance. Whenever possible the translated texts will be accompanied by videotapes of performances of plays in the original language.

LIST OF PLATES

ACKNOWLEDGEMENTS

The material by Aleksandr Gladkov included in this book has been drawn from the following published sources: "Repliki Meierkhol'da" in *Teatral'naya zhizn'*, 5, (1960), pp. 19–21; "Iz vospominanii o Meierkhol'de" in *Moskva teatral'naya*, Moscow: Iskusstvo, 1960, pp. 347–376; "Meierkhol'd govorit" in *Novyi mir*, 8 (1961), pp. 213–235; "Vospominaniya, zametki, zapisi o V. E. Meierkhol'de" in *Tarusskie stranitsy*, Kaluga: Kaluzhskoe knizhnoe izd., 1961, pp. 292–307. All of these writings plus additional material not included in the present volume were subsequently published posthumously in Aleksandr Gladkov, *Teatr: Vospominaniya i razmyshleniya* (Moscow: Iskusstvo, 1980); and more recently in Aleksandr Gladkov, *Meierkhol'd*, vol. 2 (Moscow: STD RSFSR, 1990).

During the many hours spent in conversation with Mr Gladkov in the years from 1974, when I first visited him at his apartment on Red Army Street, until his death in 1976, he was most helpful in supplying the names and background material to many of Meyerhold's observations. This information has been been included as commentary to various entries in the section "Meyerhold Speaks".

I wish to thank the following people for their invaluable help in preparing and reading over the manuscript of this book: Lisa Bornstein, Heidi David, John Freedman, Daniel Gerould, Mel Gordon, Nathan Gross, Marjorie Hoover, Rose Raskin, Margaret Smith, and Nora Szalawitz. Vyacheslav Nechaev, head of the Union of Theatre Workers Library in Moscow, and the members of his staff, are due a special word of appreciation for their invaluable assistance in furnishing me with information and material not available anywhere else; and to Maya Sitovetskaya and the former Central State Archive of Literature and Art (TsGALI) for helping me with information on the actors in Meyerhold's theatre. I also wish to thank the splendid staff of the Slavic Reference Service at the University of Illinois, Urbana for so willingly answering my questions.

Above all, I am most grateful to Aleksandr Gladkov for the hours he spent patiently answering my questions and adding information that he could not put into print at the time. And to Maria Alekseevna Valentei, Meyerhold's granddaughter, very special thanks for her permission as the sole heir of her grandfather to publish the photographs included in this book.

Note: Unless otherwise indicated, I alone am responsible for all translations from the Russian. In transliterating Russian words and proper names, I have used a dual system. In the text, I have followed more popular usage in rendering Russian names and titles. In notes and source references, I have used a modified Library of Congress system, omitting diacritical marks and ligatures. Since this book is primarily intended for theatre practitioners rather than scholars, I have rendered all titles in their English translation, except those titles – for example, *Don Giovanni* – which are most commonly rendered in the original language. In the case of Russian titles, in the Glossary of Names and Places, following the title, I have included the Russian name of the work.

The city founded by Peter the Great was called St Petersburg until August 1914, Petrograd until January 1924, and Leningrad until September 1991. For the sake of historical accuracy, I have observed these changes in the text. Dates up to February 14, 1918 are given according to the Julian (or Old Style) calendar, and after that date according to the Gregorian (or New Style) calendar. Before 1900, the Julian calendar in use in Russia was twelve days behind the Georgian calendar; from 1900 to 1918, it was thirteen days behind.

To make for easier reading, I have avoided footnotes where possible. The interested reader will find in the Glossary of Names and Places all names of people, places, and works that are mentioned in the text. In addition, for the sake of clarification, I have included within the text information in brackets where it will aid the reader in understanding what Meyerhold is talking about. In some cases at the end of Meyerhold's observations, I have also added commentary in brackets based on information furnished to me by Mr Gladkov.

INTRODUCTION

by Alma Law

It would be difficult to exaggerate the influence the Russian theatre director, Vsevolod Meyerhold, has had on the twentieth-century theatre. He was a tireless innovator with a boundless imagination who, in the words of Lee Strasberg, "exhausted almost every theatrical device and phase of theatre that could possibly be imagined".[1] Always a man in a hurry, Meyerhold never took the time to perfect what he had already invented. He constantly rushed ahead to experiment anew, leaving it to his pupils and disciples to develop further what he had already tried. "After all", as he told Aleksandr Gladkov, "life is short, and if you repeat yourself there's much you won't manage to do".

During the twenties and thirties, Meyerhold's renown spread well beyond the borders of the Soviet Union, to pique the interest of Western theatre practitioners, many of whom traveled to Moscow to see his productions and to sit in on his rehearsals. As Gladkov notes in his account of the years he spent with Meyerhold, visiting artists, writers, and musicians were also attracted to his theatre, which by the mid-1930s had became as obligatory a stop during any visit to the capital as was Lenin's tomb.

Unlike his mentor, Konstantin Stanislavsky, Meyerhold was not a theoretician. He left behind no large body of writings summing up his many years of experience in the theatre. Meyerhold did dream of one day publishing his *Collected Works*, and he often talked about writing a director's manual, saying that it would be a "very thin little volume", much on the order of Mayakovsky's *How Are Verses Made?* But the manual was never written, nor did the *Collected Works* ever get beyond the outline stage.

In the mid-thirties, as Aleksandr Gladkov recalls, Meyerhold commissioned him to put together a book of his selected writings. It was to bear the same title as his pre-Revolutionary book, *On the Theatre*, even though much of the material in that book Meyerhold now regarded as "outdated and uninteresting". The book was completed in early 1937 and turned over to a publisher. But in spite of a prior agreement for its publication, the publisher now rejected the manuscript. This rejection, which upset Meyerhold considerably, was only the forerunner of far more serious setbacks, ultimately leading to the liquidation of his theatre in January 1938, his arrest in June 1939 and execution the following February.

Nor did Meyerhold leave behind any memoirs. Although he sometimes talked about writing them, he always excused himself by saying that he was too lazy. The more likely truth, as Gladkov suggests, is that he still had not reached that point where he felt that his life was drawing to a close and that it was now time for summing up. Even in his sixties, Meyerhold had more energy and enthusiasm that most people a third his age. For him, life was a constant process of change, of new discoveries and challenges. It was not yet time to sit down and contemplate the past. As Gladkov writes, "Things were constantly changing, falling apart. There wasn't any steadiness and quiet. There wasn't any veneration, in spite of the gray hair and the international reputation".

What must take the place of Meyerhold's unwritten theoretical writings and memoirs are the reminiscences and confessions made in conversations with pupils and friends. Of these, by far the most valuable are those recorded by Aleksandr Gladkov during his years of close association with Meyerhold from 1934 to 1937. Neither his biographers nor any of his former colleagues' memoirs convey as well as Gladkov does the essence of Meyerhold's character. A talented essayist and a keen observer, Gladkov succeeded in capturing and bringing to life in his biographical essay about Meyerhold and his notes of the director's rehearsals all the complexities of Meyerhold's personality and temperament. Meyerhold's own observations as noted by Gladkov also serve to fill out the portrait of this great director.

Meyerhold could be capricious, suspicious, and unforgiving. Never one to be indifferent, his relationships with people followed a pattern of extremes from warm friendship to sharp and slanderous attack. But as Gladkov observes, even those who suffered most severely from his thrusts – and they were legion – never lost their respect for his remarkable genius. "Only those who had never known him", Gladkov once remarked, "could remain his enemy".

* * *

Meyerhold was born on January 28, 1874 (old style).[2] The eighth and last child of German-Lutheran parents, he was baptized Karl Teodor Kazimir. His father, Emil Fedorovich Meyergold, was a prominent vodka distiller in Penza, which at the end of the nineteenth century still remained a sleepy provincial town. Located about 350 miles southeast of Moscow, Penza could nevertheless boast of a lively theatrical culture. As he was growing up Meyerhold saw many of the greatest performers of his day, including Aleksandr Lensky, Nikolai Rossov, and Vasily

Portrait of Meyerhold by Aleksandr Golovin (1917).

P. Dalmatov, whom Meyerhold would direct many years later at the Alexandrinsky Theatre.

Although a rather poor student (he had to repeat a grade in the Gymnasium three times), Meyerhold avidly devoured the German and Russian books in his parents' library as well as sampling the illegal literature in underground circulation. Meyerhold's mother, Alvina Danilovna, loved music and under her influence he learned to play both the piano and the violin. In fact, for a time Meyerhold dreamed of becoming a virtuoso violinist. As a child in Penza, he was also exposed to a rich array of folk spectacle, including the *balagan*, trained bears, jugglers, acrobats, jesters, and barkers.

Meyerhold made his theatrical debut in 1892 when at the age of eighteen he played Repetilov in an amateur production of Griboedov's *Woe from Wit* staged in his hometown by the "Lovers of Dramatic Art". Performing on the stage fed a love for the theatre that had begun much earlier, well before Meyerhold was old enough to accompany his mother to sit in the family box. At the end of 1893, Meyerhold wrote in his diary, "I have talent, I know that I could become a good actor ... This is my most cherished dream, one I have thought about almost since I was five".[3]

Following the death of his father, just a week after making his stage debut, Meyerhold renounced all interest in the family vodka factory. Determined not to follow in his father's footsteps, Meyerhold announced that he was planning to take Russian citizenship and join the Orthodox church in order to marry Olga Munt as well as to avoid conscription into the Prussian army. To make the break complete, he chose the name Vsevolod in honor of Vsevolod Garshin, one of the most popular writers of his generation, and changed the spelling of his last name from Meyergold to Meyerhold.

In August 1895, Meyerhold arrived in Moscow to study law at Moscow University. But the legal profession held little interest for the young Meyerhold, and he spent most of his time going to the theatre and concerts or visiting the Tretyakov Art Gallery. In the notebook he kept at the time, interspersed among his lecture notes are lists of books on the theatre, names of plays, as well as lines from Pushkin.

By the time Meyerhold returned to Moscow in January 1896, following Christmas vacation, he had already decided to leave the university at the end of the school year. After a summer spent in Penza acting with the Narodny (People's) Theatre, in the fall of 1896, Meyerhold entered the Moscow Philharmonic Society Drama School where he studied under Vladimir Nemirovich-Danchenko. At the final examination the following year, Meyerhold was one of two students to receive a silver medal, the other being Olga Knipper, Anton Chekhov's future wife. Following graduation, the twenty-four-year-old Meyerhold was invited to join the newly organized Moscow Art Theatre (initially called the Moscow Popular Art Theatre) headed by Konstantin Stanislavsky and Nemirovich-Danchenko.

During the four years he spent with the Moscow Art Theatre, Meyerhold played a wide variety of roles, including Treplev in the theatre's historic première of Chekhov's *The Seagull* in 1898, and the title role in theatre's production of Aleksei K. Tolstoy's *The Death of Ivan the Terrible* in 1899. But by the fourth year, Nemirovich-Danchenko, who had praised his student highly when he graduated from the Drama School, now regarded him as a troublemaker. And Meyerhold, denied any major new roles, had become increasingly frustrated. The final break came when the Art Theatre's founders reorganized in 1902 and did not invite the young actor to become one of the shareholders in the new company.

Meyerhold in 1896.

Meyerhold launched his career as a director in the provinces, first in Kherson and then in Tiflis (Tbilisi). During the three seasons he spent in the south, he directed some 165 productions (the first 85 with his partner, Aleksandr Kosheverov), including all of Chekhov's plays and most of the rest of the Art Theatre's repertory. "I began", he once told Gladkov, "by slavishly imitating Stanislavsky..." But Meyerhold quickly moved on from the Art Theatre's determined naturalism to experiment with new theatrical forms.

While still in the provinces far from the center of the Symbolist movement that was sweeping through the cultural life of St. Petersburg

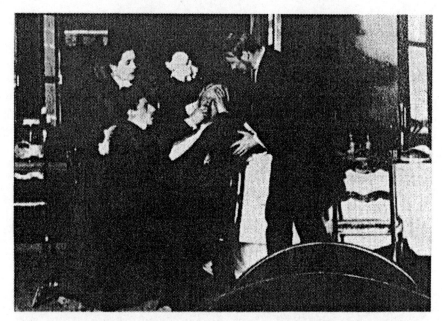

Meyerhold (kneeling) as Treplev in the Moscow Art Theatre's production of *The Seagull* (1898).

and Moscow, Meyerhold staged Maurice Maeterlinck's Symbolist drama, *The Intruder*, as an "evening of new drama". And in December 1903, he also staged Stanisław Przybyszewski's *Snow*, a production which the Symbolist poet, Aleksandr Remizov, praised as "a symphony of snow and winter".

The "unfamiliar melodies" of Symbolism also beckoned to Stanislavsky. In 1905, he invited Meyerhold back to Moscow to head a new Theatre-Studio on Povarskaya Street where the director and a select group of Moscow Art Theatre actors would explore new forms of poetic theatre. During the few months of the Studio's existence before closing in the aftermath of the 1905 Revolution, Meyerhold continued developing the experiments he had begun in the provinces. For Gerhart Hauptmann's *Schluck and Jau*, he discarded naturalistic stage settings in favor of just a few significant details, often of exaggerated proportions. And drawing inspiration from the altar paintings of Hans Memling, Meyerhold used a static bas-relief staging for his production of Maeterlinck's *The Death of Tintagiles*. Meyerhold also took his first steps toward creating a new form of theatre in which music would become an integral structural and aesthetic part of the production.

Georg Fuchs' book, *The Stage of the Future*, which Meyerhold read in the spring of 1906, opened up new vistas to Meyerhold. Inspired by it

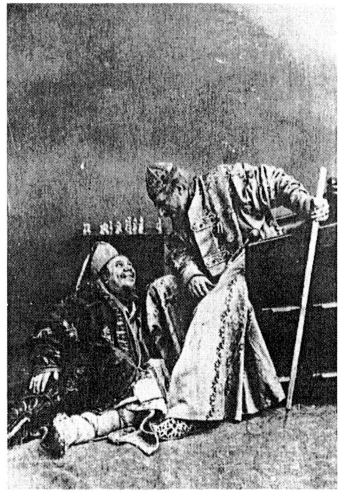

Meyerhold (right) as Ivan the Terrible and Boris Segirov (left) as the Jester in a scene from act 5 of the Moscow Art Theatre's production of Aleksei K. Tolstoy's *The Death of Ivan the Terrible* (1899).

he began moving away from the Symbolist theatre in other directions. For a production of Ibsen's *Ghosts* that summer in Poltava, Meyerhold eliminated the stage curtain in an attempt at breaking down the barrier between spectator and performer. He also started experimenting with the dance-like movements of the Japanese theatre.

More innovations followed during the two stormy seasons (1906–1908) Meyerhold spent at Vera Komissarzhevskaya's new theatre in St. Petersburg. His production of Leonid Andreev's *The Life of Man*

Meyerhold with his first wife, Olga Mikhailovna, and their daughter Mariya (1899).

introduced the use of area lighting, perhaps for the first time on the Russian stage. And his staging of Blok's *The Fairground Booth*, in which he played Pierrot, marked the beginning of Meyerhold's life-long interest in commedia dell'arte.

In 1908, following his dismissal from the Komissarzhevskaya Theatre for paying insufficient attention to the theatre's founder and leading actress, Meyerhold accepted Vladimir Telyakovsky's invitation to join the Imperial theatres in St. Petersburg. For the next decade, Meyerhold worked as director and actor at the Alexandrinsky Theatre and as director at the Mariinsky Opera where he mounted memorable productions of Wagner's *Tristan and Isolde* (1909), Molière's *Dom Juan* (1910), and Gluck's *Orpheus* (1911). In these and other productions, Meyerhold continued his experiments in theatrical stylization and the freer use of stage space.

In close collaboration with artist Aleksandr Golovin, Meyerhold created some of the most opulent productions ever seen in the Russian theatre. By eliminating both the proscenium and curtain in his production of *Dom Juan* and flooding the auditorium with light, Meyerhold joined actors and audience in a single entity. Inspired by the invisible "propmen" of the Japanese theatre, he also introduced proscenium servants into the production to carry the stage furniture on and off as needed.

For his landmark production of Mikhail Lermontov's *Masquerade*, on which he and Golovin worked for over five years, a series of exquisite gossamer curtains were created for each of the ten episodes. In addition, every single object used in the production, including the playing cards, was specially designed. This production, which opened on the very eve of the Revolution in 1917, marked the culmination of Meyerhold's pre-Revolutionary "Petersburg" period.

In 1913, at the invitation of Ida Rubinstein, Meyerhold went to Paris to stage Gabriele d'Annunzio's *Pisanelle*, which had been written

The "Ball Scene" from Meyerhold's production of *Masquerade* (1917).

Г. Аполлинер и В. Э. Мейерхольд.

Фотография 1913 г. (Париж)

Meyerhold and Apollinaire in Paris (1913).

specially for the Russian ballerina. With sets and costumes by Léon Bakst, choreography by Mikhail Fokin, and a cast including more than two hundred extras, the production was an enormous critical success. During his two months in Paris, Meyerhold acquired a rich palette of new impressions. He was enchanted by the poet Apollinaire, who served as his guide to historic Paris. Aside from a single visit to the Comédie Française and an evening spent at the Opéra, Meyerhold concentrated on acquainting himself with such popular entertainments as the Médrano Circus and the Spanish cabaret, *La Fiera*, in Montmartre. He also met and heard Marinetti lecture, visited the Paris studio of the Italian painter and sculptor, Umberto Boccioni, and saw a performance by the "Fairy of Light", Löie Fuller.[4]

In addition to directing at the Imperial Theatres, in the winter of 1912–1913 Meyerhold also organized a studio on Troitskaya Street (it moved the following year to Borodinskaya Street) where he began developing a program of actor training. Working under the pseudonym Doctor Dapertutto, Meyerhold taught a class in movement training. A course in commedia dell'arte was taught by Vladimir Solovyev; one in "Musical Reading", was taught by Mikhail Gnesin. Later Meyerhold would add Aleksandr Chekrygin, a dancer from the Mariinsky Theatre, to teach dancing, and the circus performers, Giacomino and Donat Donato, to teach acrobatics. In addition, Meyerhold published a journal, *Love for Three Oranges* (*Lyubov' k trem apel'sinam*) to promote and document the activities of his studio.[5]

Following the Revolution in 1917, Meyerhold was one of the first to join Anatoly Lunacharsky, the new People's Commissar for Enlightenment (NARKOMPROS), in reorganizing the arts. In August, 1918, Meyerhold became a member of the Communist Party, and Lunacharsky appointed him deputy head for Petrograd of the Theatre Department (TEO) under NARKOMPROS. In addition to continuing to run the former Imperial Theatres, Meyerhold also organized in collaboration with Leonid S. Vivien an ambitious program of "Courses in the Mastery of Stage Production" whose objective was "the creation of new cadres of well-prepared actors".[6]

For the first anniversary of the Revolution in 1918, Meyerhold produced in just three weeks the first Soviet play, Vladimir Mayakovsky's *Mystery-Bouffe*, with Cubo-Futurist sets designed by Kazimir Malevich. Nine days later, on November 16, Meyerhold resigned as director of the Mariinsky Theatre, thus ending his decade of association with the Imperial theatres.

In the spring of 1919, worn down by overwork and illness, Meyerhold went to the Crimea to undergo treatment for tuberculosis. Following the capture of Yalta by the Whites, Meyerhold fled to join his family, then living in Novorossiisk. But when an informer revealed his Bolshevik sympathies, Meyerhold was imprisoned by the Whites and barely escaped execution. For a time following his liberation by the Red Army after four months in prison, Meyerhold stayed on in Novorossiisk, even managing to produce one play, Ibsen's *A Doll's House*. But by late summer, Lunacharsky summoned him back to Moscow where he was appointed head of the Theatre Department for all of Russia. Meyerhold immediately took over editorship of *The Theatre Herald* and began calling for the revolutionizing of the entire theatrical system, which at the time was in a state of complete disarray.

Meyerhold also took command of the Free Theatre Company. Combining it with the remnants of two other defunct theatres, he renamed it the RSFSR Theatre No. 1 (The First Theatre of the Russian Soviet Federative Socialist Republic). As his new theatre's debut production, Meyerhold began rehearsing *The Dawns*, an epic verse drama by the Belgian Symbolist poet, mile Verhaeren. The production was staged as a political meeting with Futurist settings by Vladimir Dmitriev. Planned to mark the third anniversary of the Revolution, it proved something of an embarrassment for Communist critics, including Lenin's wife, Nadezhda Krupskaya. She felt that the production insulted the Russian proletariat by suggesting that "any self-opinionated fool can lead wherever the urge takes him".[7] Nevertheless, workers and Red Army soldiers filled the theatre at each performance. *The Dawns* ran for more than one hundred performances.

For his second and last production at the RSFSR Theatre No. 1, Meyerhold staged a completely rewritten version of *Mystery-Bouffe*, this time as a popular political revue with the clown, Vitaly Lazarenko, playing one of the devils. In spite of being roundly panned by critics when it opened on May Day 1921, the production proved very popular with audiences that delighted in the antics of the cartoon-like characters.

In June 1921, the Moscow Soviet ordered the closing of the RSFSR Theatre No. 1 as a money-losing operation. The theatre continued to struggle along for a few more months, enabling Meyerhold to direct a production of Wagner's *Rienzi*. But this "revolutionized" version of the opera, with sets by Georgy Yakulov, had to be abandoned after the second run-through when the theatre was permanently closed on September 6, 1921. Its demise, a victim of Lenin's New Economic Policy (NEP), marked the end of Meyerhold's self-proclaimed Theatrical October, and left the first Bolshevik director without a theatre.

In the autumn of 1921, Meyerhold was designated director of the newly-created State Higher Theatre Workshops (GVTM). In the former Plevako residence at 32 Novinsky Boulevard, he gathered together some one hundred young students and began training them as future actors and directors. Among his new pupils were the future film directors Sergei Eisenstein and Sergei Yutkevich as well as many other students who were destined to become prominent actors and directors in the Soviet theatre.

One of the budding actresses to join the Workshops was Zinaida Raikh, the former wife of the poet Sergei Esenin. The forty-seven-year-old Meyerhold was immediately smitten by this strikingly beautiful young woman with two small children. Abandoning his first wife and their three daughters, Meyerhold married Zinaida Raikh the following year, each of them adding the other's name to their own: Meyerhold-Raikh and Raikh-Meyerhold.

As the debut production of his new workshops, Meyerhold chose Fernand Crommelynck's farce about obsessive jealousy, *The Magnanimous Cuckold*.[8] Commissioning Lyubov Popova to design the constructivist sets for it, Meyerhold planned the production as a showcase to demonstrate the efficacy of the biomechanical exercises he was then developing in his workshops.

Stripped of the theoretical trappings Meyerhold borrowed from Taylorism and reflexology, Biomechanics was a program of actor training intended to teach all of the basic skills necessary to move properly on the stage. It came into being out of the very practical need to train large cadres of performers for the new proletarian theatre troupes that were supposed to spring up all over the country. With its emphasis on movement rather than emotion, Biomechanics was also Meyerhold's answer to the Moscow Art Theatre's school of actor training, which called for the performer to evoke an emotion or its equivalent before translating it into an appropriate action.[9]

In 1922, Meyerhold also staged Sukhovo-Kobylin's satire of Tsarist police methods, *The Death of Tarelkin*, as a montage of circus attractions with trick stage furniture designed by Varvara Stepanova.[10] This was followed in March 1923 by an agitprop production of *The Earth*

Scene from act 3 of *The Magnanimous Cuckold* (1922) showing Popova's constructivist stage set against the bare brick walls of the Zon Theatre.

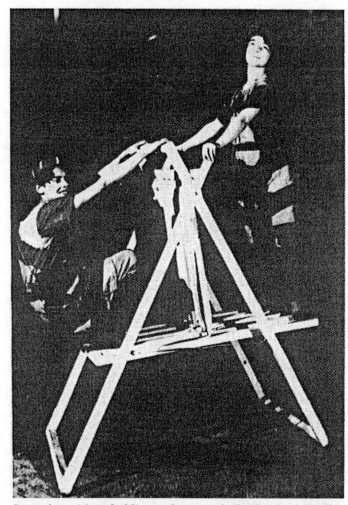

Scene from Meyerhold's production of *The Death of Tarelkin* (1922) demonstrating the trick furniture Varvara Stepanova designed for the production. Mme. Brandakhlistova's children, Kachala (Vladimir Lyutse) and Shatala (Evgeniya Bengis) on the "swing".

in Turmoil, a reworking by Sergei Tretyakov of Marcel Martinet's *La Nuit*, featuring actual machine guns, motorcycles, and mobile kitchens. Planned as a propaganda vehicle to mark the fifth anniversary of the Red Army, it succeeded primarily because of two episodes: a farcical one in which the Emperor dressed in full regalia sits on a chamber pot as the orchestra plays "God Save the Tsar"; and a second, tragic finale culminating in the death of the hero. Meyerhold adroitly constructed this scene

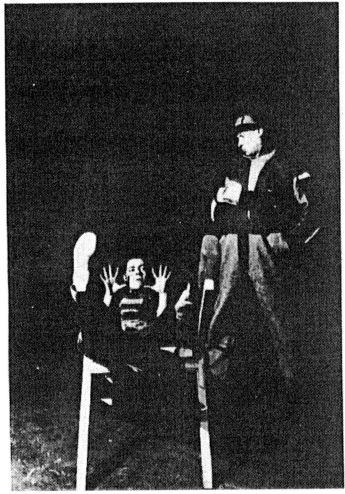

Scene from Meyerhold's production of *The Death of Tarelkin*
(1922): Varravin (Mikhail Lishin) grills Tarelkin (Maksim
Tereshkovich) who has been carried in tied to the "armchair"
with the collapsing back. He tortures Tarelkin by refusing him
the cup of water he is holding.

so that after the hero's comrades bid the fallen Red soldier farewell, the
casket is loaded on a truck, the sound of the vehicle's motor gradually
replacing the sound of the funeral music. While it may have been the first
production Meyerhold rescued by concentrating on just a few brilliantly
staged episodes, it would not be the last.

By 1924, the euphoria of the Revolution was waning. Heeding
Lunacharsky's call, "Back to Ostrovsky", Meyerhold staged the great

Episode 4, ''The Black International'', from the 1923 production of *The Earth in Turmoil.*

Episode 8, ''Father Evgeny and his Maximum Program'', from the 1924 production of *The Forest.* A rich neighbor, Uar Badaev (Sergei Martynov), shakes everyone's hand in turn leaving all of them waving their hands from the pain. He laughs.

Russian playwright's *The Forest* with Zinaida Raikh, now the theatre's leading lady, playing the role of the young ward, Aksyusha. One of Meyerhold's most enduring productions, it remained in the repertory until the theatre was closed in 1938. That same year, Meyerhold also mounted *D.E.* (*Give us Europe!*), an "agit-sketch" in seventeen episodes by Mikhail Podgaetsky loosely based on two novels by Ilya Ehrenburg and *The Tunnel* by Bernhard Kellermann, with additional material drawn from Upton Sinclair and Pierre Hamp. Just as with *The Earth in Turmoil*, the production was dedicated to Leon Trotsky, a dedication that would be used as a weapon against Meyerhold at the end of the 1930s.

Under increasing pressure to stage a Soviet play, in 1925 Meyerhold next turned to Aleksei Faiko's *Bubus, the Teacher*, which he adapted for his own use as an experiment in pre-acting. In order to make up for a lack of content, Meyerhold filled the production with extraneous activities, including a basketball game and the latest dances brought back from Paris by Valentin Parnakh. While it may have been a "valuable exercise in rhythmical discipline" for his actors, as Edward Braun observes, it was hardly what critics had in mind when they called for more plays by Soviet dramatists.[11]

Meyerhold tried again to please the critics, this time with far more success, by staging a production of Nikolai Erdman's first full-length

Scene from act 1 of *Bubus, the Teacher* (1925).

play, *The Warrant*, also in 1925. This rollicking satire of the new bourgeoisie with its subdued note of tragedy marked a significant move away from Meyerhold's previous Soviet productions. Even Stanislavsky, who had ignored Meyerhold's other post-Revolutionary productions, was prompted to remark following his first visit to the Meyerhold Theatre in October that in the final scene of *The Warrant* with its revolving stage and moving walls, "Meyerhold has achieved ... what I dream of".[12]

In the months following the première of *The Warrant*, Meyerhold left it to one of his pupils, Vasily Fedorov, to stage Sergei Tretyakov's *Roar, China!* while he concentrated on working with the Third Studio of the Moscow Art Theatre on a production (never completed) of Pushkin's *Boris Godunov* and on preparations for a production of Gogol's *The Inspector General* at his own theatre.

Drawing on all six variants of Gogol's masterpiece, Meyerhold fashioned a montage of fifteen episodes to be played out in rapid succession on a small, movable stage encircled by doors. Starring Erast Garin as Khlestakov, Zinaida Raikh as Anna Andreevna, and Maria Babanova as her daughter and rival, the production won praise from a wide array of critics when it premièred on December 9, 1926. Still, the production provoked heated controversy, much of it fed by Meyerhold's often inflammatory remarks at numerous debates following the opening. Always determined to have the final word, he called formalist critic Viktor Shklovsky "a Fascist", and so angered the distinguished critic Mikhail Levidov that he sued Meyerhold.

To see Raikh and Babanova together on the same stage, and in such close proximity, only served to draw attention to the fact that Meyerhold's wife was not a born actress. Although she was strikingly beautiful and possessed a strong voice, as Igor Ilinsky noted, her "helplessness on the stage, her physical unpreparedness, and to put it simply, her awkwardness was only too evident"...[13]

Clearly there was not room on the stage for both actresses, and while the theatre was on tour in the Crimea, Meyerhold wrote a note to Babanova saying that "he did not consider it possible to work with her anymore". Whether or not Meyerhold left the door open for her return, as he had with Ilinsky, the matter was settled by Babanova herself with a letter to the editor of the newspaper in Rostov-on-the-Don announcing that, "Following the end of the theatre's tour on June 17, 1927, I will be leaving the Meyerhold Theatre".[14] Shortly after that she moved to the Theatre of the Revolution (later, the Mayakovsky Theatre) where she remained until just before her death. To the end of her life Babanova never forgave Meyerhold for destroying her career.

Meyerhold with his stepchildren on the porch of their dacha (1926). The dacha, located northeast of Moscow in the village of Gorenki, was purchased by Zinaida Raikh with the money received from the first publication of Sergei Esenin's collected works. She had the foresight to purchase the dacha in her children's name. As a result, it was not confiscated following Meyerhold's arrest and Zinaida Raikh's murder.

The Inspector General (1926), Episode 11, "Kiss Me". To the music of "Kiss Me", a romance by Aleksandr Dargomyzhsky with lyrics by Aleksandr Pushkin, Khlestakov (Erast Garin) dances a quadrille with Maria Antonovna (Maria Babanova) and Anna Andreevna (Zinaida Raikh). At the piano is the "Officer in Transit" (Aleksei Kelberer), a figure introduced by Meyerhold.

Meyerhold originally considered staging Aleksandr Griboedov's comedy in verse, *Woe from Wit*, at the Theatre of the Revolution in 1924, the year of the play's centennial. But because of other commitments and his subsequent resignation as artistic director of that theatre, Meyerhold was forced to drop his plans. Now, three years later, faced with a serious repertory crisis following the première of *The Inspector General*, Meyerhold turned to Griboedov's classic once more.

Time and again during the 1920s and 1930s Meyerhold sought refuge in the classics when he could not find anything else to his liking. He constantly came under attack for his failure to produce contemporary Soviet plays. But as he bluntly stated in an interview just before the opening of *Woe from Wit*:

> What causes the Meyerhold State Theatre to turn to the classics? A significant majority of "contemporary" works playing in other theatres, as well as the vast majority of plays sent to our theatre, are of poor quality either from the standpoint of ideas or from the point of view of their language, dramatic construction, and as material for acting. These

plays train actors in the distortion of speech, foolish clowning, and wretchedly bad acting.[15]

Meyerhold again drew on all the extant texts, even restoring the original title, *Woe to Wit*, to create a "lyrical tragedy, where flashes of exaggerated buffoonery are used to set off more clearly the tragic note".[16] Meyerhold again divided the production into episodes, this time each set in a different room in Famusov's house. In addition, he added a prologue set in a "Small Café" where Sofiya and her fawning suitor, Molchalin, are holding a secret rendezvous. Meyerhold also made liberal use of music, depicting the idealistic Chatsky constantly at the piano providing musical accompaniment to his dialogue.[17]

Lunacharsky was right when he wrote in 1930 that Meyerhold had presented a Chatsky who was "totally different" from the usual sermonizing leading man with a pleasant baritone voice and an emotional, breast-clutching manner of declamation. Rather, Meyerhold emphasized the spiritual and biographical similarities between Griboedov and his hero. More importantly, he placed him in total opposition to the boorish society around him. Chatsky suffers the tragic fate that every creative, sensitive person suffers when he comes face to face with a solid wall of arrogant vulgarity.

Woe to Wit (1928), Episode 14, "The Dining Room". Chatsky (Erast Garin) is standing in front of the table on the left. Famusov (Igor Ilinsky) has just risen from his seat at the center of the table to join his guests in hissing at Chatsky as he finishes speaking: ". . . a million torments are in my breast..." and turns to leave. Seated on Famusov's left are Khlestova (Natalya Serebryanikova) and Sofiya (Zinaida Raikh). Meyerhold's frontal staging of this famous "slander scene", was inspired by Leonardo da Vinci's "The Last Supper" and Diego Rivera's "Feast of the Millionaires".

At the same time there was something intensely personal about this production provoking more than one critic to comment that Meyerhold closely identified with his hero. After seeing a performance, director and critic Valentin Smyshlyaev, who found the production "fresh, subtle, original, and remarkably musical", was prompted to write in his diary: "All of Chatsky's words resonated with Meyerhold's personality – right up to: 'I'm leaving Moscow, I'll go seek the world for...' And when at the end [Chatsky]-Garin (made up as Meyerhold – that couldn't have been a coincidence!) left the stage with his suitcases, I whispered to Olenka who was sitting next to me, 'There's Meyerhold leaving for America!'"[18]

In fact, talk of emigration was very much in the air at that time. In July 1928, Meyerhold and Zinaida Raikh left the Soviet Union to vacation in France. While abroad, Meyerhold sent a telegram to Moscow requesting that his visa be extended as he had fallen ill. Soon headlines in the Moscow theatre journals were asking, "Will Meyerhold return to Moscow?" In September 1928, word reached Moscow that actor-director Mikhail Chekhov, on leave at the time in Germany, had signed a two-year contract with Max Reinhardt. He was followed by Aleksandr Granovsky, head of the State Jewish Theatre. When that theatre was summoned back to Moscow in the middle of their triumphant tour of Europe, Granovsky announced that he would not be returning.

Meyerhold's telegram from Paris that fall stating that he was organizing an extensive European tour of the Meyerhold Theatre only served to feed the rumors of his intended defection. And while there were some members of the newly-formed Glaviskusstvo (Main Administration of Artistic Literature and Art) and some members of the press who were quite ready to say, "Good riddance", there were equally powerful voices, including that of Lunacharsky, who felt it was premature to write off Meyerhold and his theatre.

In the end it was agreed that any final decision about the fate of Meyerhold's theatre would be postponed until his return. In the meantime, a government commission was formed to examine the administrative and financial situation of the theatre. The theatre was also given a subsidy to cover its outstanding debts and operating costs until the end of November. As for a tour abroad, while Lunacharsky lent his support, Meyerhold was given to understand that the matter could only be settled in Moscow after his return.[19]

When Meyerhold and Zinaida Raikh arrived in Moscow by train from Paris on December 2, after an absence of five months, they were enthusiastically welcomed at the station by the entire troupe of the Meyerhold Theatre along with representatives of various military and civil organizations. And that evening Meyerhold's presence in the theatre was greeted by wild applause.[20]

Well before Meyerhold and Zinaida Raikh went abroad, it had become clear that the State Meyerhold Theatre was in serious trouble. Attendance at the theatre had dropped off and the theatre was running a significant deficit. In addition, Meyerhold seemed unable to reach agreement with Glavrepertkom (The Main Repertory Committee) as to a suitable contemporary play. In 1927 he had announced his intention to stage Andrey Bely's play, *Moscow*. There were also plans to include *The Bloody Desert* (*Morocco*), by the Armenian playwright, Stepan Bagdasaryan in the 1928–1929 season. Neither of these productions was ever realized.

Meyerhold was also negotiating with Glavrepertkom for permission to stage Sergei Tretyakov's play about eugenics, *I Want a Child*. But in spite of his enthusiasm for the play, and the support of several members of the committee, Meyerhold was turned down on the grounds that it was "premature", and that the play might provoke "undesirable responses" from the audience.[21]

In May 1928, Meyerhold had dispatched a desperate telegram to Mayakovsky pleading, "The theatre is dying. There are no plays. We are forced to reject the classics. I request a serious answer. can we count on

The Bedbug (1929), Scene 9, "A Remarkable Parasite". Igor Ilinsky as Prisypkin, who after being frozen for fifty years is now on display in a cage at the zoo as an example of *Philistinius vulgaris*.

receiving your play this summer? Wire immediately..."[22] Seven months later, on December 28, Mayakovsky read his new comedy, *The Bedbug*, at the Meyerhold Theatre. Assured that the theatre's financial crisis was at least temporarily resolved, Meyerhold immediately set to work on the production.

When this biting satire of philistinism, starring Igor Ilinsky as the smugly ignorant Prisypkin, opened just six weeks later, it was enthusiastically received by audiences. But again, Party critics were somewhat less than pleased. They were even less satisfied with Meyerhold's production of Mayakovsky's *The Bathhouse* a year later. A scathing portrait of Communist-type bureaucracy, it was vigorously condemned by critics as a "falsification of Soviet reality"[23] Although *The Bathhouse* was soon removed from the repertory, as Meyerhold later confided to Gladkov, of the three Mayakovsky productions he had staged, "I think I was more successful with *The Bathhouse* than with the others".

Meyerhold also made a valiant attempt to get Nikolai Erdman's satire of the bourgeoisie, *The Suicide*, before the public. But he fared little better than either the Vakhtangov Theatre or the Moscow Art Theatre, both of which also rehearsed but never premièred the production.

Scene from *The Bathhouse* (1930). Act 6, passengers boarding the time machine. When asked at a meeting of the Meyerhold Theatre artistic council (September 23, 1929) why he called his play "*The Bathhouse*", Mayakovsky answered, "Because it's the one thing the play doesn't have".

Meyerhold's failure to win approval for his production in 1932 following a closed late-night performance for a small audience of Kremlin officials marked the end of his efforts to stage a contemporary satire.[24]

While still rehearsing *The Bedbug*, Meyerhold also began work on *The Second Army Commander*, Ilya Selvinsky's verse tragedy about the Russian Civil War. Meyerhold saw this, his first attempt at staging a tragedy, as an opportunity to polemicize against the traditional genre interpretations of the war à la Konstantin Trenev's *Lyubov Yarovaya*. Inspired by the famous Civil War painting, *Death of a Commissar* (1928) by Kuzma Petrov-Vodkin, whom he asked to serve as consultant on the costumes for the production, Meyerhold set out to depict the bloody conflict as a legend from the remote past. He himself designed the set construction featuring a long curving stairway against high walls enclosing the entire stage, which was executed by Sergei Vakhtangov, who along with Mikhail Barkhin, would design the new building for Meyerhold's theatre in the 1930s.

Filled with long speeches and philosophical abstractions, Selvinsky's play was ill-suited for a theatre that relied on capturing its audience with a combination of boldly drawn characters and a series of striking set pieces that would overshadow the general weakness of the dramatic content, and remain in the memory of the audience.[25] In order to realize his own epic vision of the struggle for control of the army

The Second Army Commander (1929). Act 1, scene 1, "The Meeting".

between the peasant partisan, Chub, and the army clerk, Okonny, Meyerhold considerably simplified the playwright's more complex characterizations. Ignoring Selvinsky's heated objections, Meyerhold turned Okonny into an egotistical phrasemonger who in Meyerhold's more sharply drawn version faces a firing squad in the finale.

Even Selvinsky had to acknowledge that he was powerfully affected by scenes such as "Rally in the Steppe", in which one speaker after another was shouted down by the unruly crowd until brought under control by the "iron commander". Equally powerful was the chanting in the finale by the entire company using megaphones to amplify their voices as a narrator told of the Battle of Beloyarsk.

By the time Meyerhold and his theatre set off for Berlin in 1930 on the first stage of their long-awaited tour abroad, they had already been preceded by virtually all of the theatres and important studios working in Moscow, from the Moscow Art Theatre and the Vakhtangov to Tairov's Kamerny Theatre, and most recently Granovsky's State Jewish Theatre. Only now, on seeing the four productions from the Meyerhold Theatre repertory, did it become clear to Berlin critics just how much other directors, both German and Russian, had borrowed from this "resolute analyst and experimenter whose role", as one critic wrote, "could be compared to that of Cézanne in painting".[26] In the weeks following their opening night performance in Berlin of *The Inspector General* on April 1, during which the theatre toured extensively throughout Germany, probably no other Soviet theatre generated as many reviews and articles as did the Meyerhold Theatre.[27] In addition to critics, many of whom dealt very harshly with the productions they saw, the theatre attracted the attention of virtually all of the major German theatre directors, including Max Reinhardt, Leopold Jessner, and Erwin Piscator. Both Fritz Lang and Oscar Schlemmer also attended, and Luigi Pirandello came from Italy to see a performance.

No less controversial was the reception from the French press during the Meyerhold Theatre's two-week stay in Paris which began on June 16 with a run-through of *The Inspector General* for an invited audience of critics and leading members of the Paris art world (both Picasso and Cocteau were present), many of whom Meyerhold had already met on his earlier trips to Paris. While the Communist press was quick to praise Meyerhold and his theatre (*L'Humanité* hailed it as "genuine theatre"), the White Russian émigré colony took a more sober view of its role in Soviet life and of Meyerhold, calling him "not only a member of the Party, but politically and technically at the service of the Soviet rulers".[28] Nevertheless in both Germany and in Paris, the theatre played to full houses everywhere.

Meyerhold and Zinaida Raikh on their arrival in Berlin (1930).

From Paris, the Meyerhold Theatre was scheduled to continue on to the United States. But no sooner had the sets for *The Inspector General* and *The Forest* been loaded on the boat, when the company was summarily ordered back to Moscow. One can only speculate as to the reason for abruptly discontinuing the tour. Perhaps the fear that Meyerhold might defect had not been laid to rest, all the more since in addition to invitations from German theatres, Meyerhold had also received an invitation to direct in the United States. His appeals to Andrei Bubnov, the chairman of NARKOMPROS, to convey to the Politburo his request for a year's leave to work abroad, fell on deaf ears.[29]

Following his return to Moscow from Paris, Meyerhold set to work revising his 1924 revue, *D.E.*, this time calling it *D.S.E.* (*Give Us Soviet Europe*). In the new version, in addition to contrasting "the crisis of capitalism" to "the success of Socialist construction in the U.S.S.R.", the plan to build a transatlantic tunnel was replaced by a series of episodes dedicated to the achievements of the First Five-Year Plan. The revised production, intended to mark the thirteenth anniversary of the Revolution, fell far short of the success of the original.

This was also true of Meyerhold's other revised versions of earlier productions, beginning with his restaging in 1928 of *The Magnanimous Cuckold* to accommodate Zinaida Raikh as Stella. In the 1930s Meyerhold would also make revisions in *The Forest*, cutting the number of episodes from the original 33 to 16. Meyerhold also eliminated some of the more outrageous cartoon effects, including the brightly-colored wigs worn by some of the characters in order, as he told Aleksandr Gladkov, "to make it less satirical and more romantic".

In 1935, Meyerhold restaged his production of *Woe to Wit*, calling it his "Moscow version" to distinguish it from his 1928 "Leningrad version". With its more conventional staging, including the addition of a stage curtain, and the handsome, young Mikhail Tsarev as Chatsky – more matinée idol than fiery Decembrist – it might more appropriately have been named Meyerhold's "Romantic" version. As with his other revisions of productions, it paled in comparison to the daring of the original.

When the death of Mayakovsky in 1930 again left Meyerhold without a playwright he could rely on, he turned to Vsevolod Vishnevsky, whose play, *The First Cavalry Army*, had been a hit the previous season at both the Theatre of the Revolution and the Central Red Army Theatre. In staging the playwright's new play, *The Last, Decisive*, Meyerhold again dedicated himself to working in detail on several key episodes, including a long satiric prologue intended to poke fun at the Bolshoi Theatre's ballet, *The Red Poppy*. More successful were the colorful "port scenes" featuring Igor Ilinsky and Erast Garin as a pair of sailors and Zinaida Raikh as the prostitute, Carmen-Pelagea.

But none of these scenes could match the punch delivered by the final episode set in a schoolhouse under siege. One by one the remaining twenty-seven sailors perish as in the background a radio plays a foxtrot and Maurice Chevalier is heard singing. Only Bushuev (Nikolai Bogolyubov) is left. Mortally wounded, the sailor struggles to rise to his feet. He takes a piece of chalk and with excruciating difficulty writes on the blackboard the number 162,000,000 (the country's population at that time) and under it a minus sign and the number 27. Bushuev completes the subtraction, then dropping the chalk, he falls, and with a perplexed

Mei Lan-fang speaking to Zinaida Raikh backstage after a
performance while on tour in 1935. Note Meyerhold seated in
the background. Meyerhold was so taken with Mei Lan-fang's
performance that he dedicated his 1935 "Moscow Version" of
Woe to Wit to him.

smile, dies. As Bogolyubov recalled, "This was a pantomime without
words, an entire gamut of physical actions. The struggle [to write] each
number was built like a musical composition".[30]

Shortly after the première on February 7, 1931, Meyerhold wrote
Vishnevsky telling him that he had every right to take first place among
Soviet playwrights.[31] As so often in Meyerhold's past, such high praise
could only be followed by a break between the two Vsevolods. It soon
came when Vishnevsky violently protested the revisions Meyerhold

The Last, Decisive (1931). In the final episode set in a school house under siege, the mortally wounded Bushuev (Nikolai Bogolyubov) struggles to write on the blackboard the number 162,000,000 (the country's population) and under it a minus sign and the number 27. He drops the chalk, falls to the floor, and dies.

wanted to make in his new play, *Battle in the West*. Rather than finding a new playwright, Meyerhold had added yet another name to his list of enemies.

In December 1929, Meyerhold had signed a contract with Mikhail Zoshchenko to stage his play *Dear Comrade* during the 1930–1931 season. However, by 1931, Meyerhold had changed his mind, and when he assigned Nikolai Bogolyubov to direct the production, Zoshchenko withdrew the play. In its place Meyerhold set to work staging Yuri Olesha's *A List of Benefits*. As Meyerhold admitted to Nikolai Chushkin, the play was clearly inspired by Mikhail Chekhov, who was famous for his interpretation of Hamlet.[32] It tells the story of Elena Goncharova, an actress who emigrates to Paris. Although her dream is to play Hamlet, she ends up in the hands of a vulgar music hall manager who proposes that she "bare her rear and play minuets" on the flute. Filled with self-disgust and disillusionment, she joins a Paris street demonstration of unemployed workers, during which she is killed while shielding a French Communist leader from an assassination attempt by a White Russian émigré.

For Meyerhold, *A List of Benefits* marked yet another attempt to stage a contemporary tragedy. It was also an opportunity to realize in

Finale of *A List of Benefits* (1931). As the dying Goncharova (Zinaida Raikh) lies on the forestage, the striking workers seize the red flag and continue their march to meet the mounted police.

part his life-long dream to direct *Hamlet* (the Prologue includes the scene between Hamlet, Rosencrantz, and Guildenstern), and it gave Zinaida Raikh her first major role since the 1928 production of *Woe to Wit*. *A List of Benefits* was also the last production to be staged in the former Zon Theatre before it was demolished to make way for the building of the new Meyerhold Theatre. For more than a year the Meyerhold Theatre was without a permanent home. After a period of extensive touring, the company temporarily occupied a theatre on Mamanovsky Lane before moving into the theatre at 15 Tverskaya, the present home of the Ermolova Theatre, where it would remain until it was closed in 1938.

By the 1930s Meyerhold came under increasing attack, not only for the content of his productions, but also for the very essence of his artistic method which was characterized as "schematic", "two-dimensional", and "machine-like". In 1932, RAPP (The Russian Association of Proletarian Writers) published a booklet, *On the Objectives of RAPP on the Theatrical Front*, in which it judged Meyerhold's emphasis on external physical action at the expense of revealing the social essence of the characters to be "not only alien to the reconstruction of the Soviet theatre, but to be working against it".[33]

Although RAPP was disbanded shortly after the publication of this booklet, the charges leveled against Meyerhold contained in it only became more strident. In the face of growing demands to stage a contemporary play that would speak to the masses, Meyerhold was forced to admit that his once vanguard theatre was out of touch with the life around it. As part of a general purge of the Communist Party in November 1933, Meyerhold, "the most prominent representative of Soviet theatrical art", was again called upon to defend his role as a Bolshevik in the creation of the Soviet theatre.[34] After reviewing his entire career in a speech lasting several hours, Meyerhold next found himself trying to play down the importance of his system of biomechanical training as of "little significance".

In turning to a discussion of his repertoire, Meyerhold spoke in vague terms about staging a trilogy on the fate of women (he was already planning a production of Dumas' *The Lady of the Camellias*). He added that during the next Five-Year Plan, he would also like to stage *Hamlet*, a reworking of *Mystery-Bouffe*, as well as *The Ball of the Mannequins* by the Polish dramatist, Bruno Jasieński. "But", Meyerhold maintained in an appeal to speed the construction of his new theatre, "I can't express the great rise of Socialist construction with plywood sets. I need new technological facilities in a new building".[35]

After further criticism by the playwright Vladimir Bill-Belotserkovsky, who had already attacked Meyerhold in the press as early as 1928, and by the well-known cultural worker, Boris Malkin, who called upon Meyerhold to create "a major production about the Bolshevik party", Comrade Rozovsky, the chairman of the purge commission, concluded that there was ample reason to be concerned for Meyerhold's future. He warned the director of the weak state of party work in the Meyerhold Theatre, adding that it was not responding to the needs of the working class. "We are expecting from Meyerhold a decisive treatment of the theme of Socialist construction".[36]

But no such "decisive treatment" was forthcoming. Instead, Meyerhold turned to staging *Prélude*, an adaptation of Yuri German's novella of the same name about a German scientist. Yet another in Meyerhold's gallery of tragic figures, the hero, Professor Oscar Kelberg, is so horrified by the German treatment of the intelligentsia that he decides to emigrate to the Soviet Union.

On the whole, German's adaptation left Meyerhold with little to work with in terms of dramatic material. Only the second act, set in the private dining room of a restaurant where Kelberg has gathered his friends and colleagues for a farewell dinner, provided Meyerhold with an opportunity to display his mastery to the fullest extent. As critic

Aleksandr Matskin wrote in *Izvestia*, "The café [sic] scene is the height of the show from the point of view of direction. The flickering candles, the shining top hats, the actors' slow movements, the hysterical note in the dialogue – all this creates a mood of condensed despair, of genuine tragedy".[37] The scene ends with the drunken Hugo Nunbakh, an engineer now reduced to selling pornographic postcards, left alone in the empty banquet room. Slowly he climbs up on the table, embraces a marble bust of Goethe and looks into the statue's eyes as he asks, "Why am I not building houses?" The only answer he receives is silence. It was scenes like this that prompted Israel Bachelis to write, "It is time to leave behind the legend of Meyerhold as anti-psychological. His most recent work forces one to speak of his mastery of the psychological sketch".[38]

Prélude. Hugo Nunbakh (Lev Sverdlin) slowly climbs up on the table and embraces a marble bust of Goethe. He looks into the statue's eyes as he asks, "Why am I not building houses?" The only answer he receives is silence.

As with other attempts to stage a contemporary play, it became clear that, if anything, Meyerhold was over-qualified. Iosif Yuzovsky fittingly wrote in his review of *Prélude* that each time Meyerhold has encountered a contemporary play, he has pictured "a giant who is bedded down in a crib".[39] The only solution for Meyerhold was once again to immerse himself in the classics.

Of all his productions in the 1930s, including Sukhovo-Kobylin's *Krechinsky's Wedding* (1933) and Tchaikovsky's *The Queen of Spades* (1935) at the Maly Opera Theatre in Leningrad, only one, *The Lady of the Camellias*, can justifiably be considered a masterpiece. Staged in 1934, it proved to be not only an artistic success, but also a hit with audiences. Starved by more than a decade of drab austerity, they avidly soaked up every detail of the beautiful production. It brought the first full houses the Meyerhold Theatre had enjoyed in a long time.

While Meyerhold always had a ready-made justification for his productions to satisfy his critics, in this case, "an exposé of a bourgeois who corrupts a young girl of the people", such words had little to do with the director's actual decision to stage Dumas' famous adaptation of his own novel. In addition to being a loving gift to his adored wife, who would play the dying Marguerite, for Meyerhold it was also an opportunity to revel again in the kind of beautiful setting and costumes that

The Lady of the Camellias (1934), scene from act 4. Prudence (Remizova) speaks to Marguerite (Raikh) as Armand (Tsarev) looks on.

had characterized his pre-Revolutionary productions of *Dom Juan* and *Masquerade*. Perhaps it was no coincidence that he had recently revived both of these productions.

Inspired by the works of the French Impressionists, in particular Manet, Degas, and Renoir, whose paintings he had just seen on exhibition in Paris, Meyerhold shifted the period of the play from the 1840s to the 1870s. In order to set off the beauty of the elegant costumes and exquisite antiques, with the help of artist Ivan Leistikov, Meyerhold designed a setting of white walls and gossamer curtains dominated by a long curving wrought iron staircase. Against this background, Meyerhold choreographed a complex score of brilliant group compositions, lovers' duets, and highly dramatic solos for Zinaida Raikh as Marguerite Gautier.

In a masterpiece of stagecraft, Meyerhold presented Marguerite's death in the finale with only the most minimal gesture. Seated in an armchair placed at an angle to the window, Marguerite speaks her final words, "I'm not suffering!... You see, I'm smiling, I'm strong..." She suddenly rises from the armchair, and with her two hands she reaches out, grabs the shutters, and throws them open, letting in the bright sunlight. Still grasping the shutter with her left hand, she drops back into the armchair. Only her left arm is visible on the arm of the chair. She stiffens ever so slightly. An extended pause. Her hand drops from the armrest, hanging limply. This is the only sign of her death.[40]

To honor Meyerhold on his sixtieth birthday on February 10, 1934, the Soviet journal *Theatre and Dramaturgy* devoted a major part of its February issue to this "master of the revolutionary theatre". As the prominent critic Pavel Markov wrote in his "Letter about Meyerhold" in this issue, "More has been written about Meyerhold, especially in the last few years, than about any other figure in the theatre".[41] Such words of praise could not help but anger Stalin whose support was solidly behind the Moscow Art Theatre.

According to Aleksandr Matskin, Stalin had taken a dislike to Meyerhold from the earliest years of the Revolution.[42] A frequent visitor to the Moscow Art Theatre, Stalin had seen only one production at the Meyerhold Theatre, *Roar, China!* in 1926. (His reaction to it is not known.) But with the launching of the Second Five-Year Plan and at a time when the Soviet leader was doing everything in his power to win the confidence and support of the capitalist West, he needed artists and scientists like Meyerhold, Eisenstein, Gorky, and Pavlov as window dressing to impress the Western world. And so, like many of the other mannequins in Stalin's showcase, Meyerhold would be spared for a while longer.

Nevertheless the signs of official disfavor began to accumulate. In 1934, Meyerhold was refused permission to celebrate his sixtieth birthday at his theatre. Eleven years earlier on his twenty-fifth anniversary as a director, Meyerhold had been honored with a gala evening at the Bolshoi Theatre. He had also been awarded the title of "People's Artist of the Republic". But when the new award, "Honored Artist of the U.S.S.R." was established in 1936 to recognize the "most eminent figures in the art of the peoples of the U.S.S.R., particularly those who distinguished themselves in the development of Soviet theatre, music, and film", Meyerhold's name was not on the list.[43]

Pressure continued to grow for Meyerhold to stage a Soviet play. Premier Molotov had a talk with him on the subject, but Meyerhold argued that there were no suitable works worth staging. Instead, as Aleksandr Gladkov relates, he staged with little success three of Chekhov's one-act plays under the title *33 Swoons*. Meyerhold also began rehearsals of Pushkin's *Boris Godunov*, which he would rehearse on and off for the next year and a half.

On January 17, 1936, a powerful new All-Union Committee for Arts Affairs was created. For the first time it placed all of the arts under the control of a single organization, with Platon Kerzhentsev, a loyal Party member since 1904, as chairman. This announcement was followed on January 28, 1936, by an article in *Pravda* entitled "Muddle Instead of Music", attacking composer Dmitry Shostakovich and his opera, *Lady Macbeth of Mtsensk District*, which had already enjoyed considerable success since its triumphant première in Leningrad two years earlier.

This unsigned article (Shostakovich was convinced Stalin himself had a hand in writing it) and a second one on February 6, attacking Shostakovich's ballet *Bright Stream*, were an ominous sign of the significant changes in the political and cultural climate soon to take place.[44]

The attack on Shostakovich sent a chilling message to Meyerhold as well. An editorial accompanying the reprinting of these articles in the March issue of *Theatre and Dramaturgy* warned that it and similar articles attacking artists, film makers, and architects, "directly and sharply raise the question of the transference [to the other arts] of the most negative features of Meyerholditis infinitely multiplied, while at the same time Meyerhold's obedient friends have tried and continue to try to canonize any and all of his work as yet another achievement in leftist innovation".[45]

A month later, on Thursday, February 27, the Second Moscow Art Theatre, Stanislavsky's "favorite child", gave its last performance. The following day, *Pravda* published the resolution by the Communist Party Central Committee and the Council of Peoples' Commissars on the liquidation of that theatre, stating that "the so-called Second Moscow Art Theatre does not warrant the name MXAT and in fact it is a mediocre theatre whose preservation in Moscow is not essential".[46] As critic Sergei

Ignatov wrote in *Theatre and Dramaturgy* (No. 4, 1933), "The official acknowledgement of the mediocre work of the former Second Moscow Art Theatre must be seen as an alarm signal to other theatres, and as such it is a very serious warning".[47]

It is in the context of these developments that Gladkov tells of the gathering on the evening of March 5, at which Meyerhold, Zinaida Raikh, and Pasternak discussed the wisdom of Meyerhold trying to arrange a meeting with Stalin (see pp. 81–84).

As the campaign against formalism in the arts (the code word for "bourgeois ideology hostile to the Soviet people") took on a new stridency, criticism against Meyerhold in the press grew increasingly harsh. Never one to hold back when attacked, Meyerhold was quick to respond. In a speech in Leningrad on March 14, 1936, entitled "Meyerhold Against Meyerholditis", Meyerhold vigorously defended Shostakovich, arguing that there are times when it is necessary to support an artist of great talent in the certainty that he will outgrow his youthful mistakes and give us great works in the future.[48]

Turning to the attacks on himself, Meyerhold admitted that he had made many mistakes in his productions. But he justified these as experiments in his effort to convey the content of a given work. Meyerhold went on to accuse his former disciples, including Sergei Radlov and Nikolai Okhlopkov, of debasing his artistic methods by stealing his formal devices and using them out of context. In Meyerhold's view, here was the real Meyerholditis that warranted attack.[49]

At a conference of theatre workers held in Moscow on March 26 to discuss the charges against Shostakovich and to assess the implications of formalism in the arts, Meyerhold again came under heavy attack for trying to shift the blame for his own shortcomings to others.[50] Once more Meyerhold responded, again refusing to concede anything to his critics. He rejected the idea of devoting his speech to self-criticism, stating that he had spent his entire career doing just that. He also defended his experimental work as part of a constant search for new means of dramatic expression.

Meyerhold next spoke of the influence of his productions on the work of other theatres. "The Maly Theatre would never have staged *Lyubov Yarovaya* if we had not earlier staged *The Magnanimous Cuckold*", he said, adding that, "if [the Maly's production] smacked of provincialism, it was because the director failed to have his actors adapt their makeup and costumes as well as their acting style to the constructivist set". And without our *Forest*, Meyerhold pointed out to his accusers, "Konstantin Sergeevich Stanislavsky would never have produced his splendid *A Fervent Heart* at the Moscow Art Theatre".[51]

Meyerhold vehemently denied that he was trying to escape from reality by staging the classics instead of contemporary Soviet plays. He charged Soviet playwrights with trying to hide their mediocrity "behind the smoke screen of Soviet themes". Finally he warned of "throwing out the baby with the bath" in the campaign against formalism, maintaining that experimentation is vital to the theatre.[52]

In his quest for a suitable Soviet play, Meyerhold next considered staging a new version of Mayakovsky's *The Bedbug*, to be called *A Fantastic Comedy*. Meyerhold worked with great enthusiasm on this updating of Mayakovsky's comedy. But as Gladkov points out, in the course of rehearsals "it became clear that a montage of basically different excerpts along with the verses could not yield a firm dramatic basis for the production, and the work was discontinued".

In the autumn of 1936, Meyerhold, accompanied by Zinaida Raikh and her daughter, Tatyana Esenina, made his last trip to France. While in Paris, Meyerhold talked again with Picasso about the painter's designing the production of *Hamlet* he had long dreamed of staging. On this trip, Meyerhold also visited Czechoslovakia where he met Emil Burian, head of Prague's D Theatre and a longtime admirer of the Russian director. In addition he saw several productions at the theatre, including Beaumarchais' *The Barber of Seville*.

Already disturbed by the Moscow purge trials that had begun in August 1936, and the growing criticism of Meyerhold in the Soviet press, Burian now heard at first hand of the director's difficulties. Following Meyerhold's departure, Burian actively began defending him and drawing up petitions on his behalf to the point where he was accused of hysteria by local Communist critics. In Moscow, such support could only further infuriate Meyerhold's enemies.[53]

In an effort to quiet his critics, at the beginning of 1937, Meyerhold attempted to stage a realistic production of Lidiya Seifullina's *Natasha*. But its everyday picture of rural life, painfully alien to his aesthetic vocabulary, only brought new charges against the director as incapable of staging a realistic play. By mutual consent of the Committee for Arts Affairs and the artistic council of Meyerhold's theatre, the production was withdrawn and never shown to the public.

Finally, Meyerhold turned to an adaptation by Evgeny Gabrilovich of Nikolai Ostrovsky's largely autobiographical novel *How the Steel was Tempered*, entitled *One Day*. The writer, suffering from war wounds and grave illnesses and bedridden and nearly blind since 1928, had overcome virtually insurmountable odds to complete his novel in 1934. Following the decision by the Party a year later to use it as a tool for the political education of Soviet youth, the novel's protagonist, Pavel Korchagin, soon became a national hero.

Scenic design by Fyodor Antonov for the production of *Natasha* (1937).

This time remaining true to himself, Meyerhold succeeded in creating a powerful production, especially in his direction of Evgeny Samoilov as Pavel Korchagin delivering his final monologue directly to the audience. The production never went further than a general rehearsal. In addition to several members of Ostrovsky's family, among those present at this performance were film directors Aleksandr Dovzhenko, who immediately offered Samilov the title role in his new film, *Shchors*, and Sergei Eisenstein, who was stunned by Samoilov's performance: "I have just seen on the stage a real revolutionary outburst and a true revolutionary!"[54] But Platon Kerzhentsev, who attended the general rehearsal and left without saying a word to anyone, felt otherwise.

Planned for the twentieth anniversary of the October Revolution, the production's deeply tragic tone could hardly have been less appropriate. It was banned without being shown to the public, leaving the Meyerhold Theatre the only one of the 700 professional Soviet theatres without a production to celebrate this important holiday.

On December 17, 1937, an article entitled "An Alien Theatre" appeared in *Pravda*.[55] Seven years earlier, Kerzhentsev, the author of the article, had defended Meyerhold as the director who had "delivered the heaviest blow to the old theatre and was *the first one* to find the way to show on the stage our revolution and our epoch in general".[56] Now, as

Sketch by Stewart Cheney of the death of Sema (Lev Sverdlin), a young member of the Komsomol, from the production of *One Life* (1937). Of this scene, Mr. Cheney wrote that it was "certainly the finest conception of a death scene on any stage. Using orchestral music as a necessary accompaniment, Meyerhold has, with his miraculous talent, caught the essence of that moment when consciousness leaves the body, as never before conceived in a theatre" (*The New York Times*, January 27, 1938).

head of the Committee for Arts Affairs, Kerzhentsev would deliver a similar blow to Meyerhold by attacking him for having consistently "shunned real life" throughout his entire career as a director. There could be only one conclusion, Kerzhentsev maintained, after cataloging the shortcomings of Meyerhold's productions in the Soviet period:

> It has become absolutely clear that Meyerhold cannot (and apparently will not) comprehend Soviet reality or depict the problems which concern every Soviet citizen. Do Soviet art and the Soviet public really need such a theatre?[57]

On December 22, 23, and 25, at meetings of the theatre company, Meyerhold urged those present to take seriously the criticisms of the Committee for Arts Affairs. But it was already too late. "That was something terrible, the way all the actors criticized Meyerhold", Samoilov recalled. "As one of the young members of the company, all I could do was sit there silently and listen. How they treated him, though, how they

Meyerhold at the construction site of his new theatre (1937).
Although the foundation had already been laid by November
1933, little progress was made on the construction of the theatre
after that.

rejected him, it's shameful to remember... but then, everyone was afraid."[58]

On January 7, 1938, the Committee passed a resolution liquidating Meyerhold's Theatre as "alien to Soviet art".[59] "Meyerholditis Has No Place in Soviet Art", a follow-up article in *Soviet Art* headlined in endorsing the liquidation of the theatre as "expressing the will of the Soviet theatre-goer". In reviewing Meyerhold's career, the unsigned article maintained that while "proclaiming himself an enemy of empty bourgeois aesthetics, in actuality he had established his system on those very same bourgeois aesthetics, merely masking them with flashy, pseudo-revolutionary phraseology".[60] An unsigned editorial in *Art and Life* put it even more bluntly: "The failure of the Meyerhold Theatre is the failure of alien, *anti-narodny* [anti-people's] art".[61]

On Sunday, January 8, 1938, the Meyerhold Theatre gave its final performance, a matinee of *The Inspector General*.[62] The resolution liquidating the Meyerhold Theatre noted that "the question of the possibility of further work by Vs. Meyerhold in the theatre would be considered separately".[63] Shortly after the theatre's closing Meyerhold and Zinaida Raikh were offered positions at the regional Lensoviet Theatre. Zinaida Nikolaevna, who was in a state of near collapse, turned down the offer. But Meyerhold did not hesitate for a moment. Any theatre at all would be better than none. According to Gladkov there were also some vague offers from Leningrad.[64] But before Meyerhold could act on any of them, one morning a few weeks later he received a telephone call from Stanislavsky inviting him to come to his home on Leontyev Lane. The result of their many hours of conversation at this meeting and others over the next few weeks was an invitation for Meyerhold to work with him at his Opera-Drama Studio.[65]

Stanislavsky and Meyerhold at a rehearsal at the Opera-Drama Studio (1938).

Stanislavsky had already wanted to invite Meyerhold to direct at the Moscow Art Theatre earlier in the thirties, but at that time Nemirovich-Danchenko vetoed the idea.[66] Nemirovich-Danchenko and Meyerhold were barely on speaking terms. It was clear that as long as Nemirovich-Danchenko was alive Meyerhold would never be allowed to work at the MXAT. Now that he had his own studio separate from the Art Theatre, Stanislavsky could at last realize his desire to work again with Meyerhold as they had back in 1905 at the Theatre-Studio on Povarskaya Street. Even so, Stanislavsky went about it very quietly. Toward the end of 1936 Stanislavsky and Meyerhold began meeting regularly to discuss "various matters connected with the theatre".[67]

When Stanislavsky spoke of inviting Meyerhold to direct at his Opera Theatre, his sister, Zinaida Sokolova, one of the directors and teachers there, dismissed the notion as "one of Kostya's whims", and another member of the Theatre objected, "Meyerhold is alien for us, he's hostile to our traditions". But Stanislavsky simply answered, "We need Meyerhold". He was also forced to overcome the opposition of Kerzhentsev and the Committee for Arts Affairs, stating that he would take full responsibility for the decision, and they too humored the old man's "whim".[68]

At first Stanislavsky was forced to compromise by bringing Meyerhold into his Opera-Drama Studio as a teacher. Then in May 1938 an announcement appeared stating that Meyerhold had been appointed a director at the Stanislavsky Opera Theatre.[69] During the weeks remaining before Stanislavsky's death, Meyerhold provided the firm hand that the dying Stanislavsky needed to conduct the rehearsals of *Rigoletto* at the Opera Theatre. They also met frequently to discuss plans to stage Mozart's opera *Don Giovanni*. As Jean Benedetti notes in his biography of Stanislavsky, "There was a creative excitement in their talk which Stanislavsky had not experienced for many years".[70] Stanislavsky now saw Meyerhold as the only one who could take his place. One of his final instructions to the Opera Theatre's production manager, Yuri Bakhrushin, was, "Look after Meyerhold, he is my sole heir in the theatre, not only in ours, but in the theatre as a whole".[71]

Following Stanislavsky's death in August 1938, Meyerhold continued on at the Stanislavsky Opera Theatre, completing the production of *Rigoletto*. In October 1938, he was named Chief Director. In a feverish burst of activity during the 1938–1939 season, in addition to *Rigoletto* (which premièred on March 14, 1939), Meyerhold also took part in the completion of several other productions at the Opera Theatre. Working with artist Pyotr Konchalovsky, he began preparations for a production of Mozart's *Don Giovanni*. But first, Meyerhold wanted to stage a Soviet opera, and he began working on Sergei Prokofiev's new opera, *Semyon Kotko*, based on Valentin Kataev's *I Am a Son of the Working People*.[72]

In addition, Meyerhold commuted to Leningrad to direct a revival of his production of Lermontov's *Masquerade* which he had originally staged at the Alexandrinsky Theatre on the eve of the Revolution. This, the third edition of the production, was shown to the public on December 29, 1938.

But as Aleksandr Fevralsky writes in his memoirs, on January 13, 1939, Meyerhold confided to him that working at the Stanislavsky Opera Theatre was not very satisfying, and that he was considering moving to the Pushkin Dramatic Theatre in Leningrad. It was now headed by his old friend and colleague from his years at the Alexandrinsky Theatre, Leonid Vivien, who had offered him the opportunity to direct other productions there, including Ostrovsky's *The Storm* and *Hamlet*. That spring Meyerhold also had offers from Moscow directors as well, among them Ilya Sudakov, head of the Maly Theatre, and Maksim Shtraukh who proposed staging a production at the Theatre of the Revolution. But Meyerhold turned them down for lack of time. He was busy fashioning a libretto from *A Hero of Our Time* for a Shostakovich opera planned to mark the 125th anniversary of Lermontov's birth. (The opera was never completed.)[73]

Time was running out for Meyerhold when in May 1939 he was approached by Nikolai Sery, a star athlete from the Lesgaft State Institute of Physical Education in Leningrad, about directing the Leningrad contribution to the All-Union Parade of Gymnasts held each July in Red Square. This event was one of the major festivals of the year; for it each of the Republics and the major cities prepared its own program consisting of a parade, exercises on equipment, free movements, military exercises, and the apotheosis – dancing by the entire ensemble – followed by a concluding parade.[74]

Sery, who had already been working on Leningrad's contribution to the festival for three years, decided to invite a theatre director to work with him on the program in order to learn how to make the performance more theatrical. "I first approached another director by the name of Aleksandrov, but he turned me down. I then decided to ask Meyerhold. He so readily accepted my invitation when I went to see him at his apartment that I was really very surprised". He added, "The one thing Meyerhold asked was that we use his choice of composers. Before that I had been using [Issak] Dunaevsky, but Meyerhold wanted Prokofiev, and I agreed".[75]

Sery recalls that he met with Meyerhold several times at the apartment on Bryusov Lane. Meyerhold also went to see him at his apartment before going up to Leningrad to begin rehearsals. But before leaving for Leningrad, Meyerhold, as one of the major Soviet directors and a member of the Department of Directing at VTO (All-Russia Theatre Society), was scheduled to take part in the First All-Union Conference of Theatre Directors, to be held June 13 through June 20 in the auditorium at the Central House of Actors on Gorky Street.

Chairing the conference was Andrei Vyshinsky. Already famous as Stalin's Prosecutor-General, he was now making his debut as the new Deputy Chairman of the Soviet People's Commissariat. In his opening speech entitled "The Objectives of the Soviet Theatre", Vyshinsky called on all artists of the theatre to carry on the struggle to eradicate all remains of the old bourgeois consciousness.[76] Reminding his audience what a "powerful weapon" the theatre is, he urged them to fight against the last remnants of formalism and naturalism "hindering the search for new, rich, clear, brilliant forms of new, socialist art".[77]

Vyshinsky's opening remarks were followed by five days of speeches by the delegates, among them the leading figures in the Soviet theatre: Solomon Mikhoels, Nikolai Akimov, Sergei Radlov, Aleksei D. Popov, and Serafima Birman. Even at a distance of more than fifty years it is a sad experience to read the groveling praise accorded that "great

Meyerhold at the First All-Union Conference of Theatre Directors held in the auditorium at the Central House of Actors on Gorky Street in June 1939.

master of human happiness, the inspirer of the artistic growth of Soviet artists – our own beloved Comrade STALIN!" to whom the conference was dedicated.[78] Even the "wise and magical" Mikhoels, who spoke several times, could not refrain from proclaiming, "The only thing that can enlighten and renew art, the only thing that can inspire genuine enthusiasm in the genuine desire to ... turn art into a weapon in the struggle for the happiness of man ... is what the Party and Comrade Stalin teach us".[79]

On June 15, the third day of the conference, a weary-looking gray-haired man rose from a chair in the auditorium. The delegates burst into wild applause as Meyerhold approached the podium and awkwardly stood waiting for the applause to die down.

"Comrades", Meyerhold began, "we are gathered here in order that the theatre art of our country, appreciated by our people, by our government, our party, an art of the highest level – we are gathered here in order to make it, that art, an art worthy of the mighty Stalinist epoch.

"We are gathered here, comrades, in order to reveal the fundamental mistakes of the formalists and the naturalists, and to say over and over again to the people, the government and the party that we will not in the future repeat these mistakes. Life has taught us to work in the conditions of a constant analysis of our mistakes, and Comrade STALIN has given us the wisest instructions: learn to catch your mistakes, learn to reveal their roots, learn to show that you were in error, learn never to repeat your mistakes. Our leader, our teacher, the friend of workers of the entire world serves as a model to us of the greatest caution in relation to all and any mistakes on our remarkable path leading to the greatest happiness of mankind..."[80]

If anyone expected the once proud Meyerhold to deliver the kind of speech Juri Jelagin describes in his book on Meyerhold, they were doomed to disappointment.[81] The defiant words Jelagin cites from the notes he claims to have made at the conference simply are not there. Acknowledging that he as well as other artists had made mistakes, Meyerhold went on to express his appreciation that "We – I, Shostakovich, and Sergei Eisenstein – that all of us have been given the full possibility to continue our work, and only through our work to correct our mistakes. Comrades, tell me, where, in what other country on the globe, would such a phenomenon be possible".

Meyerhold next asked that "the applause, so stormy, which had filled the auditorium on the first and second day at each mention of my name – I ask you to say together with me that this, your applause was directed not at me, but at our government, our party, and above all at the one who inspires artists to great deeds in our construction, to great deeds in creating the first Communist society, at the creator of that constitution which could create the conditions for us who have made mistakes to correct them through hard work".

In the long speech that followed Meyerhold went into detail about the mistakes he had made, expressing the hope that those in the auditorium would never repeat them. Once hailed as the "Father of Constructivism", Meyerhold now acknowledged that while his "laboratory experiments" had their usefulness in liberating the actor, they should not have been "foisted" on audiences. He further admitted that in being carried away by the classics he had ignored Soviet plays and as a result many playwrights were not given a helping hand. Meyerhold also confessed that "the experimentation I did with *The Forest* and *The Inspector General* should not have been shown to the public but only to a small circle of actors, directors, and so forth". Finally, Meyerhold acknowledged that, "As sad as it is for me personally to have lost my theatre, I must consider that the order by the Central Committee and our government to close this theatre was right".

In his concluding remarks Meyerhold spoke of the need for a "heroic theatre" of the kind that "the government, the party, and the people are awaiting". He pointed out, "We often talk about the creation of a heroic theatre ... but why drag onto the stage some Hippolytuses, Oedipuses, Antigones, when heroes are walking among us. We even have a title, 'Hero of the Soviet Union'. We must, comrades, urge dramatists to write these kinds of plays".

Looking into the future, Meyerhold asserted:
We, living in the Country of Soviets, we, living in the magnificent Stalinist epoch, can with certainty say that in the Union of Soviet Socialist Republics, with the grandiose third Stalinist Five-Year Plan, art begins to become what in our epoch could be called the epoch of a new Renaissance... In educating us, Comrade STALIN, together with our party, wants to make people in the arts worthy so that their names go down in history together with the names of the leading builders of Communist society.

Meyerhold returned home after his speech feeling very depressed. He was afraid Vyshinsky would think that Meyerhold himself had organized the wild applause that had greeted the director when he approached the podium. Other directors, including Popov and Mikhoels, had also spoken warmly of Meyerhold in their speeches, Popov noting that "they were indebted to him for everything new in the theatre".

That night Meyerhold left by train for Leningrad where he spent the next several days working with Nikolai Sery and his former teacher of Biomechanics, Zosima Zlobin, on staging the Leningrad sports spectacle whose theme was "Athletes are the mighty reserve of the Red Army". According to Sery, "Meyerhold's main concern was somehow to wake up the audience, the Politburo members and all the honored guests who would have already been watching for several hours. One of his ideas, and it proved quite an innovation, was to have the sports performers come into Red Square from both sides and swoop up toward the reviewing stand rather than simply passing by in the manner of a traditional parade".[82] This presentation, Meyerhold's final work as a director, was shown on Red Square on July 18, 1939, while Meyerhold was in Butyrka Prison just a few kilometers away.[83]

Meyerhold spent the evening of June 19 at the apartment of his friends, Erast Garin and his wife Khesya Lokshina, along with their mutual friend, Elena Tyapkina, also a former member of the Meyerhold Theatre. About seven the next morning Meyerhold left for his own apartment on Karpov Embankment where members of the NKVD were waiting to arrest him. On June 22, Meyerhold was returned by night train to Moscow where he was initially incarcerated in Lubyanka Prison before being moved to Butyrka Prison.[84]

While Zinaida Raikh had been in a terrible state after the closing of the theatre, according to Maria Valentei, she was in general quite

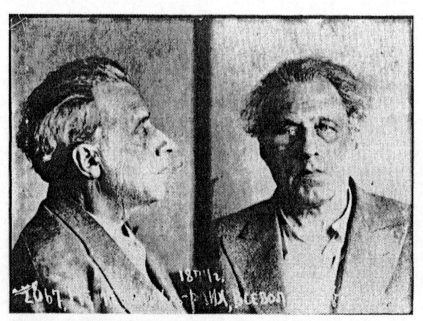

Photographs taken of Vsevolod Emilevich Meyerhold-Raikh for NKVD dossier No. 537, June 1939.

restrained following Meyerhold's arrest. "The one thing I regret", she told Meyerhold's granddaughter, "is my foolishness in writing a letter to Stalin". As Maria Valentei recalls, in the letter, apparently written after Meyerhold decided not to seek Stalin's help, and without his knowledge, Meyerhold's wife had asked, "Why, when actors don't interfere in politics about which they know nothing, do politicians interfere in theatre about which they know nothing". She finished the letter by pleading, "Come, help him".[85]

Three weeks after Meyerhold's arrest, on the night of July 14, Meyerhold's wife, Zinaida Raikh, alone with a servant in the apartment on Bryusov Lane was brutally murdered, apparently on the orders of NKVD chief Lavrenty Beria, who subsequently installed his twenty-six-year-old mistress and chauffeur in the two Meyerhold apartments.[86] After seven months of grueling interrogation and torture, Meyerhold, accused of being a Trotskyist since 1923 as well as a British and Japanese spy, confessed.[87]

Meyerhold once jokingly told Gladkov that February was his fatal month. He had been born in February, his father had died in February 1892, and that same February he had made his stage debut. Meyerhold left Moscow University in February 1896. Six years later, also in February, he left the Moscow Art Theatre. It was in February 1906, that Komissarzhevskaya invited him to work in her theatre. Gladkov recalls that Meyerhold made this observation in January 1938, right after the closing of his theatre. Noting the date, Meyerhold commented to him that this time he hadn't lasted until February. "Either that", he said, "or Fortune in her old age has become careless".[88] Unfortunately, Meyerhold was mistaken. On February 1, 1940, he was sentenced to death and the next day he was shot in the cellars of the Military Collegium. Following cremation, his ashes were unceremoniously dumped together with those of thousands of other victims in an unmarked grave, a pit five meters deep behind the crematorium at Donskoi Cemetery.[89]

Meyerhold's name was immediately removed from his theatre and opera productions, and all traces of his four decades of work in the Russian theatre were effaced. Until his rehabilitation in 1955, it was as though Meyerhold, in Lee Strasberg's words, "the greatest director in the history of the theatre",[90] had never existed.

Tombstone installed in 1991 marking Common Grave No. 1, Donskoi Monastery. On February 1, 1940, Meyerhold was sentenced to death and the next day he was shot in the cellars of the Military Collegium. Following cremation, his ashes were unceremoniously dumped together with those of thousands of other victims in an unmarked grave, a pit five meters deep behind the crematorium at Donskoi Cemetery.

Notes

1. Lee Strasberg, "Russian Notebook", *The Drama Review*, 17, No. 1 (March 1973), p. 108.

2. The account of Meyerhold's pre-Revolutionary years is based on the following sources: Vsevolod Meierkhol'd, "Biograficheskie dannie" (1921) in Meierkhol'd, V.E. *V.E. Meierkhol'd: stat'i, pis'ma, rechi, besedy*, 2 vols., Ed. Aleksandr V. Fevralsky (Moscow: Iskusstvo, 1968), Vol. 1, pp. 308–315; Nikolai Volkov, *Meierkhol'd* (Moscow: Zrelishcha, 1923); Nikolai Volkov, *Meierkhol'd*, 2 vols. (Moscow–Leningrad: Academia, 1929); Aleksandr Gladkov, *Gody ucheniya Vsevoloda Meierkhol'da* (Saratov: Privolzhskoe knizhnoe izdatelstvo, 1979); Konstantin Rudnitsky, *Meierkhol'd* (Moscow: Iskusstvo, 1981); V. Sadchikov, "Meierkhol'd v Penze", *Teatr*, No. 5 (1972), pp. 124–133.

3. Volkov, Vol. 1, p. 36.

4. Gérard Abensour, "Meyerhold à Paris", in *Cahiers du Monde Russe et Soviétique*, 5, No. 1 (April–June, 1964), pp. 5–21.

5. The first issue of *Love for Three Oranges* (*Lyubov' k trem apel'sinam*) was published in February 1914. In all, nine issues came out, the last of them in 1916.

6. "Polozhenie o Teatral'nom Otdele Narodnogo Komissariata po Prosveshcheniyu, 19 September 1918, No. 203 (467)" published in *Vremennik Teatral'nogo Otdela Narodnogo Komissariata po Prosveshcheniyu*, Vyp. 1, Petersburg-Moscow, November (1918), pp. 24–29. See also, *Leonid Sergeevich Viv'en: Akter. Rezhisser. Pedagog: Sbornik*, comp. V. V. Ivanova (Leningrad: Iskusstvo, 1988), pp. 169–175.

7. *Pravda*, (November 10, 1920), p. 2, quoted in Edward Braun, *The Theatre of Meyerhold* (New York: Drama Book Specialists, 1979), p. 157.

8. For a reconstruction of the production by Alma H. Law, see "Meyerhold's *The Magnanimous Cuckold*, *The Drama Review*, 26, No. 1 (Spring, 1982), pp. 61–86.

9. For a detailed discussion of Meyerhold's Biomechanics see, Alma Law and Mel Gordon, *Meyerhold, Eisenstein, Biomechanics: Actor Training in Revolutionary Russia* (Jefferson, N.C.: McFarland & Company, 1996).

10. For a reconstruction of the production by Alma H. Law, see "The Death of Tarelkin: A Constructivist Vision of Tsarist Russia", *Russian History*, 8, Parts 1–2 (1981), pp. 145–198.

11. Edward Braun, *Meyerhold on Theatre* (New York: Hill and Wang, 1969), p. 195.

12. Quoted in Pavel Markov, *Pravda Theatra* (Moscow: Iskusstvo, 1965), p. 43.

13. Igor' Ilinsky, *Sam o sebe* (Moscow: VTO, 1961), p. 200.

14. Maya Turovskaya, *Babanova. Legenda i biografiya* (Moscow: Iskusstvo, 1981), p. 106.

15. RGALI (Russian State Archive of Literature and Art), 998-1-393. The article as published omits this paragraph: "Kak Meierkhol'd stavit *Gore umu*", *Komsomol'skaya pravda* (March 2, 1928), p. 4.

16. N. D. Volkov, "*Gore umu* v teatre imeni Vs. Meierkhol'da", *Krasnaya panorama*, No. 15, 1928.

17. For a description of Meyerhold's production, see Alma H. Law, "Meyerhold's *Woe to Wit* (1928)", *The Drama Review*, 18, No. 3 (September, 1974), pp. 89–107.

18. Smyshlyaev Diary, entry for March 22, 1928. Unpublished, private archive.

19. A. Orlinsky, "Sud'ba Teatra Meierkhol'da v ego rukakh", *Sovremennyi teatr*, No. 41 (October 9, 1928), pp. 637–638.

20. V. M., "Vs. Meierkhol'd vernulsya", *Novyi zritel'*, No. 50 (December 9, 1928), p. 10.

21. "Vokrug p'esy *Khochu rebenka*", *Sovremennyi teatr*, No. 51 (December 18, 1928) p. 827.

22. V. E. Meierkhol'd, *Perepiska*. 1896–1929, Moscow: Iskusstvo, 1976, p. 283.

23. Particularly vicious were reviews by RAPP critic, Vladimir Yermilov (*Pravda*, March 9, 1930) accusing Mayakovsky of creating in the hero, Pobedenosikov, a "degenerate Party man", and Nadezhda Goncharova (*Rabochaya gazeta*, March 21, 1930) who called it "A tedious, confused show, which can be of interest only to a small group of literary gourmets".

24. For an account by actress Elena Tyapkina of this closed rehearsal, see Alma Law, "Pages from the Past", *Soviet and East European Drama, Theatre, and Film*, 8, No. 2–3 (December 1988), pp. 17–18.

25. For a discussion of the conflict between Meyerhold and Selvinsky, see K. Rudnitsky, *Meyerhold*, pp. 379–382.

26. "Meyerhold's Theatre", *Bravo*, No. 2, (February 6, 1929). The five productions GosTIM took abroad included: *The Inspector General, The Forest, Roar China!, The Magnanimous Cuckold,* and *The Second Army Commander. The Second Army Commander* was apparently not performed in Berlin, and of the other four, only two, *The Inspector General* and *The Forest* went on to Paris.

27. For a detailed account of the Meyerhold Theatre tour to Germany, see V. Kolyazin, "Meierkhol'd i Gropius", *Teatr*, No. 8, (August 1992), pp. 121–129. The German tour included Berlin, Breslau, Düsseldorf, Cologne, Stuttgart, Mannheim, Frankfurt-am-Main, and Darmstadt.

28. Quoted in Gérard Abensour, "La tournée du Théâtre Meyerhold à Paris en 1930", *Cahiers du Monde russe et soviétique*, **17**, No. 2–3 (April–September 1976), p. 225.

29. Kolyazin, 128.

30. Nikolai Bogolyubov, "Revolyutsionnaya deistvitel'nost'", *Vstrechi s Meierhkhol'dom* (Moscow: VTO, 1967), p. 445.

31. Letter to V. V. Vishnevsky, February 17, 1931 in *Perepiska*, p. 315.

32. In conversation with the author, March 3, 1975; N. N. Chushkin, *Gamlet-Kachalov*, (Moscow: Iskusstvo, 1966), pp. 257–259.

33. *O zadachakh RAPP na teatral'nom fronte* (Leningrad: GIKhL, 1932), p. 36.

34. Reported in: Mikhail Gliyarov, "Put' bol'shevika-khudozhnika", *Rabis*, No. 11 (1933), pp. 34–35. See also: Aleksandr Matskin, "Vremya ukhoda", *Teatr*, No. 1, 1990, pp. 34–35; and "Meierkhol'd na chistke", *Sovetskoe iskusstvo*, November 2, 1933, p. 3.

35. *Rabis*, No. 11 (1933), p. 35.

36. Matskin, "Vremya ukhoda", p. 35.

37. Aleksandr Matskin, "Vstuplenie", *Izvestiya* (March 27, 1933).

38. I. Bachelis, "Vstuplenie v Teatre imeni Meierkhol'da, *Komsomol'skaya Pravda* (March 11, 1933).

39. Yu. Yuzovsky, "Avtora, avtora! *Vstuplenie* v teatre Meierkhol'da", *Rabis*, No. 3 (March 1933), p. 33.

40. Leonid Varpakhovsky, "Zametki proshlykh let", *Vstrechi s proshlym*, p. 475.

41. Pavel Markov, "Pis'mo on Meierkhol'de", *Theatre i dramaturgiya*, No. 2 (February 1934), p. 19.

42. Matskin, "Vremya ukhoda", p. 33.

43. Maria Valentei, in conversation with the author, January 11, 1988.

44. For Shostakovich's reaction to these attacks, see Solomon Volkov, *Testimony. The Memoirs of Dmitri Shostakovich* (New York: 1979), pp. 113–115.

45. *Teatr i dramaturgiia*, No. 3 (March 1936), p. 121.

46. Reprinted in *Teatr i dramaturgiya*, No. 3 (March 1936), inside cover.

47. Sergei Ignatov, "Za sovetskuyu klassiku v teatre", *Teatr i dramaturgiia*, No. 4 (April 1936), p. 213.

48. "Meierkhol'd protiv meierkhol'dovshchiny", (March 14, 1936), *Stat'i*, vol. 2, p. 331.

49. *Ibid.*, pp. 342–344.

50. "Vystuplenie na sobranii teatral'nykh rabotnikov Moskvy", March 26, 1936, in *Stat'i*, vol. 2, pp. 348–358. For a translation of Meyerhold's speech, see Braun, *Meyerhold on Theatre*, pp. 289–298.

51. *Ibid.*, p. 354.

52. *Ibid.*, p. 356

53. Jarka M. Burian, "E. F. Burian: D34–D41", *The Drama Review*, **20**, No. 4 (December, 1976), p. 111.

54. Evgeny Samoilov in conversation, with the author October 25, 1991.

55. Platon Kerzhentsev, "Chuzhoi teatr", *Pravda* (December 17, 1937), p. 4; reprinted in *Rabochii i teatr*, No. 12 (1937), pp. 10–11.

56. Platon Kerzhentsev, "O teatre nashikh dnei", *Molodaya gvardiya*, No. 6 (1929).

57. Kerzhentsev, "Chuzhoi teatr".

58. Samoilov, October 25, 1991.

59. *Pravda* (January 8, 1938), p. 2. The resolution was also published in *Teatr*, No. 1 (January 1938), p. 1.

60. "Meierkhol'dovshchine ne mesto v sovetskom iskusstve", *Sovetskoe iskusstvo* (January 10, 1938), p. 1.

61. "Krushenie antinarodnogo iskusstva", *Iskusstvo i zhizn'* No. 1 (January 1938), p. 16.

62. Mikhail Sadovsky, "Teatral'nyi charodei", in *Vstrechi*, pp. 526–528. The theatre's final performance was to have been *The Lady of the Camellias* on Saturday evening, January 7, but since the

theatre had not yet received the official order on its closing, it went ahead and scheduled the Sunday matinee.

63. *Pravda* (January 8, 1938), p. 2.

64. Aleksandr Gladkov, *Meierkhol'd*, vol. 2 (Moscow: RSFSR/STD, 1990), p. 232.

65. *Ibid.*, p. 233. See also the chapter on "The Method of Physical Action" in Jean Benedetti, *Stanislavsky: An Introduction* (London: Methuen, 1982), pp. 315–323.

66. Boris Alpers, "Sud'ba teatral'nykh techenii", *Teatr*, No. 5 (May, 1967), p. 14.

67. Benedetti, p. 318.

68. Rudnitsky, *Meierkhol'd*, p. 421.

69. *Ibid.*, p. 421.

70. Benedetti, p. 321.

71. Yury Bakhrushin, "Stanislavskii i Meierkhol'd", *Vstrechi*, p. 589.

72. For an account of Meyerhold's work with Sergei Prokofiev on *Semyon Kotko*, see Harlow Robinson, *Sergei Prokofiev*, New York: Viking, 1987, pp. 358 ff. Meyerhold was arrested only a week before Prokofiev finished the piano score for the opera. It was ultimately staged by Serafima Birman.

73. Aleksandr Fevral'skii, *Zapiski rovesnika veka* (Moscow: Sovetskii pisatel', 1976), p. 300. See also, *Viv'en*, pp. 34–35.

74. Fevral'sky, p. 300.

75. Sery's account of his meetings with Meyerhold is based on the author's interview with him, May 24, 1991.

76. *Rezhisser v sovetskom teatre. Materialy pervoi vsesoyuznoi rezhisserskoi konferentsii*, ed. A. D. Solodovnikov, Moscow-Leningrad: Iskusstvo, 1940, pp. 16–22. See also, Arkady Vaksberg, *Stalin's Prosecutor. The life of Andrei Vyshinsky*, trans. Jan Butler, (New York: Grove Weidenfeld, 1991), pp. 177–181.

77. *Rezhisser v sovetskom teatre*, p. 21.

78. *Ibid.*, p. 7.

79. *Ibid.*, p. 82.

80. Typescript of Meyerhold's speech, private archive. All citations are from it. An edited version of the speech omitting this and subsequent excepts quoted here was published in *Teatr*, No. 2 (1974), pp. 39–44. Of other writers who have quoted from Meyerhold's speech, only Alexander Kaun seems to have seen the original text (Alexander Kaun, *Soviet Poets and Poetry*, Berkeley: University of California Press, 1943, p. 96.)

81. Juri Jelagin, *Dark Genius (Vsevolod Meyerhold)* [*Temnyi genii*], 2nd enl. ed. (London: Overseas Publication, 1982), pp. 406–410. As a Russian theatre historian recently quipped, "The only thing Jelagin got right in his book was the title".

82. Sery interview, May 24, 1991.

83. See *Sovetskoe iskusstvo*, July 18, 1939, p. 1; also Fevralsky, *Zapiski*, pp. 300–301. The program was also performed on July 6 at the Leningrad parade of gymnasts and on July 20 at Dynamo Stadium.

84. The details of Meyerhold's arrest were furnished to the author by Maria Valentei, October 24, 1991.

85. Coversation with Maria Valentei, May 20, 1990.

86. *Ibid.* When Meyerhold and Zinaida Raikh moved to Bryusov Lane in 1928, they purchased two apartments which were then joined to form a single apartment. After Zinaida Raikh's murder, they were again divided into two apartments. Beria's mistress continued to occupy the one apartment until she was finally forced to vacate in 1992 in order to make it available for the Meyerhold Museum.

87. For Meyerhold's own description of his interrogation see, "Petition". Vsevolod Meyerhold, tr. Marjorie Hoover, in *Soviet and East European Performance: Drama, Theatre, Film*, 9, No. 1 (1989), pp. 19–22.

88. In conversation with the author, February 4, 1976.

89. Alma Law, "Meyerhold's Grave Is Located", *Soviet and East European Performance*, 11, No. 3 (Winter 1991), pp. 35–39.

90. Lee Strasberg, unpublished lecture notes, January 23, 1964.

WITH MEYERHOLD

Moscow, the mid-1920s.

On Triumphal Square, next to the casino – the embodiment of NEP – in a spacious, inhospitable, and unfinished building was THE THEATRE, the most surprising, inimitable, impossible, unique theatre in the whole world.

At the entrance, instead of playbills there are laconic posters. The names of the productions sound like a password and a response: *GIVE US EUROPE!, ROAR CHINA!* Even the well-worn *Woe from Wit*, as familiar as the back of the sofa at home, or a scratched-up school desk, sounds decisive and imperative here, inarguably persuasive – *WOE TO WIT*. The everyday *The Forest* and *The Inspector General* sound and look quite different alongside the precisely defined *THE WARRANT* and *BUBUS THE TEACHER*. Here they are already *THE FOREST* and *THE INSPECTOR GENERAL*. One wants to shout these words in the bronze basso of Mayakovsky with his emphasized, rounded "eh's" and rolled "r's"...

I well remember the sensation of a kind of odd unity between these playbill-poster phonetics together with the wide, empty corridors of GosTIM and the open scenic constructions: with those stairs, bridges, moving discs, wheels, mills. There is no curtain. You enter the auditorium and suddenly see this against a background of unplastered brick wall. All this excited the theatrical youth of my generation just as our fathers had been excited by the sweetish smell of the gas lamps in the old Maly Theatre celebrated by the writers of memoirs. In all this, there was the new aesthetics of the time, the oxygen and ozone of the breath of revolution, the rhythm of the beautiful twenties, the years of our youth, of the youth of our generation.

The first production I saw at GosTIM was *The Forest*.

I wasn't surprised. I accepted everything with delighted trust.

I don't know whether I expected this or even whether I consciously expected anything. But after the performance it seemed to me that this was exactly what I had expected.

The auditorium was not full. In general, I can hardly recall a full house at GosTIM in the former Zon theatre. And this also wasn't surprising. All the spectators seemed to be friends of the theatre, and

GosTIM, the former Zon Theatre on Triumphal Square in Moscow. In 1930 the Meyerhold Theatre vacated the building so that it could be torn down to make way for the construction of a new theatre.

there are never many real friends. Auntie Manyas and Uncle Petyas didn't go to this theatre. For them, it was a curiosity, like the verses of Mayakovsky printed in the newspaper with broken lines. It wasn't any use arguing with them: a brief smile of superiority, a chair pushed back noisily, a cap pulled off a coat hook – that sums it all up.

That evening, I saw Meyerhold for the first time.

He came out during the last act from a small door on the left, and standing on the little stairs, attentively watched the stage.

It would have been difficult not to recognize his short, lithe figure and his profile, so familiar from numerous caricatures. During those years he was sketched hardly less frequently than Poincaré or Chamberlain. I was sitting on the left side of the orchestra, and in the semi-darkness of the theatre I had a good look at the shock of gray hair, the huge nose, the firmly molded lips, the curve of the shoulders, and the head proudly thrown back. I was not the only one who recognized him. A whisper of recognition ran through the audience; I remember that he did not once look into the auditorium. Not one glance. Only at the stage. He watched so attentively that it was bewitching. And although one wanted very much to look at him, one wanted even more to look together with him. He disappeared through the little door several minutes before the end of the performance, just as noiselessly and mysteriously as he had appeared.

I was lucky. On that evening I saw him twice.

The audience called for him and he came out.

I remember that the first shout of "Mey-er-hold!" came from the upper tier. The balcony joined in with it. A group of young people rushed past me, pressing toward the stage. They were university or factory students, shaggy-haired or shaved head, with KIM badges on their jackets and belted blouses. Leaning down from the balcony, the young Chinese in horn-rimmed glasses applauded fiercely. From the door through which Meyerhold had just left, a group of youths in identical blue outfits of coarse cotton ran out. They were also applauding, but with a certain sense of superiority, like initiates. I guessed that these were students at GEKTEMAS (the Meyerhold State Experimental Theatrical Workshop), future actors and directors, those who proudly called themselves Meyerholdians, and others whose still unknown names would soon comprise the group of leading cadres in the Soviet theatre.

Meyerhold also came out on stage from the left. Quickly, leaning forward slightly, he moved toward the center of the stage. But he stopped before reaching it. He bowed swiftly and awkwardly. He applauded the actors. He bowed again. And then he went out just as quickly. The audience continued to call for him. The actors also applauded. But he didn't come out again.

The spotlights humming in the side boxes were turned off. The applause died away. Arguing loudly, the audience dispersed.

I was one of the last to leave, attentively studying all the playbills and posters in the lobby, like a future traveler who studies the unknown itineraries of marvelous journeys. A plan for visits to GosTIM in the near future was taking shape. I didn't want to go home. I remember the clear sensation that something new and significant had come into my life promising to overturn everything that I presumptuously considered my established tastes. It seemed incomprehensible: how could I have lived calmly and carelessly without knowing this?

A frosty Moscow night hangs over the square. A crowd throngs out of the Gorn movie theatre which is showing *The Mark of Zorro*, thrilled by the beauties of Mexico. Near the beer hall on the corner there's a drunken scene. Some woman runs diagonally across the square chased by a cursing man in a fur coat with a briefcase. Nearer to Tverskaya, cab drivers stand in a row, clapping their mittened hands to keep warm. The entrance to the Casino glows with lights. The B streetcar makes its last circle along the Garden Ring.

I walk past the fences and gates, past the houses with their incongruous little gardens which give their names to the endless chain of streets and stop in front of all the posters, unconsciously wishing to prolong the exalted mood with which I had left the theatre that night.

I was already at Uprising Square when a couple passed by me.

I recognized both of them at once. She had played Aksyusha this evening. And he – it was HE.

The famous shock of grey hair was jutting out from under a cap pulled low over his eyes, the famous Cyrano nose protruded from behind the raised collar.

He was firmly holding his companion by the arm. She was talking loudly and laughing. I heard how he cautioned her tenderly and firmly: "You must protect your throat, it's freezing"...

There were more voices and laughter behind me. A group of young people overtook first me, then the couple.

They were all rushing along, sliding on the ice, outracing each other, filling the night with their voices. Some were without hats, others coatless, in sweaters and jackets. Everything showed that they were athletic and didn't fear the cold. Besides, they were all about nineteen years old. I recognized them: it was those who had passionately called Meyerhold out from the side stairs on the left – the GEKTEMAS students, the latest enrollment of Meyerholdians, that proud tribe as yet unknown to me.

Passing by him and his companion, they shouted to him from the square, "Good night!"... and laughing, he shouted after them, "Good night!" They were already on the side of the square where Novinsky Boulevard begins.

My way didn't lie with theirs. In order to get home, I had to turn into Vorovskaya Street, deserted at that hour.

I was pierced by something like envy.

I walked on and thought about this fortunate group of young people – his students. What I wouldn't have given to be one of them!

Yesterday's boy from the provinces, a precocious youth, a "high school" student who often cut the evening shift of classes in order to get to the theatre; who only recently stood in line for hours in front of the Art Theatre for the weekly Saturday lottery of cheap tickets; and who called for Kachalov until hoarse after *At the Gate of the Kingdom,* was returning home tonight alone, excited, captivated, wounded, betraying in one evening my former theatrical loyalties, and sickened with passionate envy of his students, the lighting crew, the ushers, and the cloakroom attendants.

At some point soon after this came the première of *The Inspector General.*

I remember the lukewarm auditorium filled (this time to capacity) with theatrical first-nighters. They wondered at the real melon; they counted Raikh's costumes; they shrugged their shoulders at the strait-jacket on the mayor and the whistles of the policemen. It was a success, but with an aftertaste of scandal. During the intermissions, jokes about the classics turning over in their graves were coined, jokes that soon became stale. But I also remember Lunacharsky's intensely attentive face, the overwhelmed look in Andrei Bely's eyes, the silent Mikhail Chekhov, and the sharp remarks and critical guns which seemed to bounce off the corridor walls.

Between *The Forest*, the first production I saw at GosTIM, and the première of *The Inspector General*, I saw the theatre's entire repertory: *The Warrant, Bubus the Teacher, Give Us Europe!, Roar China!*, and of course, *The Magnanimous Cuckold*.

* * *

And somewhat later . . . What a time it was! In the daytime at Meyerhold's rehearsals, then almost at a run on some very important business: editorial offices, exhibitions, bookstores, reading rooms. In the evening, friends without whom it seemed impossible to survive even 24 hours. Or premières, or again to Meyerhold's Theatre. At night after the end of the performances, rehearsals in Khmelev's Studio, endless meetings with high-flown sentiments, walking home in strangely beautiful nighttime Moscow . . . When did I sleep? And did I sleep? I don't remember. When did I find the time to read? I don't remember that either. But I read a lot as usual: almost all of the poetry and novels being published then, history, philosophy.

How did I live? I don't remember that very well either. At GosTIM I received a miserable salary. I wrote and published some little articles about the theatre and movies, bibliographical notes. From time to time I received an honorarium. I dressed more than carelessly. But all the same, I hung around the second-hand bookstores, I looked for the latest publications, I subscribed to newspapers and magazines. An amazingly capacious, strained existence. I greedily gulped down all that life had to offer, and spent as much as possible.

We didn't feel Moscow to be some sort of force inimical to us. And there was nothing in it to conquer because it was being created before our eyes and with our participation. The NEP way of life in Moscow had almost run out. It would be difficult to guess what it would be like tomorrow. Various innovations glided over it (such as "a continuous work week"). The construction of the subway which was then beginning (the test shafts had already been dug) was not a sign of good city planning, but a poetic subject of the time. That's why poems and plays about it soon appeared.

Of course, that Moscow was much smaller than the present-day Moscow. It had no subway or trolleys; the bus lines were rather few, while the streetcars crept along slowly and at times were overtaken by the horse-drawn cabs that still remained. We didn't always have money even for a streetcar, and besides, we often had to return home after they had stopped running for the night. Because of all this, *that* Moscow, walked all over from end to end (wherever our crazy heads would take us), even now lives in my memory as a much larger city than present-day Moscow. "I crumple the versts of streets with the sweep of my steps" ... This was the most real image, completely devoid of any hyperbole.

It's not surprising that I often went about in torn boots. Could one have enough footwear for such distances? During my entire youth I spent three seasons of the year with wet feet, and "in society" I became accustomed to hiding the toes of my boots by complicated acrobatic turns (under an armchair or divan). It was not a case of poverty. I began making money early. But already then, the money went for books, for presents to girls, for whatever you like, but not for clothing and footwear. It would happen that for months I wouldn't have dinner, subsisting on irregular meals. And that was also not because of poverty, but because of a lack of organization and of a proper way of life.

But perhaps it was easier and even healthier to live like that. There was no drunkenness either. Of course we drank sometimes, but just *sometimes* and at that, I recall, we were more concerned with the literary and ritual aspects of drinking as an attribute of a *Bohemian life*. For the entire five-year period, from 1928 to 1933, I remember only a few visits to restaurants: two or three times the Prague; perhaps the Bear down in a cellar on old Tverskaya; a restaurant on the corner of Stoleshnikov and Dmitrovka; the Livorno on Rozhdestvensky, and that's all. It's true that beginning in 1931, the cellar of the Teaklub [the Theatre Club] (the former Circle) in Old Pimenovsky came into my life, but that was something else, and there was no drunkenness there either. Spending time in restaurants began for me in 1935. I was then already 23. It was a completely different period, different in atmosphere, colors, sounds.

* * *

In Moscow during the 1920s, literally everyone knew Meyerhold's name, even those who never went to his theatre. Only Mayakovsky's name could compete with his. Vsevolod Emilevich told how once, when in the first years of NEP a bureau of newspaper clippings was organized, he stopped in to subscribe. They turned him down. It would be too big a job because of the frequency with which his name appeared in newspapers and magazines. Even if that were only a joke, still it was undoubtedly close to the truth.

I first met Meyerhold face-to-face during the winter of 1930–1931. By that time I was in love with his productions and preferred GosTIM to all the other Moscow theatres. I had already become acquainted with several actors at GosTIM and from time to time I would go backstage to see them. In my imagination, V.E. already had the aura of a legend. For some reason I had the feeling that if he caught sight of me he would ask what I was doing there. And since I didn't have any particular business backstage, I was afraid he would get angry and throw me out of the theatre.

On one of those backstage visits, I did in fact run into him in the hallway of the old Zon Theatre between the door leading from the auditorium backstage and the office of the director. Catching sight of him, I pressed up against the wall. V.E. went by me, then glancing back, noticed me. He turned, stuck out his hand and said, "Hello there". Stunned, I shook his hand. Before I had a chance to say anything, he quickly looked at me and asked, "How are you?" I didn't manage to answer before he had already gone on. He probably mistook me for someone else. After that I was even more afraid to go backstage at GosTIM. It seemed to me that if he caught sight of me a second time, he would remember how he had mistaken me for someone else and would be even more angry at me.

* * *

I spent several years with Vsevolod Emilevich Meyerhold at the theatre bearing his name. V.E. had heard a speech of mine at one of the theatrical debates and had invited me to join him. Those were the years 1934 to 1937. During that period he worked on *The Lady of the Camellias*, *The Queen of Spades*, *33 Swoons*, the second variant of *Woe to Wit*, *Boris Godunov*, *One Life*, and other productions. For three years I saw him almost every day, and sometimes twice a day. There were days when we met in the morning and did not part until late at night. Before meeting Meyerhold, I had hungrily and passionately followed him from afar. After I left the theatre, we continued to see each other from time to time. Sometimes he called and invited me to drop in, but more often, I invited myself. Those were the last years of his life. I was twenty-two years old when I first met him. I was twenty-seven when I saw him for the last time.

The differences in our ages and positions didn't prevent us from talking about many things. On the contrary, it gave me the advantage of his always being himself with me. Meyerhold knew that I was writing down our talks. But he had been famous for so long that he couldn't be upset about being observed so closely. It seems to me that he even rather liked it.

There were minutes and hours of solitude when he looked for me. There were instances when he had someone telephoning all over town for me. And when I finally showed up, it would turn out that he didn't need me for anything special, but simply wanted me with him. I always understood this immediately – no need to ask. There were evenings (especially when he wasn't feeling well) when he was at home reading and wanted me to be there with him working on something of my own. I am telling all this in order to show the degree of his trust and friendliness for it gave me the right to ask him any question at all. Sometimes he answered me with a joke, but never with silence.

I had another advantage over others who were around him. There was almost nothing I needed from him in connection with our work relationship in the theatre. My first job at GosTIM was called "research assistant". Then I was named manager of the theatre's Scientific-Research Laboratory (NIL), I was literary manager, an instructor in the Technicum [former Meyerhold State Theatre School] bearing his name, literary secretary, and assistant director. But whatever the changes in my regular duties on the official register, my main occupation all those years was to follow after V.E. with a notebook and make notes, notes, and more notes... All of our work relationships were crystal clear, and if sometimes I also brought him some paper or other for his signature, or waited for some instructions or orders like all the others, he would sign the paper, or dictate to me with the barely concealed mockery of a fellow conspirator.

And often, waving aside some report that had been the reason for my coming in, he would take off his glasses, and leaning back in his chair would suddenly begin to talk about Pushkin's theatricality, or about the three-part structure of Spanish drama about which we had spoken the night before on the brief trip from the theatre to Bryusov Lane where he lived.

Once Meyerhold invited me to deliver a series of lectures at the Technicum about his career as a director and sent a stenographer to the lectures to take them down. Later, he read the transcriptions and made a number of corrections in them as if they were the proofs of a future book. It goes without saying that at the time I took this on with all the lack of seriousness of youth – I was hardly older than my listeners, but now I don't regret it. It was these lectures that gave me the opportunity to talk with him about many things having nothing to do with the current work of the theatre at that time – about his entire life, about Chekhov, Stanislavsky, Komissarzhevskaya, Blok, Mayakovsky, and others.

Of course, I didn't succeed in writing down everything I heard or happened to observe, but even what I did get into my diaries or the notebooks I hung on to, is a whole avalanche of material. Editing them would take months and years of assiduous labor. I have countless transcriptions of various speeches Meyerhold made, notes of rehearsals and talks with the cast, director's copies of plays belonging to him and which he had given me, as well as letters and notes handwritten by him. With the help of some of this material, I want to try to portray Meyerhold as I saw him in those final years of his remarkable life.

I make no pretense at creating a definitive portrait of Meyerhold's career, or at evaluating exhaustively his activities. This is only the story of a witness, but of a witness who was not indifferent...

* * *

What was it that united Mayakovsky and Meyerhold other than the views they held in common on the goals of the theatre? In spite of various complex circumstances in the literary and political struggle during the 1920s, the shadow of a disagreement never touched their relationship. In describing his friendship with Mayakovsky, Meyerhold himself emphasized that

Photograph of Meyerhold (seated, center) and Mayakovsky (standing behind Meyerhold) together with Shostakovich (at the piano) and the artist Aleksandr Rodchenko (far right) during preparations for the staging of *The Bedbug* (1929).

the main thing in their relationship was "politics". They were allies during the October days and in the days when the country went over to the Socialist offensive. I knew them separately, but saw them together only once – at one of the debates – and I remember well how tenderly Mayakovsky put his hand on Meyerhold's shoulder next to him in the presidium. When I think of them, this is how I always see them.

It was considered that they both belonged to the "Left Front of Art". But this didn't prevent Meyerhold and the left-frontists from sharply disagreeing on several issues. Mayakovsky didn't like *The Forest*, while his comrade-in-arms in the group, Sergei Tretyakov was ecstatic over it. Mayakovsky liked *The Inspector General*, while another member of the LEF group, Viktor Shklovsky, published an abusive article about the production. The young Selvinsky excelled at making up epigrams about Mayakovsky, some of them quite crude. But when Meyerhold almost simultaneously included in his theatre's repertory Selvinsky's first play and a new play by Mayakovsky [*The Bathhouse*], the latter, in his numerous speeches at various literary debates, didn't permit himself even a single attack against Selvinsky, although he did laugh it off with a joke when he was provoked into direct discussion. He understood that Meyerhold needed new authors, and with magnificent civility he refrained from public criticism of Selvinsky's play. I heard his speech at a debate on *The Inspector General*. He said that he liked many things in the production, and then immediately added that he didn't much like this or that thing. Meyerhold didn't agree with him, but after the debate ended, they laughed and talked to each other amicably. There were few who could speak this way with Meyerhold, and few to whom he would listen like that.

They both rarely mentioned the word "creativity", preferring to it the more modest substitutes: "craft", "work", "mastery". However, Meyerhold considered even this last word too grand. In the workshop at his theatre, he forbade calling the subject of study "the actor as a master craftsman". He considered that only a few men in the country had the right to be called "masters". And when some Mr. So-and-so or his ilk taught "Mastery", it was really braggadocio. The point, of course, wasn't a matter of semantics, but of the philosophy of art. "I know that Venus is the work of hands, as a craftsman – I know craft." Probably both Mayakovsky and Meyerhold would willing have subscribed to these modestly proud lines by Tsvetaeva. They both actively fought against the tenacious, philistine idea of art as sacred ritual and mystery.

Mikhail Gnesin wrote in his reminiscences about Rimsky-Korsakov: "He possessed a kind of passion for instantly removing his poetic garb, for remaining before others and before himself as the most ordinary of mortals. He demonstrated, as it were, the absence of a poetic 'aura' around himself, and was particularly eager to preach the role of craft in art, poeticizing the prose of craft."

This definition is surprisingly appropriate for Mayakovsky and Meyerhold. Let us recall Mayakovsky's *How are Verses Made?* Meyerhold also spoke in the same way about the art of the theatre, "preaching the role of craft in art and poeticizing the prose of craft".

We were devoted to Mayakovsky and Meyerhold, but by no means blindly devoted... We looked at the objects of our admiration with enthusiastic but clear and vigilant eyes. We read with pleasure the thin volumes of *The New LEF*, with their brilliant photomontages on the covers, because we liked their militant, provocative tone. But we didn't accept everything that was written there. At that time, a new name appeared in Soviet literature – Yuri Olesha. We liked *Envy* very much, and we did not agree at all with the taunting review published in the journal *The New LEF*. We also liked Fadaeev's *The Rout*, on which Shklovsky exercised his wit in *The New LEF*. There was a lot with which we did not agree, but the journal's activist position was to our liking. Our generation had no need to agree unreservedly with one or another point of view. Arguing with each other, and sometimes with ourselves, we educated our tastes. Both Mayakovsky and Meyerhold were doubly dear to us because we had chosen them ourselves, because they were attacked, and because we constantly had to engage in arguments about them, and further because we felt that not only did we need them, but they needed us.

Our generation had a good memory, clear-sighted and sincere. The slogan, "More left than the Left Front", did not surprise us, nor did the slogan, "Amnesty to Rembrandt", for in our hearts we had already long ago "amnestied" not only Rembrandt but Blok as well. The narrow dogmatic framework of Left Front theory was too confining for us, as in the end it became too confining for Mayakovsky himself. For us the pathos of "Very Good" didn't fit the formula "...the invention of methods for the processing of topical and agitational material" – as the poet himself had defined the aim of his poem; yet, all the same, this theoretical language suited us materialists, dialecticians, and atheists much more than the lofty incantations distilled on vodka and on conversations about the Russian soul, with their frequent use of the word CREATIVITY, which filled literature at that time. Mayakovsky and Meyerhold implanted in us a dislike for artistic shamanism, and if, in fact, it were necessary to choose, then we would rather have chosen the sober schemes of the "left" theories and the merry businesslike irony of those who preferred to call themselves craftsmen and not creators, and their work, craft, and not ART.

The young actors who made up the vast majority of the GosTIM troupe were educated in the spirit of genuine and sincere love for Mayakovsky's poetry and of youthful enthusiastic feeling toward him personally. This was very noticeable at the entrance auditions for GEKTEMAS: the young people knew that they were entering a theatre organically connected to Mayakovsky, and almost every one of them recited his poetry. They say that Meyerhold once invited the poet to an audition, but he soon fled in comical horror at the gigantic portions of Mayakovsky. Mayakovsky's lines, rhymes, and witticisms were constantly heard in ordinary, everyday conversations. Receiving an advance at the accounting department was called, "Let us seize joy from future days"; it was mischievously said of someone leaving a room, "He disappeared, stinking for nothing". An invitation for a walk was called, "Let's stroll over the white curls of the day", etc. It could be said that Mayakovsky was heard continuously, subtly and gradually educating our humor and our colloquial speech. And even now, the old Meyerholdians, long ago dispersed by fate to different theatres and movie studios, upon a chance meeting automatically begin to speak the language of their youth. The vital colloquialism and peculiar energy of Mayakovsky's poetic intonations determined the language of an entire generation (as later the language of Ilf and Petrov did for pre-war youth), and the young Meyerholdians were the leaders in this. They even imitated Mayakovsky's gestures and copied them lovingly...

Meyerhold used to say that he rarely saw Mayakovsky laughing. Indeed, this man who possessed such wild humor somehow remained gloomily businesslike or somberly silent in everyone's memory. But I very well remember Mayakovsky laughing too. It was at a reading of *The Bathhouse*. During the discussion of the play, two people were sitting at a large table on the stage: the chairman of the evening (probably Litovsky) and Mayakovsky himself. The table stood not in the center of the stage, but to the left; and on the right stood the speakers who came up straight from the audience. At the end of the discussion, the chairman went out somewhere and Mayakovsky sat at the table alone. He was smoking constantly, shifting the cigarette in his mouth, and occasionally making some notes. He listened to all the remarks without looking at the speakers.

There were many who didn't like the play, and a number of the remarks were sharply critical. Two or three times Mayakovsky tossed off witty, but not very sharp replies. But then a thin, puny little fellow got up on stage and with his first words announced that Mayakovsky's new play was a "banality". He had a high voice and he lisped. Mayakovsky was sitting with his back half-turned toward him, but on the word "banality", he sharply turned, throwing back his shoulders. His motion was so powerful that the speaker involuntarily moved away to the edge of the stage in fright. The audience broke into laughter. Mayakovsky's abrupt silent turn of his whole body and the speaker's jumping away from him, as though afraid that Mayakovsky was preparing to strike him were really too funny. After he pulled himself together, the speaker began to shout out something even more impudent, but the audience continued laughing. And at this point, Mayakovsky himself laughed. He laughed together with the whole audience. At once it became clear that the overwhelming majority of the audience was on his side.

This amusing incident eliminated the tense and nervous atmosphere in which the discussion had been taking place and the last two speakers praised the play to passionate applause, and Mayakovsky was no longer looking gloomy. For a long time, remembering this incident, we said to each other, "Do you remember how Mayakovsky spun around then?" Later I told this story to Meyerhold. I think this was during a break in a rehearsal of scenes from *The Bedbug*, after V.E. had been speaking to the actors about the nature of Mayakovsky's humor. Somehow he suddenly and imperceptibly became like the poet and right there he acted this little scene for us. He wasn't present at that reading, but he acted out Mayakovsky and his movement with amazing accuracy. And right then he also acted out the speaker's fright. It was one of the most astonishing of Meyerhold's "demonstrations". A few seconds and we had an entire little sketch with two characters.

By the way, I want to correct one inaccuracy. It is known from Meyerhold's own account that at the end of the 1920s, when he was getting ready to produce a film adaptation of Turgenev's *Fathers and Sons* (a contract was already signed with Mezhrabpomfilm and the scenario was being outlined), among other candidates to play the role of Bazarov, Mayakovsky was also considered. Lately, I have encountered several times the following explanation of this fact: that allegedly Meyerhold had proposed to Mayakovsky that he play Bazarov. The whole thing was completely the opposite. It was Mayakovsky who called Meyerhold after reading in the newspaper that Meyerhold was preparing to produce *Fathers and Sons* and proposed himself for the role of Bazarov. Meyerhold was very surprised and laughed it off, saying something indefinite like, "Well, we'll see".

While he was telling me about it, V.E. smiled and spread his hands. "Mayakovsky's individuality is too sharply defined and he can only play himself," he said... And so, other than a fleeting and half-humorous conversation on the telephone, there was nothing. But all the same, this fact is very curious, if only because once again Mayakovsky's and Meyerhold's literary and ideological preferences met – in the figure of that favorite hero of revolutionary youth during the middle and end of the last century. However different the paths of both artists, which crossed only in October 1917, the genesis of their characters lies there in that world of young provincial Russia where they loved Bazarov, read Vsevolod Garshin, where they went from school benches to revolutionary groups.

In his memoirs Mikhail Chekhov expressed surprise at Meyerhold's being true to himself, the young Penza schoolboy revolutionary. But Mayakovsky was the same sort of revolutionary schoolboy. It's interesting that Mayakovsky didn't suggest himself to Meyerhold as either Zhadov [*A Lucrative Post*], or Chatsky, or Hamlet. But he did suggest himself as Bazarov. And even if V.E. gently and humorously rejected his candidacy, this unexpected telephone call surely meant for him approval of his plans.

Both Meyerhold and Mayakovsky had what I would call a sober emotional outlook. They could both be bombastic, but they feared inflated pomposity like fire.

Meyerhold was delighted by Mayakovsky's wit: "He's witty with a sullen face, while we explode with laughter," he said. It's difficult to imagine the living Mayakovsky without jest, without witticisms. But V.E.'s own sense of humor was akin to Mayakovsky's, hyperbolic and unexpected.

When the news of Mayakovsky's death came out, we spontaneously went to what was then the FOSP Club where we spent several days almost without leaving while his body lay in state in the hall which now no longer exists. (On the evening of that day, the tragic news reached Berlin, where GosTIM was on tour, and at Meyerhold's suggestion, before the beginning of the performance the Berlin audience honored the memory of the first Soviet poet by standing up. Some time later I asked V.E. if there had been any protests to his suggestion – after all, the theatre was filled mainly with a bourgeois audience. "They stood up quite nicely," V.E. said.) We each took our turn many times in the guard of honor by the coffin and formed a kind of improvised vigil...

In thinking about the main thing Mayakovsky meant for our generation, I would say that he was a great, perfect aerator; his tastes and predilections became our spiritual hygiene, our lyrical diet. The people who were in love with Mayakovsky could no longer giggle over chauvinistic anecdotes, couldn't be toadies, lickspittles, or careerists. Mayakovsky was our spiritual sanity. Therefore we were especially shocked by his death. We gazed at his features with mournful perplexity as we stood watch by his coffin. Perhaps this was our first great loss. But our generation didn't respond to this death by a "host of suicides". Our life force and the sanity of his poetry proved stronger than the example of his death.

Many years later in the Mayakovsky Museum, I was surprised to see myself next to Mayakovksy in two or three photographs, but I don't remember at all when they were taken. In them, I was not alone with him, but together with others, young men I vaguely remembered in sailor's blouses and the shirts with zipper closings that were then coming into fashion.

* * *

Like Mayakovsky, Meyerhold found humor in the most unexpected situations. One evening when we were on tour in Kiev, I told Meyerhold that I had to go to the airport the next morning to meet the poet Vladimir Pyast, who was flying in from Leningrad. He had been invited for consultation on the verses in *Boris Godunov*. That suddenly struck Meyerhold as very funny, although I couldn't understand why.

"Pyast on an airplane! Pyast is flying in!" Meyerhold repeated, laughing.

Only after meeting Pyast, who was a friend of Blok's, did I understand that, indeed, the combination of this old-fashioned figure and aviation transport could arouse humor. Pyast was a prim, refined old Petersburgian, polite and naïve in the extreme, and full of all kinds of eccentricities. For example, he always carried a quarter-liter bottle of alcohol in his pocket in the event he happened to touch a door handle or had to shake hands with a stranger, and he would unobtrusively wipe his hands with alcohol afterwards.

Pyast and Meyerhold were of the same generation. But one of them belonged completely to the nineteenth century and the other seemed like a contemporary of the very youngest generation.

* * *

Sometimes Meyerhold freely related his plans for staging a production. But other times, in answer to questions, he would make a secretive face and look around as if he feared that he was being overheard. This was a quirk of his – the fear that someone would steal something of his, present it as their own, make changes in it. Once, at the beginning of work on *Boris Godunov*, he instructed me to give a notice to the press about the coming production. I sent a short announcement indicating who was to play the major roles. Meyerhold was incensed.

"Can't you understand that when Radlov finds out who is playing who, he will immediately understand our entire directing plan?" (At the time, Sergei Radlov was also staging *Boris*.)

I don't know what provoked this mistrust. Perhaps it was because throughout his life Meyerhold was obliged to answer for his followers, among whom were some untalented imitators and vulgarizers. Meyerhold hated them almost more than his ideological enemies. But being mistrustful by nature, Meyerhold himself intensified this mistrust still more. He hyperbolized it, carrying it to the point of ridicule, a practical joke.

This was his favorite psychological trick: starting with the serious, he would exaggerate it to the point where one could no longer be sure if he were joking or speaking seriously. For a long time I could not get used to this manner he had of exaggerating half in jest, and he noticeably enjoyed my confusion. But when I became accustomed to it and could unerringly separate the serious from the joking, he stopped teasing me, and when he teased others in my presence, he only glanced at me with the smile of an augur.

Once at an important meeting where various eminent people were ponderously discussing creative methods at length, citing both Hegel and Gogol, Meyerhold took the floor and began to relate very seriously how he had discovered a remarkable work which could be of theoretical assistance in all theatrical practice. Once again he praised this work highly and again made reference to it. After arousing everyone's curiosity, he took from his briefcase a booklet wrapped in newspaper. He opened it to the title page and started reading. It turned out to be a booklet by some cabinet maker about his trade. The amusing thing was that the quotations he cited from it turned out to be no worse than all the other quotations that had been cited that evening.

Serious people without a sense of humor called this buffoonery and Meyerhold himself a buffoon, but this apparently only pleased him. He loved all sorts of poses and often adopted them, especially with people who didn't know him very well. But there was one pose I never saw – the pose of silver-haired grandeur, the pose of an oracle, the possessor of eternal truths... At one debate where for some reason he constantly said "we" and not "I" in his speech, he was accused of being egotistical. He expressed surprise. "When I say 'we' that means, not just me, Meyerhold, but me and Ivan Stepanovich, our projectionist."

Meyerhold was a very intelligent person. Another very intelligent Russian, Anton Chekhov, was one of the first to point this out in his correspondence. In the very well-educated troupe of the young Art Theatre, he particularly noted the young Meyerhold's intellectuality. The critic Aleksandr Kugel also wrote about this in his long article on Meyerhold; it was his apologia written by an enemy.

Those investigators who deduce the roots of Meyerhold's tastes only from the Symbolist art of the beginning of the century are mistaken.

For him, as for Aleksander Blok also, this was only a stage through which he passed quite rapidly. In one of Meyerhold's early diaries there is the following sentence: "I was nurtured on Gogol, Pushkin, Lermontov, Turgenev, Tolstoy, Dostoevsky, and other great Russian poets and writers"... A Lutheran by birth, Meyerhold took the name Vsevolod in honor of Vsevolod Garshin, the favorite writer of his youth.

The acquaintance, first with the works of Chekhov and Gorky, and then with the writers themselves later on, had a tremendous influence on the young Meyerhold and on the formation of his character. I had the opportunity during the winter of 1936–1937 to examine Meyerhold's personal archive, and I copied from his working notebook of the beginning of the 1900s one entry which is very typical of the young Meyerhold. It shows so clearly the formation of his character that I would like to quote it in full:

> I am unhappy more often than I am happy, but I will find happiness as soon as I gain the strength to throw myself into active struggle. In Gorky's new play, someone says, "One must become involved in the very thick of life". It's true! And the tramp, Seryozhka, in *Malva* [a short story by Gorky] says, "It is always necessary to do something so that you are in the midst of people who make you feel alive. Life must be stirred up more often so that it doesn't turn sour"... It's true! In the tragedy of Treplev, Johannes, Tuzenbach (roles which V.E. was playing at the Art Theatre), there is much that is personal to me, especially in Treplev [*The Seagull*]. In 1898, when I first played this part, I experienced much that was similar. Playing Johannes [Hauptmann's *Lonely People*] coincided with my passion for individualism, and Tuzenbach's bias [*Three Sisters*], his bugle calls to work and to active struggle are helping me to break away from the realm of passive idealism. And now I am rushing toward a vital life, toward thrilling, healthy labor. One wants to seethe, to boil, in order to create; not only to destroy, but to create in destroying. I am at a crisis now. The most dangerous moment. An acutely developed consciousness, doubts, vacillations, self-analysis, criticism of my surroundings, the passion for doctrines – all this must be only a means. All this is for something else...

Judging by the list of roles he was playing, this entry (it is not dated) precedes the young Meyerhold's departure from the Art Theatre. It is very characteristic of the youthful artist, but in it there is also the same Meyerhold I knew, with his constant self-dissatisfaction. Gorky's phrase, "Life must be stirred up more often so that it doesn't turn sour", I heard from him thirty-five years after he first entered it in his diary.

Meyerhold's library contained the first volume of Gorky's stories with the following inscription by the author: "To Vsevolod Emilevich Meyerhold. With your subtle and sensitive mind, with your thoughtfulness, you will give much more than you are giving now. Convinced of

this, I will refrain from expressing my desire to praise and thank you...
M. Gorky." This inscription was made in April, 1900.

From the days of his youth until his final years, Meyerhold always
read a great deal. His study was crammed with books. The bookshelves
ran from floor to ceiling. Once, during a conversation, talk turned to
Balzac. He wanted to quote a sentence and began to search for the book.
He squatted down, found the book on the lowest shelf, and without
getting up, began to read. It was the novel, *Splendors and Miseries of
Courtesans*. Carried away, he read several pages aloud, continuing to
squat by the bookshelf. Then I noticed that the book was covered with
penciled notes. The margins of many pages were written all over. He had
the habit of reading with a pencil in his hand. I liked to examine his notes
without his seeing and sometimes asked to read some book of his just to
look at these notes.

Meyerhold loved to write. He once said that literature was his
unrealized vocation. He loved to recall how Anton Chekhov, in one of his
letters to Olga Knipper, wrote that he liked Meyerhold's letters and that
he ought to "write". In another letter, Chekhov noted, "Meyerhold's
letters are becoming more and more interesting". Incidentally, for a long
time V.E. kept eight of Chekhov's letters written to him. Only one of them
was published. "From false modesty", V.E. said, "I published only the
one where he criticized me. But the rest, more flattering, I was embarrassed to publish"... According to Meyerhold, when he left for the
Crimea in 1919, he gave these letters to one of the Petrograd museums
for safekeeping. It is possible that they may still be found. It is interesting
that on Meyerhold's employment form preserved in his theatre, Meyerhold wrote in the "profession" column: "Director, teacher, littérateur".

Pushkin was Meyerhold's Bible. He knew him brilliantly and
freely quoted from memory not only what everyone knows, but little-
known critical excerpts and unfinished sketches. Meyerhold was a good
speaker and he loved to speak in public. But most of all he was proud of
his lecture in Leningrad on Pushkin as a dramatist and his address at the
Pushkin conference at VTO [the All-Russia Theatre Society] in 1937.

Meyerhold loved poetry. Blok, Esenin, and Mayakovsky were all
friends of his. During his final years, young poets were often in his home.

Even more, Meyerhold loved music. In his youth, he played the
violin. He once said that he went into the theatre only after he had failed
the competitive exams for first violin in the student orchestra at Moscow
University when he was a law student there. He knew music as well as a
professional. He could be seen at all the important concerts at the Conservatory. He was friendly with Sergei Prokofiev, Dmitri Shostakovich,
Vissarion Shebalin, Gavriil Popov, Lev Oborin, and others.

Meyerhold often maintained that theatre people shouldn't live in their own narrow world, and rarest of all was it possible to meet actors or directors in his home. I remember how once when it was necessary to consider an important matter concerning the fate of his theatre, he invited Ilya Ehrenberg and Boris Pasternak to help advise him. Among his guests were architects, artists, and military men.

One morning before a rehearsal Meyerhold met me with the question: had I read that day's *Architectural Gazette*. He was genuinely surprised to learn that I rarely looked at it.

"But what's the matter with you! You must read it! Today they printed the most interesting remarks by Vasily Bazhenov"...

Meyerhold subscribed to a number of newspapers. Every day he glanced through them and put them into a pile. Twice a week he would take them up again and read them almost from cover to cover.

Individual scientific problems interested him. Thus, for example, he carefully followed the experiments and work of Ivan Pavlov, and after the scientist's death he maintained connections with his followers. He believed that Pavlov's work could at some stage of its development help in the creation of a genuinely scientific theory of the art of acting. Once I saw that he had an article by Aleksei Gastev on the problems of the organization of work processes in a factory, and it, too, was all marked up with pencil notes.

Meyerhold's professional curiosity was truly limitless. Once during a walk with him I was struck by the freedom and ease with which he became engaged in a conversation with some deaf mutes. It turned out that he knew their sign language very well. I asked when and why he had learned it, offering the guess that this had been necessary for his work with Zaichikov on the role of Estrugo in *The Magnanimous Cuckold*.

"Nothing of the sort", he answered. "It's simply that it's very interesting." Even now, I still have his gifts: an old letter-writing manual, a guide for revealing the deceptions of horse dealers in buying horses, and a beautiful edition of the *Dueling Codex*. Each of these books was presented to me with a sharp and unexpected jest.

Older people's attachment to "old ways" has its charm, but it was completely foreign to Meyerhold. More than anyone else in the art world of his generation, he was in all his interests a modern man. He was always surrounded by people much younger than he was. With young people, he behaved in a simple and friendly way.

Meyerhold was in love with life: he loved nature, flowers, animals...

I remember long excursions when the theatre was on tour: on a launch along the Dneper in Kiev, to Peterhof and Pushkin in Leningrad.

Meyerhold loved to point out places he liked. Once in Leningrad in a cold drizzle he twice turned off to the side when we were on our way from the Astoria Hotel to the Conservatory in order to point out a city landscape he loved – a canal, a bridge, streetlamps. He would not move on until he was convinced that his companions had enjoyed the fantastic effect of the evening light. Another time, on a day filled with unpleasantness he dragged me several blocks out of the way in order to see a magnificent iron grating in front of an ancient private residence, and looking at it, he seemed to forget all about his worries.

But with all the breadth of his aesthetic interests, Meyerhold could not be called omnivorous. In art, he could both love and hate. He had a good understanding of painting and could not stand what he called "naturalism". Of Shishkin's paintings he said, "Only his bears believe in his trees". Among Russian artists he liked Serov, Fedotov, and Kiprensky. On the wall in the dining room of his apartment hung a large composition by Fernand Léger – a gift of the author, a French Communist artist.

In 1938, after the closing of his theatre, Meyerhold regretted bitterly that he didn't have the extra money to go to Leningrad specially to hear the first performance of Shostakovich's new symphony. But he didn't hold back when it came to fighting with second-rate composers.

Meyerhold's enemies called him a "decadent". It always seemed to me that this was either slander or a misunderstanding. I spent several years alongside him and I don't remember his even once, either publicly or in a private conversation, aloud or in a whisper, expressing his predilection for depressing, vapid, misanthropic, decaying art, that is for anything that might be called "decadent". He who was passionately in love with life, in love with Pushkin, Gogol, Lermontov, Griboedov, Balzac, Stendhal, Tolstoy, Chekhov, Mayakovsky – a decadent! It was characteristic that he was somehow indifferent to Dostoevsky.

* * *

Meyerhold was too great and complex a person to be depicted as idealized and slicked up. The soaring grey mane, the slightly hoarse voice, the quick, sharp movements, the huge Cyrano-like nose – he was both externally and internally angular, sharp, unexpected. Such was his character as well, full of unique contradictions. They shouldn't be ignored. They are inseparable from him, and without drawing them, we won't see his living image.

It is impossible to pass over his personal attitude toward his students. It is too characteristic of him and can hardly be called idyllic. This passionate and complex man often deeply hurt his devoted friends and students. With almost every one of them, his relationship passed through the same cycle: infatuation, trust and closeness, jealousy and suspicious wariness. In the last stage, he was often grossly unjust.

Sometimes Meyerhold returned to a former attachment or attraction, but very rarely. That wasn't characteristic of him. More often, it was the opposite – a total break, and only later at a great distance, a certain softening. The initiative for the aggravation always came from Meyerhold himself. Thus, for example, Meyerhold's relationship with Babanova or Garin – these are whole complex psychological novels. How can this be explained? Perhaps by his jealousy at the growing independence of his students? Or by Meyerhold's characteristic gravitation to new people? But with time these new people also gradually passed through this same cycle from infatuation to distrust. This explains the constant human storm around him: all those rejections, breaks, departures. His suspiciousness aggravated everything; each person insulted by him soon became an enemy in his imagination. "I love passionate situations and create them for myself in life", he once said to me. Indeed, he built them in abundance.

Perhaps he was always attracted to new people because of his avid and boundless curiosity about life, which did not at all weaken in him with the passing years. Everything well-known, familiar and habitual bored him and seemed insipid. His main character trait was a constant striving for the new in himself, in his life, in his art. Perhaps it also demanded new surroundings, new enthusiastic eyes, new voices, new characters, and new collisions. "Life must be stirred up more often so that it doesn't turn sour." Perhaps these ebbs and flows, these changes, this constant novelty were necessary for him in order not to get tired, not to grow old, not to become indifferent.

The rejected and insulted students, however, rarely became his enemies. Even at a distance, the fascination of his inordinate temperament and his sharp mind left its mark on those who had broken with him, bruised by unjustly attributed offenses. On the contrary, at a distance, his influence even increased. His contribution to the personalities of all who were near him even for a short time was too great to be renounced inwardly. It would have meant renouncing one's own self. Among his many talents, Meyerhold possessed the ominous gift of acquiring enemies. But their circle did not coincide with the circle of people personally offended by him. Meyerhold's enemies were always those who didn't know him.

* * *

In 1931, Meyerhold staged Vsevolod Vishnevsky's play, *The Last, Decisive*. The production proved to be very interesting. Vishnevsky was satisfied with it. He argued at numerous debates side by side with Meyerhold. It seemed that the theatre had found its own author, for whom a need had been sharply felt – Mayakovsky had just died. However, Meyerhold did not stage Vishnevsky's next play, *The Battle in the West*. It was shown in another theatre (The Theatre of the Revolution). There was a falling out, and after writing *An Optimistic Tragedy*, Vishnevsky gave it to Aleksandr Tairov. The rift was transformed into a gulf when, after the première of *The Lady of the Camellias*, Vishnevsky came out with a sharply critical article. For a time, Vishnevsky occupied in Meyerhold's eyes the never vacant role of "Enemy No. 1". But the repertory portfolio of the theatre was empty. There was no Mayakovsky, no Sergei Tretyakov; Nikolai Erdman and Yuri Olesha were silent. Ilya Selvinsky withdrew after the failure of *The Second Army Commander;* there were no new plays from the playwrights Meyerhold considered close to him.

At this time, Vishnevsky returned from a trip to Spain. He had already produced a film, *We Are from Kronstadt*. In the theatre the idea was born of convincing Vishnevsky to write a play about Spain and of reconciling him with Meyerhold. At first this project seemed absolutely Utopian. After all, not long before that Meyerhold and Vishnevsky, both temperamental people, had rained insults upon each other at the debate about *The Lady of the Camellias.* I was entrusted to make the first reconnaissance. The difficulty of my position was aggravated by the fact that during the bitter skirmish at the debate about *The Lady*, I had heard several irritated remarks from Vishnevsky and had paid him in kind...

But there was nothing to be done. We wanted him to return to the theatre, and, gathering up my courage, one fine evening I picked up the receiver and dialed Vishnevsky's number...

What occurred later that evening proved convincingly that "Enemy No. 1" was very well-disposed toward Meyerhold, and if he didn't make the first step himself, it was only because he was afraid that his extended hand would be left hanging in mid-air.

I will never forget the long conversation with Vsevolod Vitalyevich in the little apartment in the writers' annex on Kislovsk Lane. It was the evening of January 15, 1937. Without a second thought, he expressed his agreement to collaborate with the theatre, to write a play, to be reconciled with Meyerhold. Without naming any conditions, he agreed to take the first step himself in a form that would best suit Meyerhold. We discussed in a friendly way how we should begin. In the first twenty minutes of the conversation, we were transformed from yesterday's enemies into allies. He spoke of Meyerhold with great affection. And of course, it wasn't my eloquence that accomplished this, but Meyerhold's tremendous charm. No one could resist the opportunity to collaborate with him. That evening, Vishnevsky expressed this in plain terms. It wasn't his fault if this didn't come about.

* * *

Meyerhold possessed the most brilliant director's vision of a future play; it almost approached hallucination.

How did he produce this vision?

He thought that just as a writer nourishes in his imagination a future novel before he sits down at his desk, so the director must for a long time nourish in his imagination the image of a future production. "Not less than a year," he said.

The director must know the play well enough before he begins to stage it to even have the right to forget it.

It seems like a paradox, but V.E. insisted on this.

He said that only at the junction of memory and free imagination could the image of the production be born.

While listening to his stories of the various interpretations of scenes in a future production, his collaborators sometimes caught him inaccurately describing the action of the play. Once he began to describe how Chekhov's *The Bear* would be staged. Zinaida Raikh suddenly interrupted him with the remark that in this vaudeville there were no such monologues, the interpretations of which V.E. was describing. V.E. was at first surprised and began to argue; the book was brought in. Convinced that he was mistaken, and not at all embarrassed, he began to fantasize aloud about how to reconcile and combine the fruits of his imagination with the text of the play. It was at this point that his best ideas were born.

In his final years, Meyerhold never sketched the future plans for his productions or how they would be staged. "To sketch them means to stop up the imagination," he once answered when I asked him about it. What he called "forgetting the play" didn't at all mean, of course, to free his memory from it entirely. More likely, it meant the need to traverse, as it were, in his director's imagination the path which the play had traversed from conception to realization in the creative consciousness of the author, thus making it "his own", sensing it as the author did. In "forgetting" the play, Meyerhold evidently unshackled and freed his imagination which then began to work parallel to the author's creation of the play. In conversation with V.E., I once attempted to decipher this paradox of his: "To know well, in order to have the right to forget." He agreed that this was correct.

"I'm afraid to clutter up the play within me by frequent re-reading"...

"When I die, they'll poke in the cupboards of my study (a sly glance at me) to find out what little secrets are there, but there will be nothing. They'll be almost empty. Some odds and ends and scribblings. When I was younger, I used to write things down, but as I mastered my craft, I stopped. If I devise a staging and sketch it on a scrap of paper, it becomes static. Everything that I devise and forget because I didn't write it down is worthless, since what is good doesn't get forgotten. One shouldn't clutter up one's mind...

"When I am asked at rehearsal, 'Did you devise this earlier, or did it come up just now?' I always answer, 'I don't know'. Often what seems to be a sudden improvisation is in reality the result of a broad plan worked out in its entirety. The general composition worked out before a rehearsal sets up firm points of stability, solid posts which determine the ideas arising along the way. In the art of directing, improvisation is obligatory, just as in acting, but always within the limits of the general composition. All possible improvisational variations must be self-limited by the feeling for the composition. People possessing that ability have the right to improvise"... (Note of February 11, 1936)

* * *

Although Meyerhold possessed enormous professional experience and practice, he nevertheless wasn't able to stage just any play at all. Sometimes he tried to do it, but the productions, although they shone with his genius, were as a whole, unsuccessful. But when the play rested on one of his themes, no matter how dissimilar they were in genre, plot, place and time of action, his artistic talent began to glitter in all of its aspects.

Take, for example, the famous scene, "In the Restaurant", from the production of *Prélude* (based on Yuri German's novella). In Berlin, in an atmosphere of economic crisis due to unemployment, old friends meet in a private room in a first-class restaurant. Life had thrown them in different directions. Some had been fortunate, others were on the edge of poverty. On that evening, everyone is trying to be respectable, and they agree not to speak of anything unpleasant. At first, the scene is worked out almost as a comedy. Drunken men in smoking jackets organize a "water" game. They try to joke and laugh.

Hugo Nunbakh, a former engineer and now a seller of pornographic postcards (Lev Sverdlin played him remarkably), also tries to forget himself. To the melancholy strains of a violin playing a foxtrot, the sound of which is coming from the main hall of the restaurant (this tragic dance was written by Vissarion Shebalin), he tries to dance... It is difficult to describe further that stunning dance of despair which

Meyerhold brilliantly demonstrated and Sverdlin brilliantly performed...
All that could also be given the name of Pushkin's "little tragedy" – *A Feast During the Plague:* a tragicomedy, a tragicomedy of a generation of people who are doomed. In many of Meyerhold's productions there are individual episodes or entire acts of this nature. Would it have been difficult for him, in the course of several hours, improvising almost aimlessly to find the theatrical form for Pushkin's brilliant play? It was one of the leitmotif themes of his artistry, the artistry of a great poet of the theatre.

One could identify several other constant themes, the revelation of which Meyerhold returned to in various productions. There was, first and foremost, the theme of the present and the future. It concerned him in Mayakovsky's plays. He even saw that theme in his discoveries in *Hamlet*. One time Meyerhold told how together with Lunacharsky he dreamed of the appearance of a great poetic "utopian" play which would "look ten years into the future"

In the finale of *Prélude*, during the departure of the famous German professor–engineer, Kelberg, to work in the Soviet Union, the wind suddenly tears into the room and the brightly colored curtains billow like sails. That wasn't just the usual realization of a Meyerholdian metaphor for a theme (here, the theme of departure, the theme of a journey); it was "the fresh wind from the world of the future", about which Meyerhold spoke in attempting to define the essence of Mayakovsky's dramatic poetry...

Remember also the extraordinarily poetic, joyfully lyrical "departure into the future" of Aksyusha and Pyotr in *The Forest* along the road going off into the distance...

Still another constant theme of Meyerhold's was the social and psychological unmasking of the bourgeoisie in all its aspects. A frightening panorama of philistines and bourgeoisie of various periods – from Famusov's guests in *Woe to Wit* and the provincial officials in *The Inspector General* to the philistines of our day in Erdman's *The Warrant*, in Mayakovsky's *The Bedbug* and *The Bathhouse*, and in Bezymensky's *The Shot* – were shown by Meyerhold in these and other productions with colossal artistic force.

Meyerhold didn't know any limit to expressing his hatred and contempt for the bourgeoisie. There was something very personal in the satirical, lampooning masks of the bourgeoisie which he created in many of his productions. He modeled these masks with such passion that it seemed he was battling with his own enemies...

The heroic theme in Meyerhold's art is almost always decided tragically. Take, for example, the astonishing finale to *The Last, Decisive* by Vsevolod Vishnevsky. Not long ago the three-volume works of Vishnevsky were published, in which are collected his diaries from the wartime years. In one of the notes about the heroic defense of Leningrad, Vishnevsky recalls that finale. The art of Meyerhold–Vishnevsky was prophetic.

In the uneven and contradictory *The Second Army Commander*, a tragic scene of a meeting, mighty as Shakespeare, was created. That was one of those fragments from a production of Meyerhold's which must be artistically described and studied in detail. While working on the second director's edition of *Woe to Wit*, which V.E. called the "Moscow" edition, in distinction to the first which he called the "Petersburg" edition (both editions were realized in Moscow; the difference between them was stylistic), Meyerhold worked out the final, fourth act as a tragedy. At rehearsals he spoke a great deal about the devices for performing a Greek tragedy, "a tragedy with dry eyes", as he called it. He selected as an epigraph for that act a line from Sophocles' *Oedipus Rex:* "Oh wretched one, in equal measure from wit and misfortune," which so remarkably coincided with the name and the theme of Griboedov's "comedy". The scene "At Gantske's", in which Gantske-Bogolyubov reaches a genuinely tragic pathos, and the tragic final scene "In the Restaurant" (Sverdlin-Nunbakh's dialogue with the bust of Goethe), also from *Prélude*, and many more were by V.E.'s own admission "bridges, ladders to tragedy"... (Note of March 4, 1936)

* * *

There was nothing out of the ordinary in the presence of foreigners at a rehearsal during the 1930s. Meyerhold was famous and well-liked. People in the arts tried to get into his rehearsals. V.E. turned these rehearsals into lessons in wise mastery. Sitting in the dim auditorium of GosTIM watching his "demonstrations" could be found young actors and directors as well foreign visitors to Moscow. During those years Julius Fučik, Léon Moussinac, Louis Aragon, Gordon Craig, Saint-Exupéry, Rafael Alberti, María Teresa León, Bertolt Brecht, André Malraux, and others came. These were famous people and V.E., who knew several languages, spoke with them himself, but with the Spaniards he conversed with the assistance of Aleksandr Fevralsky. Guests of a different rank also came, most often journalists accredited to Moscow with their interpreters. The night before, they would call from VOKS and notify me, and before the rehearsal I would meet them, find places for them, and explain what was going on during the course of the rehearsal. During the break, Meyerhold himself would come up and greet them affably. They would look at him wide-eyed: he was known all over the world, and a small amount of his fame rubbed off, even on me, his assistant. Probably it was this way on that particular occasion too.

March 4th and 5th, 1936. A ride in a car with V.E. He asked me to come to his house that evening. In the evening there was the most interesting, informative conversation on many subjects: about the right to experiment, and on Hokusai, about the kinship with "left art", about the accordion in the theatre (V.E. dreamed of staging a show where the accordion would play the role of a Greek chorus), about Malraux's novels, about dialogue and monologue in the modern novel, about "internal monologue" and whether it could be realized on the stage, about "Meyerholditis", about how the pose of a conceited *metteur en scène* would be improper for V.E., about modern trends in psychology. I told him about Hemingway, whom he knew only by hearsay, and he asked me to bring him *Fiesta* [*The Sun Also Rises*] the very next day.

V.E. said that the French avant-garde writer André Malraux had arrived in Moscow the night before. Meyerhold was planning to adapt one of his novels for the theatre. He suggested that I take part in this work... It was the novel *Man's Fate*, about the Shanghai uprisings. Ilya Ehrenburg was to translate the novel. The next day Malraux was to dine with V.E. and he also invited me. A dinner at Meyerhold's with Malraux. My heart immediately began to beat faster...

On the fifth, V.E. asked me to come to his house at 5 o'clock. I arrived at five on the dot. And, of course, I was the first of the invited guests. I sat in the dining room for about twenty minutes with V.E. and Z.N., and we talked about the theatrical news of the day in Moscow: what was going to happen to the actors at the Second Moscow Art Theatre, about Vishnevsky's film, etc. The table was already sumptuously laid in the dining room: each place setting had a number of wine glasses, forks, knives.

A knock at the front door (the Meyerholds didn't have a bell for some reason). And at once a well-known, nasal, droning voice was heard from the hall... A tremendous surprise! It was Boris Leonidovich Pasternak and Zinaida Neigaus. I wasn't aware that they were also coming. V.E. introduced us. The conversation was still about the same thing: the struggle with "formalism", about "Meyerholditis"... Surreptitiously, I studied Pasternak's face: he was youngish, but seemed tired. V.E. noticed this too. B.L. complained of insomnia. Another knock. No, it was not yet Malraux, but a photographer from the *Journal de Moscou*. Before Malraux arrived, he took a picture of V.E., B.L., and me, the three of us sitting on a little couch. I tried to move away, but V.E. pulled me in by the arm.

Malraux didn't come alone, but with his younger brother. During dinner, Pasternak and Malraux talked the most. Malraux was nervous,

Photograph of Pasternak, Meyerhold and Gladkov taken on the evening of
March 5, 1936.

purposeful, dreamy, a man of monologues. It was characteristic of his
manner of speaking that he didn't directly address the person he was
talking to. He didn't take part in a dialogue or a general conversation, but
spoke as though to the side, in bits of monologue. His brother was silent
or made polite remarks. Pasternak's speech, as in his public addresses
which I had heard (this was the first time I saw him up close), was
complex, even florid, often obscure, passionate ...

After dinner, Malraux and his brother left for the Kursk Railroad
Station to catch the train to the Crimea; their luggage was being brought
right to the station from the hotel. Together with Isaac Babel and Mikhail
Koltsov, they were going to Tesseli to see Gorky who was ill. After their
departure I also wanted to leave, but they wouldn't let me go. We sat for
several more hours, until almost midnight. Over coffee, excellently
prepared by Meyerhold, V.E. began to "demonstrate". He acted out for
us waiters of different nationalities, going out and coming back each time
as a new "character", pouring out liqueurs and cognac, doing tricks with
a napkin, and so forth.

The conversation over coffee was confidential and interesting, but
almost completely concerned with Meyerhold and his situation at the
time. The matter was as follows. A highly-placed comrade from among

Stalin's closest personal assistants had come to see three performances of *The Lady of the Camellias* practically one after another. One evening he dropped in on Zinaida Raikh, or maybe sent a message (by now I don't remember exactly), saying he was very sorry that in the building at 15 Gorky Street where GosTIM was then located there was no official box, and that therefore Stalin couldn't come to a performance; otherwise he was certain that Stalin would without question like it, and that could have major consequences for Meyerhold's Theatre and for Meyerhold himself. He added that there might be a possibility of Stalin receiving Meyerhold in order that V.E. might express to him his needs and so forth. He, of course, couldn't promise anything in advance, but he was ready to try to organize such a meeting, if, of course, Meyerhold himself wished it.

This was soon after the appearance of the notorious article "Muddle Instead of Music" (*Pravda*, 28 January 1936) and the banning of Shostakovich's opera, *Lady Macbeth of the Mtsensk District*. Meyerhold deeply sympathized with Shostakovich and refused to write an article hailing the criticism of the opera, which at that time was an act of great civil courage. Almost two years remained until the closing of GosTIM and the general situation didn't yet seem hopeless to us. In the theatre, a production in memory of Mayakovsky was being rehearsed and work on *Boris Godunov* was gradually getting under way.

And so on this day (March 5) which is so memorable for me, over coffee after dinner Vsevolod Emilevich told us about the proposal by Comrade X, emphasizing that he regarded all those present as his friends whom he trusted completely. And he asked for advice: should he seek a meeting with Stalin, and in the event of an affirmative answer, what questions should he put before him? Should he ask something for the theatre, or should he attempt to defend Shostakovich and touch on other general topics?

It would be difficult to choose any more unlikely advisers: Zinaida Raikh's boundless emotionality; Pasternak's subjectivity, noble but somewhat cut off from everyday life; and my own complete inexperience. What could Meyerhold, who himself was far more experienced in life and politically wiser than all of us put together, glean from all this. We sincerely loved him, he could be certain of that. But even the greatest love isn't the best advisor in such a serious and delicate matter.

As at a council of war, the youngest in rank, that is me, was to speak first. I of course said that he certainly must try to achieve that meeting, and that V.E. must talk with Stalin not only about GosTIM and himself, but about all of the vital problems concerning art. "Who if not you, a Communist and a leading director in our country, can tell the entire truth to Stalin about how his incompetent assistants are compromising the true meaning of Party directives in the realm of art?" I said with a naïveté of which very soon not a trace was left. Zinaida Nikolaevna supported me, but cautiously added that it would be better for Meyerhold to limit himself to the question of Meyerhold's own efforts and not touch on Shostakovich whom only time and his own work could help.

But Pasternak didn't agree with either of us. In a long and complex speech, as always with a multitude of digressions and long subordinate clauses, but nevertheless very categorically, he advised not to seek a meeting with Stalin because nothing good could come from it anyway. He told about the sad experience of his telephone conversation with Stalin after the poet Mandelshtam was arrested, when Stalin, not hearing him out, hung up the receiver. Heatedly, Pasternak pointed out to V.E. that it was unworthy of him, Meyerhold, to go to Stalin as a petitioner, and he couldn't be in any other position at that time. He argued that people such as Stalin and Meyerhold must either speak as equals or not meet at all, and so on and so forth...

It seemed to me that Zinaida Raikh's instinctively practical advice as a woman was closest of all to reality. But to my great amazement, Meyerhold agreed with Pasternak: he said that he understood that right now, indeed, was not the time to seek such a meeting and he asked all of us to forget this conversation. He in fact refused to take steps to be received, although of course, hypothetically there was some chance for success. And who knows... after all, not all of those in disgrace perished. Perhaps...

There's no point in useless speculation, and I recall all this only in order to add one more feature to the complex and contrasting portraits of Pasternak and Meyerhold. They didn't resemble each other, but still they understood each other better than we understood them. Besides, the atmosphere of those years is strongly reflected in this strange episode.

At that time, Pasternak's arguments seemed to me lofty, but not practical, something like a high-minded, poetical Don Quixotism, which I was ready to praise, but was not in sympathy with since I wanted so terribly for everything to work out all right for Meyerhold. When many years later I reminded Pasternak of that conversation, he moaned as if from a sudden twinge of toothache and started to blame himself for being naïve and romantic.

But in looking back I believe that Pasternak was completely right. What he didn't put in words (although he spoke long and heatedly), Meyerhold understood and actually agreed with. After all, a similar meeting didn't help Babel when Gorky took him to see Stalin. They say that when he returned, in answer to the question, "Well, how did it go?" Babel answered tersely, "Very badly!..." He was asked, "You think he didn't like you?" "No", Babel answered, "It's much worse. I didn't like him"... More precisely, one could say that they didn't like each other.

Meyerhold and Stalin met occasionally at Kremlin receptions. They had a short conversation after Stalin saw a performance of *Roar China!*, but that, it would seem, was all. I think that they also might not have liked each other. I remember how Pasternak, as an example of an unworthy manner of talking to Stalin, mentioned that one time when Aleksei Tolstoy was telling funny stories to Stalin, he complained without being very subtle about the poor condition of his dacha. And I remember very well how Meyerhold listened to Pasternak. At first he looked at him, then he seemed to retreat into himself as if lost in thought, the cigarette between his lips gone out...

After that, we remained there for a long time talking about various things, but unfortunately, the unusualness of the situation, my extreme tenseness, and several overly large portions of cognac which V.E. generously poured out, and which I was too embarrassed to refuse, resulted in my remembering far from all that was said then, for which I mercilessly reproached myself the next day...

＊ ＊ ＊

On the instructions of Vsevolod Emilevich, I was at one time putting together a book of his selected works. The book was compiled. Its volume was much greater than the old, pre-revolutionary book *On the Theatre*; and although much from that book was rejected by him as outdated and uninteresting for republication, he wanted the new book to have the same title.

The old book had an epigraph that now sounds sufficiently clear:

> Even if you eat me to the very root, I will still bear enough fruit to make a libation from it to pour on your head when you, the goat, are sacrificed.
> Even – The Ashkelonian

Once I asked him who this Even was.

Meyerhold looked at me slyly and began to laugh.

"Vyacheslav Ivanov is the only one in the whole world who knows that", he said. "He found it for me. Well? Is it good?"

I asked him if we should keep this epigraph for the new book as well.

"No, we need something new. You find something."

I suggested a line from *Hamlet* to him: "Armed at point exactly cap-a-pie" (I.ii.200).

Hamlet was his favorite play.

At first he liked it. He asked me to type it out on a separate sheet of paper. He looked at it for a long time, then folded it carefully, and put it in his briefcase.

A few days later, however, he brought me another paper. On it was one sentence written in his hand:

> They will accuse me of boldness until they have understood me completely, and then they will accuse me of timidity.
>
> Anatole France

"Where is this from, Vsevolod Emilevich?"

"From the introduction to *Joan of Arc*. Well? Is it good?"

He looked at me triumphantly.

"Type it out. Let's see."

I typed it. I still have this paper even now.

Work on the book was finished toward the beginning of 1937. But it didn't get published. The advance agreement given by one of the publishing houses was withdrawn. Meyerhold was very upset by this. This setback was the forerunner of other major setbacks which culminated in the closing of the theatre.

At the same time he was working on this book, Meyerhold was also dreaming of publishing *The Collected Works of Vsevolod Meyerhold*. In addition to his previously published works, it was to include stenographic records of rehearsals for productions in the previous several years, and a *Director's Manual*. I remember that to my questions about the nature of the *Manual*, he said it would be a "very thin little book, almost a brochure", where only a very few, but mathematically precise and clear laws of "scenometrics" (Meyerhold's term) with the simplest examples would be collected. He saw it as similar to Mayakovsky's *How are Verses Made?*, and in his work, V.E. constantly referred to that book. There were to be eight volumes in the *Collected Works*. Its outline has been preserved.

Meyerhold didn't leave behind any memoirs. He sometimes said that he wanted to write them, but that he was too lazy. But Meyerhold and laziness are a combination hard to imagine. I think it was because he still hadn't yet reached a point in his life when one writes memoirs. There wasn't any feeling of life coming to an end. It wasn't a time for summing up. Things were constantly changing, falling apart. There wasn't any steadiness, any quiet. There wasn't any veneration, in spite of the gray hair and world fame.

Individual reminiscences and confessions came out at rehearsals and in conversations with pupils and friends and were written down by stenographers, myself included. But they were always used as an example for something right then: "And once when I was" ... And they almost always had a humorous twist to them. In telling about himself, Meyerhold always made himself out to be more naïve, more eccentric than he was, and we, listening to him, almost always laughed. He added to the comical effect with gestures.

* * *

Meyerhold's acquaintance with Nikolai Ostrovsky in 1936 made an enormous impression on him. In an unpublished jotting titled "He Knew How to Inspire Courage" (December, 1936), he wrote:

> In this man, one is struck by the fortunate combination of extraordinary determination and steadfastness of spirit with extraordinary sensitivity and tenderness.
> He possessed an almost unbelievable wisdom for his thirty-two years of age. Such wisdom is characteristic of a person who has traveled far along life's route and who has had a great deal of experience in life...
> This remarkable person lived only with his mind. Those who performed the post mortem on him were astonished by the fact that his entire body was completely disintegrated. Only Ostrovsky's brain was in remarkable condition.

Meyerhold's failure to produce *How the Steel was Tempered* was pre-ordained by the weakness of the dramatic adaptation of the novel. When it became clear that the first adaptation ordered by the theatre was unsuccessful, a second was ordered. But it was also unsuccessful. The mature and refined mastery of the director couldn't replace the absence of a dramatic text. This production, brought along as far as the dress rehearsal (it was titled *One Life*), was the last production Meyerhold directed at the theatre named after him.

* * *

Meyerhold could enjoy art wherever he found it. When he was delighted, he became ecstatic and eloquent. When he spoke about Pushkin or read the poet's verse, his low and slightly hoarse voice climbed upward and began to vibrate. I remember that in my presence he spoke on the telephone with Stanislavsky in that same uncharacteristic high voice.

I remember one time – that was, indeed, only once – V.E. asked me to show him my notes. It was under very strange circumstances, in the lobby of our theatre on New Year's Eve in 1937. The night was drawing to a close. The merriment was already dying down. Meyerhold and I sat together at a table, and as always in those days we talked about the work on *Boris*. One of the actresses came toward us carrying a goblet (she was an official worker inside the theatre). She overheard us and with coquettish familiarity began to reproach V.E. for talking business "on such a night".

V.E. frowned and I was afraid he would answer her with something sharp, but she didn't wait for an answer and disappeared, calling to someone else.

"About business!" Meyerhold said very angrily. "And what else is there for us to talk about?"

Then suddenly without any transition:

"Give me your notebook!"

I was embarrassed. I was certain that I was the only one who could make out my notes. They suddenly seemed to me pitifully amateurish. And besides – my handwriting!...

V.E. looked at me rather severely.

Taking the notebook, he silently leafed through it, stopped at something, read through one page carefully, then suddenly slammed it shut, gave it back to me, and unexpectedly covered with his hand mine which was lying on the table:

"Thank you!"

It seems to me that even now I can feel the warmth of his hand.

* * *

Meyerhold was prickly, sharp-tongued, mistrustfully proud, rancorous. He was involved in a variety of complex relationships with the entire theatrical world. He actively protested against everything that he disliked. He quarreled over trifles with his followers and friends. But throughout his entire long life, he retained an almost childlike admiration for Stanislavsky. It was more than respect; it was love. He was happy and elated when he was told things about Stanislavsky with which he himself could agree. He was silent when someone reported some rumor from Leontevsky Lane [Stanislavsky's home], and he tried to convince himself that it was a lie he didn't have to believe. He never allowed anyone to speak badly of Stanislavsky in his presence and sharply cut off anyone who did not in his opinion regard Stanislavsky with sufficient respect. His first teacher in the theatre was not Stanislavsky, but Nemirovich-Danchenko. They had come to the young Art Theatre together, but Meyerhold's attitude toward him could not be compared to his attitude toward Stanislavksy.

In February 1935, a seminar for directors from outlying districts was held in Moscow. The participants in the seminar were present at rehearsals in GosTIM and expressed a desire to ask Meyerhold several questions. One of the questions concerned Meyerhold's relations with Stanislavsky. Here's what Meyerhold answered:

> The assertion that Meyerhold and Stanislavsky are antipodes is wrong. This notion is meaningless in such a static, ossified form. Neither

Stanislavsky nor Meyerhold represents something completed. Both are in a state of constant change. As a wise artist, Stanislavsky listens intently to everything, carefully follows everything that takes place on the art front. And I myself am not the same as I was during the period of *The Earth in Turmoil* (1923). During the first Five-Year Plan, I was one person, and in the second, another. The same is true of Stanislavksy. The fascination of art lies precisely in the fact that at every stage of one's creative life one feels oneself to be a student again... I'm called a master, and no one suspects that before each first night I tremble like a student. Stanislavsky taught me this...

The many mishaps and failures Meyerhold suffered in later years were offset and compensated for by the renewal of his friendship with Stanislavsky in 1938. I once saw them sitting together at one of the exams at the Stanislavsky Opera Studio, and knowing V.E. as well as I did, I couldn't help but notice that he, a world famous director, was nervous.

I also remember a very lengthy conversation, almost an hour long, on the telephone (I was sitting in V.E.'s study), during which Stanislavsky did most of the talking and V.E. listened. They were discussing the projected staging of Mozart's opera, *Don Giovanni*, at the Stanislavsky Opera Theatre. When the conversation was over, V.E. was in a highly excited state. He seemed almost happy.

I remember (this was earlier) Meyerhold's laudatory review of Stanislavksy's production of *Carmen*.

In 1938, Meyerhold more than once mentioned that Stanislavsky's "system" in its latest stage of teaching about "physical action" was close to his own objectives in directing and teaching. With great pride, he would repeat that now nothing divided Stanislavsky and him.

At our last meeting, Meyerhold spoke with enthusiasm about his upcoming work with the artist Pyotr Konchalovsky on *Don Giovanni* at the Stanislavsky Opera Theatre. It seems to me it was at that time that he said jokingly, but with a certain secret pride, that he had uncovered something else he and Stanislavsky had in common. He said that, like Stanislavsky, his grandmothers were also French...

* * *

Meyerhold could be nasty and gloomy, but I don't remember him ever depressed. His outward cheerfulness, optimism, and unwavering tenacity didn't desert him even under the most difficult circumstances.

During the final performance of *The Lady of the Camellias* [the evening of January 7, 1937], when the theatre's closing had already been announced and the auditorium was packed full, after each act Meyerhold was summoned by an ovation. But he didn't want to come out as he didn't wish this to turn into a demonstration of sympathy. During the performance, after which Zinaida Raikh immediately fainted onstage, V.E. sat backstage with me on some boxes and broken scenery (he no longer had an office) and ... joked.

Several days later, I again dropped by the theatre. In the administrator's room there was already some kind of commission meeting to assign the actors to other theatres. V.E. had been summoned "for consultation", but that was, evidently, just a formality. No one consulted with him. I saw a crowd of actors standing by the coat room. Someone told me that V.E. was walking alone out in the lobby. I must say that already for a half-year I hadn't been working in the theatre. I went to the lobby. V.E. was silently walking around with a fur coat thrown over his shoulders. He seemed to be happy to see me and asked, "What's new?" But he didn't listen to my answer very attentively. He took me under the arm and we continued to walk in the foyer together.

I tried to distract him, told him something funny, asked him which opera he was going to stage in Leningrad – the day before he had told me on the telephone that he had received an invitation from the former Mariinsky Theatre. I told him about Nemirovich-Danchenko's sharp answer to the invitation of some editorial staff to give them an interview about the closing of the theatre. But each time Meyerhold answered me with just a word and didn't sustain the conversation. He held me firmly under the arm and we continued to walk. Finally I also fell silent. We both walked in silence. It was a heavy silence. V.E. was smoking a cigarette. When he finished it, he turned and threw the butt in the urn. The urn was standing rather far away, but since V.E. had a remarkable eye, the butt landed right in it. And suddenly I sensed that this trifle – how the butt landed exactly in the urn from afar – heartened him. He seemed to straighten up immediately; he laughed at something and began jokingly telling me about how the porter of the house on Bryusov Lane where he lived then regarded the closing of the theatre...

Incidentally, it's worth recalling Nemirovich-Danchenko's remark. Although he was V.E.'s first teacher, they were not inclined to be friendly toward each other and that was widely known. That was why the journalist had sought out Nemirovich-Danchenko's response. It is said that when he heard the request to express his opinion on the closing of the Meyerhold Theatre, V.I. silently stroked his beard for several moments and then answered, "Do you know, I find that to ask me about Meyerhold is the same as to ask the Grand Duke Nikolas Nikolaevich his opinion of the October Revolution" ...

Meyerhold at his desk in his apartment on Novinsky Boulevard, January 1928. Shortly after this picture was taken, there was a fire in the building. Meyerhold then moved to the apartment on Bryusov Lane where he lived until his arrest in 1939.

MEYERHOLD SPEAKS

About Myself

The theatre has been the main interest in my life since I was seven years old. Already at the age of seven, grown-ups would find me before the mirror trying to transform my childish little face. Later, there were other powerful attractions: to music (the violin), literature, politics, but the attraction to the theatre proved to be the most powerful of all. What has had the greatest influence on my life? There have been many influences: first, great Russian literature, personal acquaintance with Anton Chekhov and Konstantin Stanislavsky, the remarkable masters of the old Maly Theatre, Blok, Maeterlinck, Hauptmann, the study of the old theatrical epochs, the study of Eastern theatre, again a return to the creative works of the great Russian poets – Pushkin, Lermontov, Gogol – the storm of the October Revolution and its stern beauty, the new young art of the cinema, Mayakovsky, Pushkin again, and with ever-increasing force... Can one really enumerate everything? An artist must be attracted by many things, respond to a variety of things, rejecting some, keeping certain ones within himself... You just mentioned Ernest Hemingway... I've already heard his name and will certainly read him.

* * *

There was a crossroads in my life when I almost became a musician, a violinist. In the middle of the 1890s, Moscow University had a magnificent student orchestra. They gave full-fledged concerts. I was studying law, but adored music. Perhaps, even more than the theatre. The violin was my passion. And then they announced a competition for second violin in this orchestra. I dreamt about this position. I worked hard for it, abandoned even Roman law and... failed the competition. In my disappointment I decided to go into acting. I was accepted. And now I wonder: I might be a second violinist playing in a small orchestra in a theatre headed by Bendersky or Ravenskikh; they would be attacked as I am now, and I would scrape away on my violin and smile to myself... [In fact, Meyerhold hadn't practiced for almost a year. While he was upset at the time, later he was glad. Soon afterwards he dropped the violin. For a time, Meyerhold also considered switching from law to medicine.]

* * *

In Nikolai D. Volkov's detailed and exact biography of me, there are still gaps. For example, such an important moment in my development as my acquaintance in Italy, in May 1902, with Lenin's "The Spark" and his book, *What Is To Be Done?* which had just been published abroad. I went to Milan in order to see cathedrals and museums and all day long wandered through the streets watching the Italian crowds. And then I returned to my hotel and buried myself in illegal newspapers and pamphlets and read and read endlessly. There were already some vague rumors then of the dissension between Lenin and Plekhanov, and my student-émigré friends argued breathlessly about the tactics of the R.S. D.R.P. [Russian Social Democratic Worker's Party]. The term "Bolshevik" and "Menshevik" didn't yet exist, if I'm not mistaken, but the differentiation was already palpable...

* * *

In my life, before each new creative upsurge, there have been tragic pauses full of hesitations and doubts, sometimes almost to the brink of despair. Only two – and the most important! – decisions in my life did I make without hesitation: when, after finishing the Philharmonic Drama School, I rejected the advantageous and flattering proposals of two prominent provincial impresarios, and for a small salary joined the newly opening Art Theatre (from a Philistine point of view, it was a risk!); and again, when I immediately understood the significance of the October Revolution and threw myself into it. I was prepared for adopting these decisions by my entire inner development, and they came to me naturally and simply.

But I will never forget my emotional turmoil in the autumn and early winter of 1905. There was a powerful revolutionary ferment in the country, but we were preparing to open the Studio on Povarskaya Street. Then the scandalous première of *The Children of the Sun* in the Art Theatre. Stanislavsky decided not to open the studio. I was no better off than before. At Konstantin Sergeevich's suggestion, for a while I again played Treplev in the revival of *The Seagull* at the Art Theatre. It was a kind of bridge to my possible return to the Moscow Art Theatre, about which K.S. hinted to me. But there were obstacles as well: Nemirovich Danchenko had a more than cool attitude toward this. And at the time I didn't know myself what I wanted. I had completely lost my bearings. [Meyerhold always called Treplev his "most favorite role," perhaps because it was more than a role for him, but was also a reflection of his own dissatisfaction with the state of theatre at that time.]

But I didn't have to decide anything. Everything was decided for me by the complete absence of friendly contact with my former colleagues, the cast of *The Seagull*, whom I met backstage during performances.

They irritated me, and I seemed strange to them. This was during the armed uprising in Moscow. I was living in a neighborhood covered with barricades. I'll never forget the terrible impressions of those days: Moscow dark, the Presnya District broken and bleeding. The tragedy of the crushed revolution somehow overshadowed everything personal then, and the pain at the death of the unborn theatre passed very quickly. Soon I genuinely stopped regretting it. And then the trip to Petersburg, new meetings and acquaintances, the attempt to revive the Fellowship of New Drama in Tiflis, and finally, the unexpected letter from Komissarzhevskaya...

* * *

For me, Stanislavsky's closing of his Studio on Povarskaya Street in 1905 was a personal tragedy, but in essence he was right. Because of my characteristic haste and lack of caution, I strove to unite there the most heterogeneous elements: Symbolist drama, artist-stylizers, and young actors trained in the school of the early Art Theatre. Whatever the objectives, all this didn't go together and, to put it crudely, called to mind the fable of the swan, the crayfish, and the pike [a fable by Ivan Krylov]. With his flair and good taste, Stanislavsky understood this. And for me, when I came to my senses after the bitterness of failure, this became a lesson: at first it is necessary to train the new actor and only then put new goals before him. Stanislavsky also drew the same conclusion and in his mind the features of his "system" in its first version were already forming.

* * *

The Ministry of the Court to which the Imperial theatres were subordinate until the Revolution tried several times, under pressure from the Okhranka [see *Glossary*], to dismiss me from the Alexandrinsky and Mariinsky Theatres. Only Golovin's unlimited influence on Telyakovsky, the director of the Imperial theatres, saved me.

* * *

If you like, I'll tell you what sharply divided artists when the Revolution arrived. It's naïve and superficial to think that all the writers, musicians, and artists who emigrated were thinking only of their lost bank accounts or their confiscated dachas [summer cottages]. In fact, the majority of them didn't have these things. Chaliapin loved money. Everyone knows this, but even for him it wasn't the main thing. The main thing was what Gorky, Mayakovsky, Bryusov, and many others including myself understood at once: that the Revolution was not only destruction, but creation as well. Those who thought the Revolution was only destruction absolutely rejected it. Mayakovsky and I belong to different generations, but for both of us the Revolution was a second birth.

* * *

For Pavlov's anniversary, I sent him a telegram in which I somewhat flippantly wrote that I greeted in him the man who finally had done away with that mysterious and dark thing, "the soul". In reply I received a letter from Pavlov in which he politely thanked me for my congratulations, but noted: "As for the soul, let's not hurry. Let's wait a little before we make any assertions"... I'd like to say the same to everyone who thinks that Stanislavsky or I know all the truths about the mysteries of the actor's creative work. Follow the work of Konstantin Sergeevich, and you will see that he is constantly introducing corrections into his "system". At one time I maintained that man is a "physio-chemical laboratory". Of course, this is very primitive. In my Biomechanics, I was able to define in all 12–13 rules for the training of an actor. But in polishing it up, I'll leave perhaps not more than eight.

* * *

If I had some free time, I would like to rewrite certain of my articles in the book *On the Theatre*. Without fundamentally changing them, I'd like to free them of the modernist terminology popular at the beginning of the century. Now, this terminology only keeps them from being properly appreciated. Wouldn't it be nice to be slightly ill and, while slowly recuperating, work on this at leisure? As it is, I still get in trouble from certain of my old-fashioned and unsuccessful formulations. [*On the Theatre* was a collection of articles by Vsevolod Meyerhold presenting his views on the development of the theatre as reflected in his work as a director from 1905–1912. Published in St. Petersburg in 1913, it was the only book Meyerhold ever wrote. Meyerhold often talked about writing more, but as Gladkov commented, he wrote almost nothing in his later years, leaving it to his assistants to write articles for him. Aleksandr Fevralsky had many examples in his files of articles he had drafted for Meyerhold in the 1920s.]

* * *

When life deals me another blow, I know by now I must calmly and patiently wait for a miracle – the salutary hand of a friend. After the closing of the Studio on Povarskaya Street, it was the letter from Komissarzhevskaya. After I left her, there was also at first an impasse, and then suddenly the letter from Telyakovsky, prompted by Golovin. And now, after the closing of GosTIM, Konstantin Sergeevich's telephone call... (Written in 1938 – A.G.) [While it is true that Meyerhold always waited for a miracle, Gladkov said that his waiting was neither calm nor patient.]

* * *

When you see a tree lose its leaves in autumn, it seems to you that it is dying. But it is not dying, it is preparing for its revival and future blooming. There are no trees that bloom the year round, and there are no artists who do not experience crises, decline, doubts. But what would you say of gardeners who in the fall cut down trees that were losing their foliage? Shouldn't artists be treated as patiently and carefully as trees?

* * *

All my life I have had good luck with teachers. Stanislavsky, Fedotov, Nemirovich-Danchenko, the masters of the Old Maly Theatre, Chekhov, Gorky, Dalmatov, Golovin, Varlamov, Savina, Blok, Komissarzhevskaya – I learned from all of them as best I could. I can, if you like, add another dozen names. You'll never become a master if you cannot be a pupil. I was avid and curious. And I'll give you one piece of advice: be curious and appreciative, learn to wonder and to admire.

* * *

I maintain that we have the best spectators in the world. And we have the very best readers! They are above comparison with those in Western countries and with our former Russian intelligentsia as well. Can you believe that in the days of my youth, in the general opinion of the intelligentsia, Boborykin, for instance, seemed a more serious and idea-oriented writer than Balzac? And Balzac was considered comparable to a Paul de Kock. Spielhagen was rated more highly than Stendhal. Sheller-Mikhailov was held up to Chekhov as an example. (Small wonder that this indiscriminate lack of taste made us plunge into decadence.)

* * *

In my opinion the explosive period in art hasn't yet passed. But tears dampen the gunpowder. That's why I don't like sentimental art.

* * *

Beware of using metaphors with pedants! They take everything literally and later give you no peace. Once I said that words are a pattern on the canvas of movement. This was an ordinary metaphor, such as one often tosses out when speaking with students. But the pedants understood it literally and now for two decades have been scientifically refuting my light-winged aphorism.

Similarly, for a long time every sin has been laid at Gordon Craig's doorstep because he compared actors to marionettes. Goethe (who, by the way, I don't like) once said that actors must be like tightrope walkers. But does this mean he was advising actors playing Hamlet to walk a tightrope? Of course not! It was simply that he wanted to advise them to achieve on the stage the same unerring precision in each movement. [In his article, "Balagan" (1912), Meyerhold wrote, "How long will it be before they inscribe in the theatrical tables the following law: *words in the theatre are only a pattern on the canvas of movement?"* In the context of his thinking at that time, these words could hardly be dismissed as some offhand comment to a group of students. More likely this observation from the 1930s was motivated by a need to downplay his interest in movement in the aftermath of the introduction of Socialist Realism, just as in the 1930s Meyerhold also referred to Biomechanics as a "pedagogical fiction", even though it continued to be taught in his theatre school right up to the closing of the Meyerhold Theatre.]

* * *

The basic law of Biomechanics is very simple: the whole body takes part in each of our movements. The rest is elaboration, exercises, études. Tell me, what is there in this that could disturb people, provoke protests, seem heretical, unacceptable? Probably it's something in my personality. Even the simplest things I assert for some reason seem to be paradoxes or heresy for which I should be burned at the stake. I'm sure that if tomorrow I announced that the Volga flows into the Caspian Sea, then the day after tomorrow they'd start demanding an admission from me of the errors contained in this statement.

* * *

It's not necessary for the artist to know who he is: a realist or a romanticist. Besides, everyone understands these concepts differently. You have to bring to art your own vision of the world, whatever it might be. Later you'll be placed in a definite slot, and what's more they'll move you several times from one to another. With us, these attributes are used not so much to explain, but as an award. When they once wrote about me that I had finally staged a realistic production, I was pleased. Actually, not because it was true, but because I understood that they wanted to pay me a compliment. Well, it's as if someone were a cavalry general and then were promoted to full general...

* * *

When I argue with the people from RAPP [Russian Association of Proletarian Writers] about whether Igor Stravinsky's *The Rite of Spring* is a great work, it always seems to me that they are very insincere about the fact that this astonishing music is alien and incomprehensible to them.

* * *

Who says I'm old? I'd like to go to SOVNARKOM [Council of People's Commissars] and say, "Since I didn't return in a lead coffin after a cure aboard, sing to me today the praise that is being saved for the obituaries".

In an obituary for Khlebnikov, Mayakovsky wrote "Bread for the living! Paper for the living!" I would add, "And respect for the living!"

* * *

Picasso promised me he would be the designer for our *Hamlet* when we have time to do it... When we have time to do it... All my life I've been dreaming of *Hamlet* and have put off this work now for one reason, now for another. Frankly, in my imagination I've already staged several *Hamlets*. But you know this. I told you about it... And now I've definitely decided that *Hamlet* will be our first production in the new building. We will open with *Hamlet*! We will open the new theatre with the best play in the world! A good omen. [According to a letter from Paris written by Zinaida Raikh on December 16, 1928, Meyerhold first discussed *Hamlet* with Picasso when he visited the artist at his atelier in Paris on that trip. The two artists again talked about a production of *Hamlet* when Meyerhold was in France in the autumn of 1936.]

* * *

My theatre and the Moscow Art Theatre are considered to be the two poles of theatrical Moscow. I agree to be one of the poles, but if you're looking for the second, then, of course, it's the Kamerny Theatre. There is no theatre more opposed and alien to me than the Kamerny. At one time the Moscow Art Theatre had four studios. I can let my imagination roam freely and admit that my theatre is also one of the Moscow Art Theatre Studios. Only, of course, not the fifth, but say, considering the distance separating us, the two hundred fifty-fifth. After all, I'm also a student of Stanislavsky's and the Moscow Art Theatre was my alma mater. I can find bridges between my theatre and the Moscow Art Theatre, and even the Maly. But between us and the Kamerny Theatre there's an abyss. It's only the Intourist guides who put Meyerhold and Tairov side by side. But then they are ready to put St. Basil's next to us as well. I would sooner agree to be St. Basil's neighbor than Tairov's.

* * *

When I happen to read obituaries and various memorials about famous people whom I've had the good fortune to know personally, I'm always surprised: were they like that or not? Reading the elegiac pages about Anton Chekhov, Vera Komissarzhevskaya, Aleksandr Blok, Evgeny Vakhtangov, who would say that they were in life very cheerful people? But I remember that they were, because I myself laughed a lot with them. I remember once on tour in Poland when Komissarzhevskaya and I laughed all day over every trifle – such was our mood. Chekhov I remember as almost always laughing. And when I would meet Vakhtangov, there would be more wit and joking than solemn discourse about something highly significant. Or maybe it's because I myself am such a frivolous and light-hearted person that they behaved that way with me.

If after my death you happen to read reminiscences where I am portrayed as a priest puffed up with his own importance, intoning eternal truths, I beg you to declare that this is all lies, that I was always a very cheerful person. First of all, because more than anything I love to work. And when you work, you are always happy. And second, because I firmly believe that what is said in jest is very often more serious than what is said seriously...

* * *

For some people the sight of a chasm evokes the thought of an abyss, for others, a bridge. I belong to the second group.

* * *

You speak of "theatre science", but I don't know what that means. Scholars argue among themselves about the ultimate, future goals of science, but they all agree that at one hundred degrees centigrade water boils. We have not yet established similar basic truths. There is complete disagreement about everything! The first goal of a so-called "theatre science" is the establishment of a uniform terminology and the formulation of basic truths. But I fear that we are still far from even that.

* * *

You are waiting for me to produce a thick tome about my work as a director, but I am dreaming of a thin little book, almost a brochure, in which I will attempt to set forth certain basic truths. And in this booklet I will gather together the sum total of my "enormous" experience. Of course, only if I have time to be brief, as someone once put it so well.

* * *

(To a young actor during a rehearsal break.)
Did you happen to catch *The Queen of Spades* yesterday? You couldn't get a complimentary ticket? Well, well, well!... And the scalpers wanted a lot for tickets? Ah-ha! And, of course, you had no money? A long time to payday? And so you passed it up? But don't you know how to get in without a ticket? When we were young, we knew how. There was a time when they threw me out of the Maly Theatre almost every evening. One evening you'd see the first two acts, and another, two more... Of course, it was embarrassing when they threw you out in front of respectable people, but what wouldn't you do to see Ermolova!... And so, they didn't give you a complimentary ticket and you gave up. What? You went home? Oh, to the skating rink!... Well, that's a different matter!

That's perhaps even better than *The Queen of Spades!* You were right! Good for you!

* * *

Probably no director in the whole world has been abused as much as I have. But will you believe me if I tell you that no one has judged me as severely as I have myself? True, I don't much like self-deprecation. I believe that in the final analysis, it's a matter between the two of us: me and myself... But internal criticism is a strange thing. There are victories you are almost ashamed of, and failures you take pride in.

* * *

When they say to me, "You are a master!" I'm inwardly a little amused. Do you know, I'm worried and excited before each première as if I were again taking the competitive exam for the position of second violin.

* * *

Critical direct hits at me have been rare, not because there have been none who wanted to shoot, but because I'm a target that moves too quickly.

* * *

To maintain that stylization is an inherent characteristic of art, isn't that after all the same as defending the thesis that nutritiousness is characteristic of food?

* * *

I love to rework my old productions. I'm often told that in so doing I spoil them. Perhaps, but I've never once been able to see a production I've done without the desire to change something.

* * *

I constantly hear about my "mistakes". And just what is a "mistake" in art? A person makes a mistake when he enters one room and finds himself in another. But in order to make that mistake, you must have two rooms to go into. If somewhere alongside one of my productions, there were another one which was a model in every respect, then I might be reproached for staging my production differently. But, you see, there is no other production, no other room. In art, one can make mistakes in one sense only: to choose for one's objective unsuitable means and consequently to ruin one's own idea. But that's not what all those who shout about my "mistakes" mean. Oh, if only they would judge me by Pushkin's rule, that is, by the rules which I set for myself! But how rarely do I hear such criticism.

* * *

I often wake at night in a cold sweat thinking that I have become banal, that everything in life is going too well for me, that I will die under a thick quilt, that I have stopped being an innovator.

* * *

I'm often reproached because I don't develop my own discoveries and findings, but always hurry on to new work: after one production I put on another seemingly completely different in style. First of all, life is short, and if you repeat yourself there's much you won't manage to do. Second, where a superficial glance sees a chaos of different styles and manners, my collaborators and I see the application of the very same general principles to different material, a diverse reworking of it depending on the author's style and present-day objectives. And furthermore!... The biographer of the Renaissance masters, Giorgio Vasari wrote in characterizing the highest achievement of an artist, "In a manner unknown until now"... Doesn't this phrase excite you? Isn't that the highest honor for an artist, to produce a work "in a manner unknown until now"...?

* * *

The so-called "success" of a première should not be the main goal of the theatre. Sometimes you have to go with eyes open even when approaching the failure you anticipated. When I was staging Selvinsky's *The Second Army Commander*, I was convinced of an inevitable "flop", but this didn't affect my determination. Besides short-term tactical goals, I had long-range strategic goals. I wanted the magnificent poet, Selvinsky, to smell the theatrical gunpowder, and I hoped that in the future he would give us a new, remarkable play.

In *The Second Army Commander* there were powerful scenes and energetic verse. But there was also one fatal mistake: the main character, Okonny, could not be the hero of a Soviet tragedy. He was too insignificant for that. But all the same, I'm not sorry I staged this play. Without "flops" there can be no successes. In the production there were discoveries I value greatly, and several first-class acting performances. Is this really so little? I think in certain circumstances the theatre must boldly risk a "flop" and not retreat. This was precisely such a case. [*The Second Army Commander* was first performed in Kharkhov on July 24, 1929. Selvinsky started out with great promise – he was even compared to Mayakovsky – but that promise was never realized. And as was true of a number of playwrights who worked with Meyerhold, Selvinsky resented the way Meyerhold reworked his play, though he admitted later that the production significantly influenced his subsequent works.]

* * *

With me, anger is often a creative incentive. Thus, I wanted to stage *The Queen of Spades* after I saw and heard Nikolai Pechkovsky as Herman. I was so angry with him that if we'd met at night in a dark alley, it would have gone badly for him. I felt angry, I grumbled for a while, then I began to think and dream, and thus arrived at my production of the opera.

* * *

When I see a brawl on the street, I always stop and watch. In street scenes and brawls, you can observe the most varied and hidden human traits. Don't listen to the policeman when he says to you, "Come on, get moving citizen!" Circle the crowd and stand on the other side and watch. When as a young man I went to Italy for the first time, I planned to make the rounds of most of the museums and palaces. But I soon threw that over, because I was carried away by the animated street life in Milan. I wandered open-mouthed, intoxicated by it. If I should be late for rehearsal, and you see through the window that there's some kind of incident on Gorky Street [formerly Tverskaya Street], then you may be sure, Meyerhold is certain to be there. [Gladkov recalls the time when an actor arrived late for rehearsal, excusing his tardiness by saying that he had stopped to watch a street brawl. "How did it come out?" Meyerhold eagerly asked. When the actor answered that he didn't know because he had left to get to the theatre, Meyerhold exclaimed, "How could you! How could you not stay and see how it came out!"]

* * *

The critics would like very much for the maturation of an artist to take place somewhere in a laboratory behind curtained windows and locked doors. But we grow, mature, seek, make mistakes and discoveries in full view of everyone and in collaboration with an audience. Great generals are also taught by the blood shed on the battlefields. But an artist is taught by his own blood... Besides, what is a mistake? Tomorrow's success sometimes grows out of today's mistake.

* * *

Ferruccio Busoni interprets Bach, Chopin, and Liszt in his own way, and his interpretations are even called "Bach–Busoni" or "Liszt–Busoni". No one but a vulgarian would even think of beginning to compare in importance Bach and Busoni and of reproaching Busoni for immodesty and usurpation. But how many critical shafts have been thrust at me because I interpreted Ostrovsky and Gogol in my own way. It's curious that this in no wise disturbed Lunacharsky, or Mayakovsky, or Andrei Bely. But on the other hand Metalnikovs of all sorts literally foamed at the mouth... It seems that Mérimée in *Carmen* cites the Spanish proverb:

"The daring of a dwarf lies in how far he can spit"... [*Metalnikovs*: According to Gladkov, this was Meyerhold's way of referring to the reactionary critic, David Talnikov, and other critics like him.]

* * *

I love passionate situations in the theatre and often create them for myself in life.

* * *

I would have been stepping "on the throat of my own song", in Mayakovsky's words, if I had disavowed my *Magnanimous Cuckold*.

* * *

In revolutionary times people live at an accelerated pace. Remember 1893–94 in France, remember our own 1917, completely unbounded and embracing whole decades. All the changes in these periods take place at the same breakneck speed. I'm told, "But look, last year you maintained thus and so". "Not last year", I answer, "but ten years ago according to my inner calendar".

* * *

Well, tomorrow I'm going to my dacha to rest... You're also going to the country? Where do you live out of town? On the Yaroslavl line? Somewhere near Pushkino? Ah, on another branch! (Pause.) Yes, Pushkino... I remember how once on a dusty summer day Moskvin and I arrived by cab at the Yaroslavl Station, boarded the train, and set off for Pushkino. And with that, it all began. As Stephen Zweig says, a fatal moment!... I hear that recently Moskvin has been ill. Do you know how he is? All right?... (A long pause.) Yes! A fatal moment!... [Meyerhold is recalling the train trip in June 1898 to Pushkino where the newly-born future Moscow Art Theatre would spend the summer rehearsing in a house and barn belonging to Nikolai Arkhipov, a lawyer and would-be actor. Stanislavsky's summer home was conveniently located at nearby Lyubimovka.]

* * *

On V.E.'s desk, Romain Rolland's book on Beethoven is lying open. In leafing through it, I see a phrase of Beethoven's underlined: "There is no rule that cannot be broken for the sake of the more beautiful"...

On the Art of the Actor

The theatre has one amazing characteristic: the talented actor, for some reason, always finds an intelligent spectator.

* * *

Don't try so hard! Trust the spectator! He's much smarter than he seems to us to be.

* * *

It's essential that the actor find pleasure for himself in executing a given movement or action pattern [*risunok*]. If you find that pleasure, then everything will work out. Victory awaits you.

* * *

Stop! (To the actress S.) You are terribly tense. I could barely budge you from your place just now. The actor in a production must have the kind of tension a *Lezginka* dancer has. The slightest effort and there he is flying across the stage.

* * *

Don't deny drunk scenes their internal logic! The only thing about the behavior of drunks that is different is that all their segments of acting are unfinished as it were. You begin a movement and suddenly break it off. Or in the movement more energy is expended than necessary, or less. Therein lies their comic essence. But it must be light. The lighter, the funnier, and the more finesse there is. I would assess the taste of an actor based on how he plays a drunk.

* * *

In a tail coat one must keep to half movements. Elbows have to be held closer to the body. Gestural thrusts must be short, movements light. When Dalmatov made his entrance in a tail coat, it was already a whole production number. It was worth paying money to see. I remember one time Stanislavsky silently walked before us for two hours in a cloak. He turned, he sat down, he lay down, and after that I couldn't fall asleep all night. That too you must love in the theatre. [Throughout his life, Meyerhold kept an old-fashioned photograph of Dalmatov which the actor had autographed for Meyerhold's father. Not long before his death, Dalmatov rehearsed the role of "The Unknown" in Meyerhold's production of *Masquerade* at the Alexandrinsky Theatre. Following his death, Meyerhold wrote an article about this remarkable actor, signing it "Doctor Dapertutto".]

* * *

Get closer to the door before you exit! Even closer! That's axiomatic. The closer you are to the door, the more effective your exit. In moments of climax, the seconds of stage time and centimeters of stage floor decide everything. This algebra of stagecraft wasn't scorned by Ermolova or Komissarzhevskaya, or Lensky or Mamont Dalsky.

* * *

Don't shout like that! Everything must be done more quietly! When actors shout like that it's impossible to bring out the nuances. When as a young man I worked with Konstantin Sergeevich, he also considered me a terrible shouter, and he continually made me speak more softly. But I didn't understand and robbed myself...

* * *

The voice of tragedy must be detached. Tears are inadmissible.

* * *

In tragic art all the scenes are crescendo, but in sentimental art, diminuendo.

* * *

If the spectator is bored, it means the actors have lost the substance of the scene and are playing out the dead form of it.

* * *

Whatever you do on the stage, always keep to half-measures, both in voice and in movement. The spectator always notes the tension and strain of an actor who is trying too hard.

* * *

One of the things I hate most of all in the theatre is when the text of a role is littered with all sorts of unappetizing interjections and prepositions: "Oh", "Well-well", "Yes, siree", "That's it", and so on... It's usually second-rate actors who are prone to that.

* * *

Even in the pauses you have to know how to maintain the tempo of the dialogue.

* * *

Easier! Don't sit on the spectator's neck!

* * *

Training! Training! Training! But if it's the kind of training which exercises only the body and not the mind, then No, thank you! I have no use for actors who know how to move but cannot think.

* * *

The swifter the text, the more distinct the breaks must be: the transitions from one segment to another, from one rhythm to another. Otherwise the motivation is lost, the living breath of meaning vanishes.

* * *

A line has to be served up succulently, as though to arouse the appetite, like a cook serving up a tasty dish. He doesn't raise the lid of the saucepan right away. First enchant us with the aroma of the line and then treat us to it.

* * *

A goal to strive for during rehearsals is to make the play with objects become automatic, so that it isn't done each time as a fresh stunt.

* * *

An object held in the hand is an extension of the hand.

* * *

A distinctly spoken line will pierce a wall of any thickness.

* * *

Don't overdo the exposition of the play. The exposition must be precisely and clearly "announced".

* * *

In order to cry real tears on the stage, one must feel creative joy, internal elation, that is, the same feeling as is necessary in order to sincerely burst out laughing. The psycho-physical nature of stage tears and stage laughter is absolutely identical. Behind them are the joy of the artist and his creative elation – that's all. Any other means for evoking tears are neurasthenic and pathological, hence inadmissible to art.

* * *

Creative work is always a joy. The actor playing the dying Hamlet or Boris Godunov must tremble with joy. His artistic elation will give him that internal voltage, that tension which will make all his colors glow.

* * *

An actor must know the composition of the entire production, must understand and feel it with his whole body. Only then does he make himself a component of it and begin to sound in harmony with it.

* * *

Strive to get pleasure from carrying out acting instructions. That's axiom number one!

* * *

You play very well in the Korsh style and badly in the Meyerhold style. You're playing only for yourself, forgetting the general compositional plan. In Korsh's theatre you also weren't supposed to upstage your partner, but that was all they demanded. But with us, if you change the layout by half a meter, everything is lost. There must be the artistic discipline of feeling a part of the overall composition. Otherwise switch from me to Korsh! One or the other! [Founded in 1882, the Korsh was a typical commercial theatre with a new production opening every

Saturday night. It was characterized by a total absence of directorial control with the actors themselves setting the mises en scène.]

* * *

Play this segment differently at every performance! (To the actor playing the role of Krechinsky [the hero of Sukhovo-Kobylin's *Krechinsky's Wedding*] in the scene in which Krechinsky is awakened with a pistol.)

* * *

I don't like makeup. I loved it as a youth and then that passed. Now I can't stand it. Actors often argue with me about this when, before a première, I begin removing their makeup. But I keep silent, as I know the time will come when they too will cease to like it. Makeup must always be at a minimum. Lensky brilliantly did a minimal and completely convincing makeup. A lot of theories were concocted about there being almost no makeup used in my production of *Cuckold*. I also composed them. But the explanation is quite simple: I don't like makeup, that's all. And why would the young Ilinsky, Babanova, and Zaichikov need makeup? All great actors used little makeup. It hampered them. A passion for makeup is a childhood illness for an actor.

* * *

The actor must possess the ability always to mentally *mirrorize* himself. In general, everyone possesses this ability in rudimentary form, but in the actor it must be developed.

* * *

At the beginning of Chekhov's *The Bear*, Smirnov is a Vesuvius still gently smoldering...

* * *

Allow for a short break! For the members of the audience it will indicate the end of a segment. Let them, together with you, catch their breath. And then a new segment begins. You must feel the breathing of the audience and sense where it needs to catch its breath. When you act well, the audience breathes along with you.

* * *

If you can't rid yourself of some defect in speech or movement, then force the spectator to come to love this defect. Andreev-Burlak lisped, Rossov stuttered, Leonidov spoke with a whistle. Savina and Sarah Bernhardt spoke nasally, but their stage presence was so powerful that these traits seemed to be virtues. [Vasily Andreev-Burlak made his stage debut in 1868 and became famous on the provincial theatre circuit as a character actor. Meyerhold, who was only fourteen when the actor died, saw him perform in Penza. Nikolai Rossov was one of the last of the old-time touring actors in Russia. Meyerhold first saw him in Penza and even wrote a review of his performance. In the 1930s, Rossov sometimes came to see Meyerhold at his theatre. Although they were from two completely different theatrical epochs, Meyerhold always treated the old actor very kindly. Leonid Leonidov made his debut at the Moscow Art Theatre as Pepel in Gorky's *The Lower Depths* in 1903. His whistle was probably the result of ill-fitting false teeth, a common problem among older actors on the Russian stage. Maria Savina joined the Alexandrinsky Theatre in 1874. She was one of the leaders of the opposition against Meyerhold when he became a director at the Alexandrinsky Theatre in 1908. In 1915, Meyerhold directed her in the role of Elena Ivanovna in Zinaida Gippius' *The Green Ring*.]

* * *

Aside from the great works of dramatic literature, there are plays which in themselves are nothing remarkable, but which grandly bear the traces of great performances. They are like a canvas for stunning improvisations by the actor, just as many of Anton Rubenstein's piano pieces are outlines for a virtuoso performer to fill in. But only very rich and talented acting can endow these outlines with a fullness of content. Thus, Eleanora Duse gave a performance of genius in *The Lady of the Camellias*, and Chaliapin sang divinely in the weak opera, *The Demon*. [The most celebrated of Anton Rubinstein's operas, *The Demon* is based on Lermontov's poem of the same name.]

* * *

Apollon Grigoriev praised the scene of Kudryash and Varvara in *The Storm* as one of the most remarkable in terms of airy transparency and lyricism. But in the Art Theatre's production, I saw with horror that they had turned this scene into something like a European music-hall number – disgusting pornography. Putting aside the violence done to the author, I was hurt and offended for the sake of the actors: for the talented Livanov and for the actress whose name I tried not to remember from an innate sense of modesty. [Meyerhold is speaking of the 1935 production of *The Storm*, directed by Nemirovich-Danchenko. The actress was Klavdia Elanskaya. Meyerhold characterized her to Gladkov as "a boring actress who delivered her lines in a weepy mono-tone".]

* * *

The great Italian comedian Guglielmo demanded from an actor the ability to adapt himself to the playing area. An actor's movements on a round platform are not the same as on a square one. They're different at the proscenium than at the back of the stage.

Here, only directors think about this, and not always, at that. Yet, the ability to position one's body in space is a fundamental law of acting.

* * *

An actor must study as a violinist does, for seven to nine years. You can't make yourself into an actor in three to four years.

* * *

The good actor is distinguished from the bad by the fact that on Thursday he doesn't play the same way he did on Tuesday. An actor's joy isn't in repeating what was successful, but in variations and improvisations within the limits of the composition as a whole.

* * *

I hate to think that the art of such a remarkable actor as Igor Ilinsky will disappear with his death. Ilinsky ought to train a pupil. Not ten or twenty depersonalized pupils as produced by almost assembly-line methods in the so-called theatre institutes, but one or two real pupils. It's the duty of a master craftsman personally to train apprentices who would have to help him, live with him, eat with him, like the students of the Renaissance masters or the actors in the Japanese theatre. Each great master has a duty to train a pupil, irrespective of whether he's engaged in teaching. And he should take full responsibility for him.

* * *

In his personal relationships the actor shouldn't lock himself into a narrow professional circle as has been customary up to now. A closed actors' circle is a terrible professional evil. Shchepkin was friends with Herzen and Gogol, Lensky with Chekhov. All my life I've also tried to make friends with writers, musicians and artists. It broadens the horizon and gets you away from the conservatism of parochial interests.

* * *

The genuine master-actor reaches his prime at forty to forty-five years. By this age professional experience has been strengthened by the riches of life's accumulations.

* * *

Many times I've observed that when a talented actor violates an action pattern I've set, it's not that I close my eyes to it, usually I simply don't notice it. Sometimes later on I'm told, "V.E., look, X has broken the established action pattern". And I'm honestly surprised. "Really?" Usually it even seems to me that I had set it or thought it up myself.

* * *

I would most strictly forbid actors to drink wine, or coffee, or take valerian drops. They all shatter the nervous system. An actor's nervous system must be the very healthiest. A certain poet wrote Flaubert that he had composed his poem while sobbing, and Flaubert laughed at him. Contrary to accepted opinion, Sergei Esenin never wrote poetry while drunk. That I know. Acting, as well as all other creative work, is an act of clear and joyous consciousness, of a healthy, clear will. At the beginning of the century a type of actor appeared called a "neurasthenic-hero" (Orlenev and others). But, characteristically, no one so quickly became disqualified professionally as actors of this type. By forty-five, they were almost all spiritual and physical wrecks. And yet, that age is the zenith for a dramatic actor.

* * *

The most valuable quality for an actor is individuality. In even the most skillful stage transformation, individuality must shine through. There was an actor named Petrovsky who had a striking technique of transformation, but he never did become a great actor: he had no individuality. Perhaps it existed at one time in the embryo, but he not only didn't develop it, he completely erased it. It seems to me that individuality exists as a starting point for everyone. After all, children don't all resemble one another. Any kind of upbringing erases individuality, of course, but the actor must defend his individuality and develop it.

I have a habit when I meet a new person: I always ponder what kind of a child he was. Try it. It's very interesting and instructive. Now there's one actor in our troupe who with all my imagination I can't possibly picture as a child. He's like an onion: beneath each little stage image there is another and another, right to the end ... He has completely erased his individuality; and in spite of his excellent technique, he's mediocre in every role... You want to know who it is? Oh no, nothing doing!... [According to Gladkov, Meyerhold had in mind Pyotr Starkovsky, the actor who played the mayor in Meyerhold's production of *The Inspector General*. In addition to numerous secondary roles, he also played Famusov in the 1935 version of *Woe to Wit*.]

* * *

Gorky wrote the most profound observations about people when they are alone with themselves. When I visited him in Sorrento in 1925, and he read them to me himself, I was struck by their subtlety and acuity. The theatrical nature of human life is more apparent in them than in Evreinov's posturings and flowery treatises. In every person there is a quality that makes him an actor. Observe yourself at home. You have returned from a meeting where you made a speech, or from a date, or from a river where you helped rescue a drowning child – and even in your own home, for some time you'll be an orator, or a lover, or a hero. People would not love actors so much if they all didn't have a little bit of the actor in themselves.

* * *

Practically speaking, an actor's work begins after the première. I maintain that a production is never ready by its première. Not because we were "short of time", but because a production ripens only in front of an audience. At least in my experience I've never seen a production that was ready by the première. Salvini said he understood *Othello* only after the two-hundredth performance. Nowadays, time moves at a different pace, and so shortening it to one tenth of that number, let's tell the critics: judge us only after the twentieth performance. Only then will the actors' roles sound as they should. I heard that Nemirovich-Danchenko recently maintained the same thing. He and I may say that, as well as Stanislavsky, Craig, Mei Lan-fang and Moissi, but just the same, the pig-headed theatre administrators will go on inviting the critics to the première... [The truth is, according to Gladkov, Meyerhold's productions tended to be at their best at the première. Once a production was staged, Meyerhold lost interest in it and moved on to something else, rather than spend time improving what he had already done.]

* * *

Training and creativity are two different things. The person who receives top grades in acting school doesn't always become a great actor. I'm even afraid he'll never be one. Penmanship lessons are not at all needed in order to write later on like a calligrapher. Only army clerks write like that. However, that doesn't mean penmanship lessons aren't needed at all. While calligraphy doesn't create handwriting, it gives the correct foundation, as does any training.

But Serov was right when he said that a portrait is good only when it has a magical flaw in it. I've talked with many people whose portraits Serov painted. I was interested in the process of their creation. It's curious that each of the subjects believed that it was just in his portrait that something unexpected and unusual happened with Serov. But since this something unexpected happened in all of them, it means that this was Serov's method of working. At first he spent a long time painting simply a good portrait. The client was satisfied, and so was the client's mother-in-law. Then suddenly Serov would dash in, wipe off everything, and paint on the canvas a new portrait containing that very magical flaw of which he had spoken. It's curious that for the creation of such a portrait he first had to sketch a "correct" portrait. It's amusing, by the way, that some of his clients liked the "correct" portrait better.

* * *

The rank of Soviet actor should be just as honorable as the rank of Red Army soldier.

* * *

The actor must not rivet his role hermetically tight any more than a bridge builder his metal constructions. You have to leave slots for bits of extemporaneous acting, for improvisation. [Meyerhold didn't like an actor who wasn't good at improvising. Lev Sverdlin, for example, was incapable of improvising at rehearsal; he couldn't even repeat what Meyerhold would demonstrate. Instead, he would wait until he got home and then work on his role. Meyerhold didn't like this.]

* * *

The costume is also a part of the body. Look at the mountain dweller. It would seem that the *burka* [felt cloak worn in the Caucasus] must conceal his body, but usually it's sewn in such a way that when worn by a real Caucasian, it's all alive, all pulsating, and through the *burka* you can see the rhythmic waves of the body. I saw Fokine in a ballet and purposely went backstage later to see how his costume was made. He was wearing a lot of heavy cloth, wadding, and the devil knows what. But during the performance I saw all the lines of his body.

* * *

Stop! (To the actor K, who is sitting on a high ladder.) Change your posture! Sit more firmly, more comfortably. (Actor: "I'm comfortable, V.E".) I don't care so much if you are comfortable. I care much more that the spectator doesn't fear for you, that he doesn't worry about your being uncomfortable. This pointless worry distracts him from the scene we are playing... That's it! Good! Thanks!

* * *

"*The director's basting threads*"... take out the director's basting threads!... Hide the basting threads of my instructions. (To the actress T.) I asked you to sit down at this point, but you do it too obviously, revealing my design. First sit down lightly, and then settle more firmly! Conceal my director's plan, my basting threads!

* * *

In each role the actor acquires new nuances and they remain with him forever. Suppose you play Armand Duval [Marguerite's lover in *The Lady of the Camellias*] and then a series of other roles. After three years you'll no longer play Armand Duval as you did earlier, but will in some measure enrich him with these new nuances.

* * *

Shchukin plays Lenin not badly, but his imitators will be unbearable. He somewhat sentimentalizes Lenin, but they'll make him saccharine sweet. It seems to me that Shtraukh plays him more correctly: more manly and more intelligent.

* * *

You know, someone once told me how Lenin, during a very serious political argument (can you imagine how he could argue?) petted a dog under the table while listening to his opponent. With that detail, for the first time I understood with absolutely clarity the power of Lenin's inner composure and his spiritual serenity. For an actor, such a detail is invaluable. Once he has heard that, he's set. The role is ready. For the skilled actor, of course...

* * *

I have seen fifteen to twenty Hamlets in my lifetime, and they were all different. The only thing they had in common was that they all wore black.

* * *

I love the theatre and I sometimes feel sad because leadership in the art of acting is beginning to be taken over by movie actors. I won't speak of Chaplin, who by some magic premonition we loved even before we saw him. But remember Buster Keaton! When it comes to subtlety of interpretation, clarity of acting, tactful characterization, and stylistically restrained gesture, he was an absolutely unique phenomenon. [Meyerhold was a fan of both Chaplin and Keaton and knew their movies well. Meyerhold first saw Chaplin in person in Paris in the 1920s.]

* * *

The actor of the future will have before him for a given part of a production exact director's instructions. But he will also have certain voids, gaps, places for "*ex-improvisio*" acting which he must fill, not with previously prepared, but with freshly-created stage business.

* * *

I have noticed in our company the beginning of a tendency to disdain small roles. An actor appears in a minor part and we feel that with his acting he is saying, as it were, "Well, this isn't much of a role!" But Atyasova, I notice, has a true artist's attitude. Her role may be small, yet she plays it at full strength. For that I now stand up and bow to her. Thank you, Atyasova! [Meyerhold highly valued the minor actresses like

Antonina Atyasova in his troupe and was always extraordinarily attentive to them. For them, being a part of Meyerhold's theatre was the high point of their lives.]

* * *

I don't like Isadora Duncan. One gesture with five variations... [Meyerhold first saw Isadora Duncan perform in St. Petersburg in 1908. At that time he wrote in a letter that he was "moved to tears". But by 1915 Meyerhold was already speaking of the necessity for the actor to eliminate "all traces of Duncanesque balleticism". Meyerhold also dismissed as "unnecessary for actors" Jaques-Dalcroze's "eurhythmics", which he saw demonstrated in 1911 when Dalcroze and a group of his students came to Moscow and St. Petersburg.]

* * *

Every morning, from my window on Bryusov Lane, I watch as the famous actors pass by on the way to their theatre. There goes M., there's L., and here comes K. It is us, their manner of walking says. Look at us; you are lucky that you are seeing us, we are famous... And I look at them and think: How on earth are they going to rehearse and perform with such an unwavering sense of their superiority. You couldn't even shake them... Chekhov once rejoiced that the actors at the Art Theatre didn't look like actors but like ordinary educated people. Not one bit! Life has put everything in its place! Stanislavsky lives on Leontyev Lane and almost no one passes his house, and so he doesn't see that. Otherwise he would doubtless raise an uproar. I know that much about him... [Meyerhold is referring to the Moscow Art Theatre actors, Ivan Moskvin, Leonid Leonidov, and Vasily Kachalov; they lived further down on Bryusov Lane and would have passed Meyerhold's apartment on their way to the Moscow Art Theatre.]

* * *

The basic quality of the Kabuki players' acting is the same as Chaplin's: their naïveté. Naïveté in everything they do: in tragedy and in comedy. That's why the stylized form of their productions seems natural. Without the naïveté in acting, the stylized devices of a director seem stiff and strange.

* * *

The variety theatre is very harmful for Kachalov. In my opinion he is becoming worse and worse as an actor. The variety theatre accustomed him to declaiming, and that has already begun to seep into his roles on the dramatic stage. He has a velvet voice, a good build, his hair is blonde and wavy, he has languishing eyes, a nasal tone that makes his voice firm. He's not a person, but an oboe. You watch when he goes out on the concert stage. But he can no longer act. The same thing happened with Yurev. On the variety stage, an actor shows off his own "self". But in the theatre, through this "self" he builds an image. Since our Gorsky began working as a reader in a variety ensemble, he has become noticeably weaker as an actor. At first, I didn't understand and wondered: what's happening to Gorsky? And then I learned that he's working in an ensemble. Well, now it's all clear...

* * *

The difference between acting that relies only on words and the acting of our school is like that between an express telegram (ours) and a telegram taken by wagon to a village sixty miles away from the telegraph office (the word-actors). Our acceleration comes from the stylized elements of our stagings, the pantomime acting of the players, and so forth.

* * *

The funnier a comedy, the more seriously it must be played.

* * *

The skilled professional can be distinguished from the novice by the fact that nothing in his work is neutral. Each detail contributes (even if imperceptibly) to the whole.

* * *

Moskvin is an outstanding Khlynov [in Ostrovsky's *A Fervent Heart*], a magnificent Zagoretsky [in *Woe from Wit*]. I can't imagine a better one. But then he played the mayor [in *The Inspector General*] in a heavy style, verging on tragedy, and not only in the finale where it's permissible, but also earlier.

* * *

An actor arrives at the theatre in the evening. He hangs up his coat and an hour later he is already a different person. He's not yet Othello, but he's already made up as Othello. Although he still chats about this and that with his dressing room neighbors, he's no long Ivan Ivanovich, but halfway to being Othello. Most of all I love to watch a good actor when he's halfway to the character he's going to portray: still Ivan Ivanovich and a little bit Othello.

* * *

I can always distinguish a genuine actor from a poor one by his eyes. The good actor knows the value of his gaze. With only a shift of his pupils from the line of the horizon to the right or the left, up or down, he will give the necessary accent to his acting, which will be understood by the audience. The eyes of poor actors and dabblers are always fidgety, darting here and there to the sides.

* * *

An actor must know how to act "with the music" and not "to the music". There is a colossal and not yet completely understood difference.

* * *

It is ten times easier for me to work with an actor who loves music. Actors should be trained in music while they are still in school. All actors like music "for setting the mood", but very few understand that music is the best organizer of *time* in a production. Figuratively speaking, the actor's acting is in single combat with time. And here, music is his best helper. It doesn't even need to be heard, but it must be felt. I dream of a production rehearsed to music, but performed without music. Without it, and yet with it, because the rhythm of the production will be organized according to the music's laws and each performer will carry it within himself.

* * *

My favorite actor, Mamont Dalsky, said that there must never be any correspondence between the personal mood of the actor and the mood of the character being portrayed. That kills art. He always played Hamlet in complex opposition to the mood in which he arrived for the performance. If he felt energetic and full of life, then he played him as dreamy, tender, hesitant. If his mood was meditatively lyric, then he played him with power and fervent passion. This is indeed the basis of artistic reincarnation.

* * *

I fell in love with Mamont Dalsky when I noticed the light and immediately interrupted movement of his hand toward the dagger in the scene where the King, cloyingly friendly and almost lovingly, first speaks to Prince Hamlet. Actually, with this half-movement, fleeting, barely noticeable, but expressive, the actor has already drawn us into the heart of the play and promised us all that we are now going to follow with such emotion.

* * *

Do you know, Salvini and Rossi played Hamlet differently almost every time, sometimes leaving out the philosophical monologues, sometimes putting them back in, depending on the makeup of the audience!

* * *

We are justifiably proud of our theatre. But when I'm abroad, I always try to spot there, too, something good that should be borrowed. Yes, worthless little plays, old-fashioned stagecraft, but in the actors, I'm always won over by their particular musicality, high professionalism, discipline, and that sense of responsibility for each rank-and-file performance that is disappearing with us. At the Parisian Théâtre de la Madeleine, I admired the performance of one actor and was taken backstage to meet him. Can you imagine – after a very difficult performance he wasn't resting, he was in no hurry to run off for supper. Instead, he was preparing coffee on a spirit-lamp and rehearsing one place in the production that he thought hadn't gone well that evening. No one forced him to do that. He understood it by himself.

* * *

We are somewhat weak in professional discipline. We're getting slack. We're becoming dependent. We don't attend performances and rehearsals, and we try hard not to express sharp opinions. I consider Oblomovism in our troupe enemy number one. [A reference to the hero of Ivan Goncharov's novel, *Oblomov*, who was so consumed by inertia that his name became synonymous with laziness.] One needs constant discipline, upward drive, energy in one's work! Our performances must be saturated with will! The principal purpose of the theatre, like music, ·is to be a stimulus for an active life. Living conditions? Forget it! In 1920, half-starving and tubercular, I felt fine and even fell in love... [Meyerhold is referring to his meeting and falling in love with Zinaida Raikh. In 1921, she became a student in his Workshop. A year later Meyerhold took her as his second wife. Following her debut as Aksyusha in Meyerhold's 1924 production of *The Forest*, Zinaida Raikh played in virtually every one of Meyerhold's productions. Without question, her greatest role was Marguerite Gautier in *The Lady of the Camellias*, which Meyerhold staged in 1934 as a gift to her.]

On the Art of the Director

As a director I began by slavishly imitating Stanislavsky. Theoretically, I was no longer accepting many of his earlier methods of directing; I was critical of them. But in practice, when I began my work, I at first timidly followed in his footsteps. I don't regret it because this period wasn't prolonged. I swiftly and intensively went through it. It was, all the same, an excellent school of practical directing. In a young artist, imitation is not dangerous. It's almost an unavoidable stage. I would even say that in youth it's useful to imitate good models: it polishes up one's inner independence, provokes its clear development. Earlier, no one was ashamed of the word "imitation". Remember Pushkin: "Imitation of

Parny", "Imitation of Chénier", "Imitation of the Koran". Mayakovsky said he began by imitating Balmont. Later he imitated Whitman and Sasha Cherny, but this didn't interfere with his becoming his own self. I'll say it even more definitely: imitating an artist you feel close to enables you to define yourself completely.

* * *

A director must always work confidently at rehearsals. It's better to make mistakes, erring boldly, than to crawl uncertainly toward the truth. You can always reject your mistakes the next morning, but nothing can restore the actors' loss of faith in an uncertain and vacillating director.

* * *

If today I say to an actor, "Good!" this doesn't at all mean that I will be satisfied with him when he repeats this place exactly the same way the next day.

* * *

I regret very much that I didn't stage Shaw's *Heartbreak House*. I've thought a great deal about that remarkable play. With good actors I could stage it now in three weeks. Why are you smiling? Not enough time? The young Stanislavsky wouldn't have been surprised. We've gotten lazy. We've forgotten how to work intensively, under pressure... Yes, yes, and I too...

* * *

Prior to *The Inspector General* I staged twenty productions which were examinations for staging *The Inspector General*.

* * *

In our *Forest*, at first there were 33 episodes, but because the performance ended very late and the spectators missed the last streetcars, I heeded the management's pleas and abridged it to 26 episodes. The performance, which had lasted more than four hours, now ran 3 hours and 20 minutes. Time passed, and the management informed me that the performance was again taking four hours. I concluded that the actors, on their own, had put back some of the scenes I'd cut. I came and watched, but nothing of the sort! It was simply that they were overplaying the remaining 26 episodes. I reprimanded them. It didn't help. I arranged a rehearsal and with aching heart cut the production to 16 episodes. For a time the performance ran two and a half hours, but then again grew to four hours.

Ultimately, the show half fell to pieces, and we had to rehearse it anew, reestablishing all the rhythms and temporal proportions within the production. Once I had to post an order that if the scene between Pyotr and Aksyusha, which was to last two minutes, ran a minute longer, I would impose a penalty on the actors. Actors must be taught to be aware of time on the stage, as musicians are aware of it. A musically organized production isn't a production where music is being played or sung all the time behind the scenes, but rather a production with a precise rhythmic score, with precisely organized time.

* * *

When the architects, Mikhail Barkhin and Sergei Vakhtangov, and I began working out the project for the new building of our theatre, I suddenly understood to my own surprise that the structure of my so-called "landmark" productions had unconsciously reflected my quest for new stage architecture. Take a look at the plans. What does this row of doors in a semi-circle, opening directly onto the stage through two little balconies suggest to you? They are actors' dressing rooms. Aren't they just like the doors in *The Inspector General?* And I put the orchestra above the stage, as in *Bubus*. And the stage area itself is almost the same as in *The Warrant*. And so forth. This is how you live, staging now one thing, then another, seemingly without any connection or consistency. And then it turns out that all your life you've been erecting the walls of one huge building.

Recently, I was rereading Balzac's *Splendors and Miseries of Court-esans* and thinking about how Balzac discovered one fine day that all his novels were fragments of one great epic. If you write about me after my death, don't get carried away hunting for contradictions, but try to find the common connection in everything I have done. Although, I must confess, even to me it hasn't always been apparent.

* * *

In the good director there is a potential dramatist. After all, at one time it was a single profession. Only later was it split, just as science is gradually being divided up. This wasn't a fundamental division, but a technical necessity because the art of the theatre had become more complicated. One had to be a Leonardo da Vinci in order both to write the dialogue and handle the lighting. (I'm speaking, of course, in rough terms.) But by nature they are one! And therefore the art of the director is an authorial art, not a performing art. But of course, one must have the right to do that. And are the pianists Neigauz or Sofronitsky merely performers? Who will dare to say that?

* * *

You can astonish the spectator as much as you want in the first act, but he must believe you completely in the last.

* * *

Beethoven said that he achieved mastery when he stopped trying to put into one sonata contents that could fill up ten. If this is true, then I'm still far from mastery.

* * *

I think a "claque" of sorts is permissible in the theatre, if it facilitates the correct understanding of a production. You've noticed, of course, how sometimes a little group of spectators greets with applause a favorite actor appearing on stage and how the whole audience at once joins this little group. Visual emotion is a very infectious thing. When everyone around you is laughing, you can't help laughing; when they yawn, you also begin to yawn. Therefore, to insure that a performance will "take hold", we always try to fill the theatre with spectators in a friendly mood. And taking into account the infectiousness of the spectators' emotions, why should we exclude the device of active arousal in the audience of the emotions we need? It may shock the theatrical puritans, but I confess that in *The Last, Decisive*, I placed an actress in the audience who began to sob at the right moment. At once, as if by command, everyone around her reached for their handkerchiefs. This was timed with Bogolyubov's line, "Who is crying there?"... All means are good, if they lead to the necessary result! [According to Mikhail Sadovsky, "Meyerhold not only couldn't bear a calm audience, he simply feared it. He was ready to do anything to create a conflict." (Sadovsky, p. 515.) *The Last, Decisive* had its première on February 7, 1931. The title of the play comes from a line of *The International* in Russian, "The last, decisive battle..." The scene Meyerhold is describing comes at the very end of the play. As the dying Bushuev (Bogolyubov), the last of a group of sailors holding out in a schoolroom against the enemy, falls to the floor, he looks out at the audience, smiles, and asks, "Who is crying?"]

* * *

When I read a play I like, I automatically compose juicy annotations the whole time.

* * *

The most difficult thing of all is to stage poor, shallow plays. I would pay directors double the usual fee for staging bad plays. And for the chance to stage *Hamlet* or *The Inspector General*, I would make them pay.

* * *

The problem of the intermission in the theatre isn't so much a question of a break to give the spectator a rest, as it is a question of the comsitional division of the performance. A play consisting of one enormous act is unthinkable, as would be a speech without pauses or a symphony consisting of one movement. And it would be preferable if the breaks between the acts of scenes in a performance were no longer than the pause between the movements of a symphony. But that is a goal not so much of the technique of drama as of the technique of theatre.

From my point of view, a performance must be constructed in such a way that the spectator rests right there sitting in his seat, watching a quiet scene after a loud one, a calm scene after one full of movement. (Ideally, it should be possible to change the angle of the seat back. Without fail, I'll try to get that from the builders of our new building.) Hasn't psychology long ago come to the conclusion that rest isn't idleness, but a change of activity? Shifts in the intensity of the spectator's attention are also a concern for the director.

* * *

When I was staging *The Lady of the Camellias*, my dream was that a pilot who attended a performance would fly better afterwards.

* * *

Shakespearization is not at all the restoration of the theatrical techniques of the Shakespearean age; it is the mastery in new material of his use of multiple levels, broad scope, and monumentality.

* * *

When I have had to stage two productions at one time, as, for example, *Boris Godunov* and *Natasha* right now, I've always been amazed that what I found working on one was bound through a complex process to find its way into the other. The scene of the "Religious procession" in *Natasha* will not at all resemble the crowd scenes in *Boris*, but it's inspired by them. However, this is productive only if you are working on plays remote from each other. I could not stage Gogol's *The Inspector General* and his *Marriage* at the same time. In my opinion, it's good to stage a classic masterpiece and a modern play simultaneously. [Meyerhold staged Lidiya Seifullina's *Natasha* in 1936, but it was never shown to the public. Even Meyerhold could not breathe any life into a work that was, in Gladkov's words, "so artistically false".]

* * *

The various arts have much in common, in spite of all the differences in the material used. If I were to study the compositional laws of painting, music, literature, I would no longer be helpless in the art of stagecraft. I omit the self-evident thing, a knowledge of the nature of the actor: that is the raw material of the theatre.

* * *

The director must believe in his actors the way Pavlov believed in his monkeys. When he was carried away, he would so overrate their abilities that sometimes it began to seem to him they were pulling his leg. He told me that himself.

* * *

The art of the theatre doesn't progress, but only changes its means of expression, depending upon the character of the period, its ideas, psychology, technology, architecture, its style. I think that to the audiences of Euripides and Aristophanes, our best actors would seem without talent, just as Karatygin would probably surprise us if we were destined to see him. Each period has its own code of conventions which must be observed in order to be understood. But we shouldn't forget that conventions change. When I watch some performance in the Maly Theatre, it seems to me that I'm watching some old Bolshevik women making a curtsy, or a Civil War hero kissing the hand of a young girl in a leather jacket. In life we easily sense the falsity of antiquated conventions, but in the theatre we often applaud them out of habit.

* * *

I always know when I have failed. For example, *The Proposal*, [from the Chekhov production *33 Swoons*, so-named because there were 33 fainting spells in the production, each signaled by a burst of music] on which we all worked with such pleasure and so lovingly, turned out to be an experiment that failed. The audience didn't take to it. We over-intellectualized it and as a result lost the humor. One has to look truth in the eye: they laughed more at any amateur production of *The Proposal* than at ours, even though Ilinsky played in it and Meyerhold staged it. Chekhov's light and transparent humor didn't support the weight of our philosophizing, and we flopped. It's never necessary to deceive oneself. You can not tell the truth to the critics, but to yourself, you must tell everything... [While Meyerhold had staged all of Chekhov's plays when he was working in the provinces at the beginning of the century, following the Revolution, *33 Swoons* was the only time he returned to his favorite author. According to Gladkov, Meyerhold always observed rather disingenuously, "Chekhov belongs to the Moscow Art Theatre, so why should I stage him?"]

* * *

A director's inexperience is most often felt in his inattention to the clarity of exposition. If you don't "announce" the exposition with utmost clarity, the spectator will understand nothing that follows, or he will still be only guessing when he should already be carried away.

* * *

No, I don't like to work around the table! I don't like it, period! And now they say that lately Konstantin Sergeevich has also come to dislike it...

* * *

Around the table there may be agreement between the director and the actors, and that's all. You can't come out on the stage confidently with feelings worked out around the table. All the same, you have to begin almost everything anew. Often there is little time left for this because the management is hurrying you along. And so productions appear that are full of rhythmic and psycho-physical falseness. All this only because you sat too long at the table and became strongly attached to what you found there. With directors of Sakhnovsky's type, actors in effect create a role twice: around the table and onstage. And these two interpretations collide and interfere with each other. I advise young directors to try from the very beginning to rehearse under conditions approaching those of the future performance. My *Masquerade* would have failed if I had agreed with management's requests to begin rehearsals in a small foyer. I had to accustom the actors from the very beginning to the rhythms of broad expanses. Such a wise and skilled actor as Yurev understood this perfectly and supported me.

* * *

When I was rehearsing almost simultaneously two of Lermontov's plays, *Masquerade* and *Two Brothers*, I got so deeply immersed in the 1830s, that once in answer to an insult in the press, I attempted in all seriousness to challenge my offender to a duel. It's not surprising that those productions were a success.

* * *

If it seems to you that some scene fell into place all at once at rehearsal, then you must know that, in my imagination, I had already staged it in many variations. Actually, experience lies not in the fact that you do less trying and rejecting, but in the fact that you gradually learn to do an ever greater portion of this work when you're alone with yourself.

* * *

It is incorrect to juxtapose the stylized theatre to the realistic theatre. Our formula is a stylized, realistic theatre.

* * *

Zola said that a writer needs as much courage as a general. So does a director!

* * *

I am often asked what I think about Okhlopkov's productions where the spectators sit around the stage, etc. I haven't seen these productions, but

I think the artist-director has the right even to such an arrangement of seats in the theatre if he needs it. I am only somewhat concerned because this experiment is being done in a small theatre. From my point of view, a layout like that demands a great volume of air space above the stage, a special placement of the orchestra, and special acoustical conditions in the theatre. A good idea, when carried out in a tiny location where these conditions are lacking, can be compromised in practice. [Although he was a former student and actor at his theatre, according to Gladkov, Meyerhold didn't like Okhlopkov; he considered him insincere. He also resented Okhlopkov's use of many of his ideas and devices.]

* * *

When I watch a production staged by the very youngest of my pupils, my head begins to spin from the constant changes of the mise en scène and the transitions. I ask myself in alarm, "Did I really teach them that?" And then I comfort myself, "No! Their youth and inexperience exaggerate my shortcomings, which they have mastered to a T, and then some". After that I want to stage a performance even more calmly and with greater reserve. Thus I learn from my own pupils.

* * *

It's not true that the contemporary director doesn't need the concept of the "emploi". The only question is, how to use this concept. Here, if you like is another paradox: I must know who in my theatre is a "lover", so that I don't assign him the roles of "lovers". I've observed many times that an actor unexpectedly reveals himself in an unusually interesting way when he is working somewhat against his innate gifts. They won't be lost anyway, but will accompany, as it were, the image he has created. There's nothing more boring than the provincial heroine playing Katerina [in Ostrovsky's *The Storm*]. Komissarzhevskaya's charm lay precisely in the fact that she played heroines without at all being a "heroine".

An actor is so constituted, alas, that when he's cast according to type, he stops working at all, as if counting on his voice or his figure to carry it off. In order to give an actor an incentive to work, it is sometimes necessary consciously to give him a paradoxical task, so that in dealing with it he'll have to upset his "ways". In my experience, such a method for distribution of the roles has almost always been justified. I don't like sweetly declaiming Ferdinands [in Schiller's *Kabale und Liebe*], Katerinas with throaty voices [in *The Storm*], and Khlestakovs who chatter [in *The Inspector General*].

* * *

I'm convinced that an actor placed in the correct physical *raccourci* [see *Glossary*] will pronounce the text correctly. But after all, the selection of the correct *raccourci* is also a conscious act, an act of creative thought. *Raccourcis* may be incorrect, approximate, close, almost correct, happenstance, precise, etc. The range of selection is huge. But just as a writer seeks the precise word, I seek the most precise *raccourci*.

* * *

The mise en scène is not at all a question of a static grouping, but a process: the influence of time on space. Besides the plastic element, there is also in it the time element, that is, rhythm and music.

* * *

When you look at a bridge, you seem to see a leap imprinted in metal, that is, a process and not something static. The dynamic tension expressed in the bridge is the main thing, and not the ornamentation that decorates its railings. The same is true of the mise en scène.

* * *

Using a different type of comparison, I can also say that if the acting is the melody, then the mises en scène are the harmony.

* * *

A director mustn't be afraid of creative conflict with an actor at rehearsal, even to the point of fisticuffs. The strength of the director's position lies in the fact that he, as distinguished from the actor, always knows (must know!) the future course of the production. He is in charge of the *whole* and therefore he is stronger than the actor anyway. So don't be afraid of quarrels and fights!

* * *

It's very bad when a director works with the blinders of a preliminary plan on his eyes and doesn't know how to use what the course of a rehearsal sometimes brings about by chance. Often some chance occurrence can prompt a completely unforeseen effect, and you must know how to make use of it. In my experience such things have happened constantly. I'll cite two examples from work on our most recent productions. At one of the dress rehearsals of *The Lady of the Camellias*, in the second scene of the first act, the actors by chance began to toss the carnival streamers up so high that they didn't fall back, but hung on the cables. This was so unexpectedly beautiful that a little whisper of delight ran among those present. Strictly speaking, this was an "embellishment", but it gave us a marvelous touch. The actor playing Gaston made use of this and without instructions from me, took the ends of the streamers in his hand and absent-mindedly fingered them during the scene with Marguerite. It remained only for me to approve, and develop and complicate it a little.

At a rehearsal of the scene "In the Restaurant" in *Prélude*, there was also such an unforeseen occurence. One of the actors who was not in the rehearsal and was sitting backstage on some construction piece, jumped heavily onto the floor. The impact of this jump coincided so rhythmically with the *luft-pause* in the music of the dance composed by Shebalin, that I sensed the possibility of changing Hugo Nunbakh's movement which I'd thought out earlier, from upstage to downstage right. And so I staged a dance for Sverdlin which in his rendition at a performance always draws applause.

* * *

In my first version of *Woe to Wit*, I made a great many mistakes, with a lot of help, it's true, from the artist, [Viktor] Shestakov. It was oozing with pseudo-erudition. Individual episodes grew all out of proportion and weren't linked with each other. In 1935, I did a new version in which I corrected some of my mistakes. The revisions hardly affected the actors' interpretations (not counting the usual polishing). In that respect, we were on the right track in 1928. Only Shestakov and I are to blame for the mistakes in that first production. I don't blame the actors at all.

* * *

A director must be able to read correctly the play he is staging. But this isn't enough. He must be able to construct in his imagination what I call for myself the "second level of the play". Whatever you say, a play is only raw material for the theatre. I can read through a play in a spirit opposed to the author's, without changing a letter of it, just by using directorial and acting inflections. Therefore, the fight for the preservation and embodiment of the author's intention isn't a fight for the letter of the play.

* * *

In the first half of the nineteenth century, there were cases in Russia where censorship removed from the repertory plays the reading of which had provoked no apprehensions and so had been passed. But talented actors like Mochalov went beyond the text by introducing mime play, pauses, stops, gestures, *raccourcis*, and various inflections into their performance. The audience understood perfectly and reacted according-ly. That is what I call the "second level of the play". But it was still by chance, half-improvised, since the art of directing didn't exist. After seeing such a production, the censors clutched their heads, and the play, previously passed, was forbidden following the performance. In this case, they understood the nature of theatre better than some of our critics who are still appealing for the letter of the text.

* * *

The contemporary director must know not only the direct impact of an actor's emotion – he steps to the footlights and brilliantly delivers a soliloquy – but also the complex and peripheral turns of associative imagery.

* * *

A director must have a sense of time without removing his watch from his waistcoat pocket. A production is an alternation of dynamics and statics as well as of varying degrees of dynamics. That is why a gift for rhythm seems to me one of the most important qualities in a director. Without a keen sense of stage time, it is impossible to put on a good production.

* * *

When I divided the text of *The Forest* into episodes, everyone cried out that I was imitating the movies. No one remembered that Pushkin's *Boris Godunov* and almost all of Shakespeare's plays are constructed this way.

* * *

Igor Ilinsky in *The Forest* is the most logical continuation of the great tradition of Mikhail P. Sadovsky. From him comes that quality of the *gracioso*: lightness, impetuosity, frivolity, bravado. Sadovsky in his turn caught this line from an expert on the Spanish theatre, Aleksandr Ostrovsky. But Ilinsky is a contemporary actor, and he has not bypassed Chaplin's influence. The fusion of the Ostrovsky-Sadovsky tradition and the influence of Chaplain – this is the genealogical image created by Ilinsky.

* * *

In my production of *The Forest*, certain things now seem a little crude, primitive, blunt, emphatically tendentious. But compare a newspaper page from 1924, an issue of *Crocodile* or *The Atheist* of that time, with a present-day newspaper and today's *Crocodile*. The worker-students of the twenties also don't resemble the university students of the thirties. Our *Forest* was aimed fully at the contemporary audience, that is, the audience of the mid-twenties. It's not surprising that the production has aged in some respects. One might be surprised at something else – that it has aged comparatively little, and that it still provokes a stormy reaction in the theatre. But this is explained by something else: by the fact that besides being contemporary, the production embodies the traditions of the best theatrical ages. And so, let's remove from the production everything that was "topical" then, but which is no longer relevant. In my observation, after the many changes in the production during more than ten years, it has become less and less satirical and more and more romantic. This has occurred almost by evolution, and seemingly quite naturally. (Written in 1936 – A.G.) [One of Meyerhold's must successful and durable productions, *The Forest* remained in the repertory from the time of its première in 1924 until the closing of the theatre in 1937. It played more than 1500 times, setting a record as yet unmatched in the Russian theatre.]

* * *

Before the première of *The Lady of the Camellias*, I was in a state of extreme anxiety. And with reason. At the dress rehearsal, the performance ran about five hours. The management looked daggers at me. I hurriedly shortened some things, but all the same it was still very long. And what complicated matters was the fact that this feature of the production corresponded to its style. An attempt at excessive abridgement would have resembled the condensed American versions of Tolstoy's great novels, those fictional canned goods. I awaited the encounter with the audience with extraordinary excitement. Would it agree to listen to my unhurried tale? At the première, I was moved to tears (these "tears" are not at all a figure of speech, but fact!) when I saw that the audience watched and listened without any apparent strain. This was the moment of my greatest joy and triumph. Later such thoughts as these came to me: the spectator in a hurry is an enemy of the theatre. We quickly swallow a bitter medicine, but slowly savor a tasty dish. The spectator's patience shouldn't be abused. But it's equally wrong to indulge the kind of spectator who always "has no time". If a theatre can't force the spectator to forget about this "no time", does such a theatre have the right to exist?

* * *

A director must know all the spheres that make up the art of the theatre. I had the opportunity to watch Edward Gordon Craig at rehearsal, and I was always won over by the fact that he didn't shout "Give me a blue light!" but indicated precisely, "Switch on lamps No. 3 and 8!" He could even speak professionally with a carpenter, although he probably couldn't build a chair himself. One must sit for hours in a lighting technician's booth in order to have the right to give him orders. When the wardrobe mistress brings the newly finished costumes, the director mustn't hem and haw, "Here a little tighter, and here a little looser", but indicate precisely, "Rip out this seam, and put a wire in here". Only then will lazy assistants not argue that it's impossible to alter anything, as they usually do, and you won't have to take them at their word. Stanislavsky studied pattern cutting in Paris in order to understand the nature of the art of the stage.

* * *

A director must know how to stage everything. He doesn't have the right to be like a doctor who specializes only in children's ailments, or in venereal diseases, or in the ear, nose, and throat. A director who claims he can stage only tragedies and doesn't know how to stage comedies or vaudevilles, is certain to fail, because in genuine art the high and the low, the bitter and the funny, the light and the dark always stand side by side.

* * *

You simply can't imagine how the receptivity of audiences has changed before my very eyes. Even in *The Fairground Booth*, the spectators didn't yet accept the rapid change of scenes and lighting effects. And an episode like "Penki in an Uproar" in *The Forest* (with the throwing of chairs), which today provokes stormy applause, at the beginning of the century would have provoked bewilderment.

* * *

The argument still continuing on the pages of the theatre journals seems to me extremely naïve: who is the leading figure in the creation of a production, the director or the playwright? In my opinion, the leader is the *idea, no matter* to whomever it belongs. Of the two members of the partnership (author–director), the one whose thinking is more significant, more active, more acute is the "leader" in that particular case. With respect to Faiko and perhaps Erdman, I was the "leader", but when it came to Mayakovsky, I must honestly say, it was a different matter... I see nothing insulting here for either the playwright or the director in both the first and second cases.

* * *

I was an actor with a broad range: I played both comic and tragic roles, and nearly even women's parts. I studied music and choreography. Besides this, I studied law, wrote for the newspapers, and translated foreign languages. I consider myself a littérateur and a teacher. All this has been useful to me in my work as a director. If I knew still other specialties, they also would be useful. A director must know many things. There is an expression: "a narrow specialty". Directing is the broadest specialty in the world.

* * *

The spectator's impression is richer when it's perceived subconsciously. I myself hide certain of my devices from the audience. In the scene, "The Hostel", in *The Bedbug*, Ilinsky's stage business as Prisypkin gives the effect of a tightly stretched string all through the scene and creates the necessary tension. But I certainly don't want the spectator to notice this.

* * *

Recently I saw a production where the director competently constructed the mise en scène, the artist made excellent stage settings, fine actors took part, and the play wasn't bad. But the spectators responded with sympathetic laughter to all the lines of the negative character, who was interpreted scandalously wrongly by a good actor; and they listened indifferently to the monologues of the positive characters. I said to myself: such a director should be kicked out of the theatre. He's a wretched mediocrity, a dangerous fool who's worse then an enemy! You want to know which production it was? And are there so few such productions?

* * *

I'm very much afraid we've taught audiences to laugh thoughtlessly and foolishly, to laugh no matter what. Isn't there too much laughter now in our theatres? Won't the moment soon arrive when audiences, corrupted by our contrivances to make them laugh at all cost, will greet with a roar of laughter or with cold silence a subtle, complex, intelligent play? It's for this very reason that I always so passionately attack the playwright X. He may be a capable person, but he's actively taking part in corrupting audiences with stupid laughter. For this alone, I hate him with all my heart!

* * *

If you start to read a play, don't take a break. But if this should happen, then when you pick it up again, begin once more from the first page. I've noticed that you can correctly evaluate a play only when you read it straight through, in one gulp, at one sitting.

* * *

Nothing on the stage occurs by chance. At one performance I saw an actor inadvertently drop a flower as he was exiting. The actress remaining on stage unobtrusively picked it up. This would seem to be a mere trifle! But I saw that the spectators were already whispering to each other. Lord knows what they now concluded about the relationship between these two characters, and they expected something from them in the future.

* * *

At the dress rehearsal the old prompters always noted in their copies of the play how long each act should run: let's say, the first – 34 minutes, the second – 43 minutes, the third – 25 minutes ... I saw these notations in old prompters' copies of plays that have been preserved. For a long time I didn't understand why that was done, until old-timers in the theatre explained it to me. It turned out that the good, experienced prompter was obliged to keep a record of how long a performance ran.

Now, we speak of chronométrage and we think we've discovered America. But this was already being done in the old days. It was the prompter's duty to report after the performance: today the act ran this long, because this actor overplayed in a minor scene, or that actress rushed through such and such scene, or the director's assistant was late in cueing an entrance... That was an extremely important function. By slowing down or speeding up an act we can completely distort a performance. Play Maeterlinck quickly and you get vaudeville. Play *The Neighbor Lady and her Neighbors* [a French vaudeville] slowly and it will seem to you that it's Leonid Andreev.

* * *

The director must sometimes know how to use cunning for the sake of results. When I produced [Hardt's] *Tantris the Fool* at the Alexandrinsky Theatre, there was a big crowd scene that the supernumeraries trained by Sanin constantly spoiled with their excessive overacting. They went all out: each of them strove to impress with his acting his girlfriend sitting in a complimentary seat in the thirteenth or sixteenth row. I couldn't do a thing with them. Then I made all the participants in the crowd scene join hands. I don't remember how I explained it to them. (This was the crowd of "guards".) As soon as they joined hands I no longer had to restrain them. I even had to call out, "More energetically! Livelier!" while I smiled to myself. But if I had told them categorically, "Quieter! More restrained!" they would have stood stock still, just like that...

* * *

I don't like to begin work on a new play from the first act. I like to do as certain French dramatists did. They started their work from the end, with the culminating scenes, and then brought the play from exposition to climax. First tackling the most difficult episodes, they then moved on from them to the easier ones. I have done most of my work in exactly this way.

* * *

There was a time when I staged a play in small segments and polished each of them for a long time. Then I noticed that this led to overgrowth and disproportionate swelling. Now I'm returning to the way I worked a long time ago: after resolving two or three major culminating scenes and staging all the rest in outline, I try to run through all the acts swiftly in succession. When you run through everything in sequence, the whole becomes visible more quickly. I don't know Wagner's technique, but I'm convinced that it wasn't a mosaic of work on little pieces. Otherwise, his "endless melody" would not have been born. The unity of a production is most easily found through dynamics.

* * *

The best of what I devise beforehand rather than during rehearsal nevertheless always comes to me, not sitting at my desk, so to speak, but in the presence of others, in noise and movement when it seems you aren't thinking at all of work. One mustn't forget that the artist works constantly. Mayakovsky wrote beautifully about that in *How are Verses Made?*, that thin little booklet which contains all his experience. When I get ready to write about directing I will strive to write just as briefly and succinctly.

* * *

If I manage to live a little longer, I am going to try to achieve by theatrical means what in literature is now called "internal monologue". I have some notions about that. No, I can't tell you anything. Not yet. What's more, there are no suitable plays! And adaptations are always a palliative! [In 1936, Meyerhold discussed with Gladkov collaborating on a dramatized adaptation of André Malraux's novel, *Man's Fate*, with the idea of using internal monologue in staging it.]

* * *

The most difficult thing in staging a play is the distribution of the roles. When I have to assign roles, I don't sleep for several nights and almost become ill. If I can cope with that without obvious compromises, then I can look ahead with confidence.

* * *

The new technique in the theatre was dictated by the dramatist. In Maeterlinck's *The Death of Tintagiles*, there are acts lasting ten to twelve minutes that take place in a medieval castle. But in order to change the scenery for the castle, it would be necessary to make the intermissions twice as long as the acts, and this is absurd. Willy-nilly, we had to invent a "stylized castle". Thus the dramatist pushed the theatre into new techniques.

* * *

Ibsen's plays seem calm only to poor directors. Read them carefully and you will find as much movement there as on a roller coaster.

* * *

All my life I've dreamed of staging a Greek tragedy on the square in front of Kazan Cathedral in Leningrad. Even in Greece itself there isn't such a suitable, and I would even say, ideal place: colonnades enclosing a central square, (two wings), a great depth between the columns making it possible for the performers to conceal themselves until their entrance.

* * *

In one type of theatre (for example, in the Art Theatre) the première of a production is the high point in its life: the culmination of a long period of rehearsals. But with us, it is only a step, a moment when, in the process of creating a production, the audience enters. The high point, the zenith of the production's life, is still far ahead.

* * *

The use of lighting in the contemporary theatre is akin to the use of music. Aside from the purely technical goal of illuminating the actors and the stage, the combination of blue and yellow spots (as in our production of *The Lady of the Camellias*) enables us to underscore individual lines by creating individual emotional waves, sometimes highlighting the text, sometimes shading it. The audience perceives this unconsciously. But gradually, as they become used to it, theatregoers will begin to read the lighting score just as connoisseurs of music read the musical score. In my work on the lighting for a production, I am interested not in the impressionistic treatment of light and shadow, but in the creation of a lighting score.

* * *

I am an enemy of long periods of reading at rehearsals, or as they say, "around the table preparation". When actors scan the lines with their eyes, they unwittingly begin to declaim, as is natural for people who are reading a text. I want to snatch the parts from the hands of the actors as quickly as possible and therefore I hurry to move on to the staging of the scenes. I would even rather have the actors speak with the aid of a prompter than follow the parts with their eyes.

* * *

A director must be a dramatist and actor and artist and musician and electrician and tailor.

* * *

There are directorial devices which must take effect not immediately but slowly, like the poison the Medicis used on their enemies, after a certain amount of time, at a suitable moment chosen beforehand. The audience notices such devices only after the performance has ended, or doesn't notice them at all, which is even better.

* * *

A theatrical performance knows neither "yesterday" nor "tomorrow". The theatre is an art of today, of just this hour, just this minute, this second. "Yesterday" in the theatre is traditions, legends, texts of plays; "tomorrow", the dreams of the artist. But the reality of the theatre is only "today". The poet and the musician can work for the future reader and listener. Baratynsky dreamed of a future friend in posterity. For the actor such dreams are meaningless. His art exists only while he breathes, while his voice vibrates, while his muscles are strained in acting, while the audience is listening to him with bated breath. Precisely for that reason the theatre is the ideal art of the present. When the theatre breathes of the present, then it can become the great theatre of its time, even if it plays Shakespeare and Pushkin. The theatre that doesn't breathe of the present is an anachronism, even if it presents plays dramatized from today's newspaper.

* * *

When I think about Chaplin, I am struck by the fact that in his films there is nothing artistically neutral. They are not at all like the productions of former times featuring famous visiting stars where, along with the brilliant acting of the leading actor, the rest was almost second-rate. As an actor, Chaplin is great, but you need only recall the rowdy newsboys at the beginning and ending of *City Lights*, or the boxer with the amulet, to understand what a great director he is. From him one can learn how easily and offhandedly it is done.

* * *

Each author must be staged differently – and not only in the style of the production, but also in the way it is rehearsed. When we asked Mayakovsky about the biographies of his characters, he got angry, shouted at us, and banged his walking stick. His plays demand one type of approach, Olesha's plays another, Erdman's plays still a third. We must be flexible in this; otherwise, in our theatre all the authors will resemble the one who is our special favorite.

There is such a theatre where this always happens... but, silence. I'd rather not ruffle anyone's feathers! Even so, all my life I've never been able to stay out of polemics. I've had enough! I feel like working and not arguing! [Meyerhold's remark is aimed at the Moscow Art Theatre.]

* * *

If I had to put a prompter into a production, then I would not hide him in the prompter's box, or in the wings, but would seat him at a reading stand in front of the orchestra. He would sit there wearing glasses, a starched shirt front, a bow tie, and with a fat folio edition of the play. I see no logic in the fact that we don't conceal the orchestra conductor and he never annoys or interferes, but we hide the prompter. The spectator will willingly accept any technical stylization. We don't have to be ashamed of it and mask it.

* * *

A number of devices from Symbolist art live on in our cinema. This is obvious from Eisenstein's films. The apples in Dovzhenko's remarkable film, *The Earth*, are not simply apples, but also distinct symbolic images, like Blok's street lamp and pharmacy sign [in *Dances of Death*].

* * *

While working at the Alexandrinsky Theatre, I learned to be a little crafty in order to gain adherents among the actors of the old school, like Yurev. They always needed steps and columns. Earlier, in *Hamlet* there were always steps and in *Othello* too, along which the hero could run while killing himself. Sometimes you'd put up steps and columns and Yurev would move heaven and earth for you. But I just couldn't capture Apollonsky, although I put up eight columns for him.

* * *

The ultraviolet rays of a production's main idea must be invisible and penetrate the spectator in such a way that he does not notice them.

* * *

By the time Selvinsky brought us *The Second Army Commander*, a lot of plays about the Civil War had already been staged in the theatres, and almost all of them were yet another variation of [Trenev's] *Lyubov Yarovaya*. But we didn't need a hundredth play about the breakup of the family under the influence of the class struggle. We wanted a deeper penetration into that amazing and heroic time. When I received *The Second Army Commander*, I rejoiced. It seemed to me that I would come out of the repertory crisis without lowering my standards to the level of authors who follow the line of least resistance. At that time, as now, I strove to draw into the theatre dynamic poets who would bring to the stage in their plays the major problems of the time.

Selvinsky presented in his play an almost philosophical problem (similar to Ibsen in his remarkable play, *The Pretenders*) about who has the right to be a leader. And that appealed to me. I always dreamed about the appearance of new dramatists who would consider the common masses ready for great, complex art, instead of those dramatists who imagined the level of that public a low one, and, what's more, themselves descended to it.

* * *

I was once asked: did our *Magnanimous Cuckold* grow out of Bio-mechanics, or the other way around, Biomechanics out of it? Both one and the other... *Magnanimous Cuckold* was our practice work which went on parallel with our studies. It was needed so that our studies would not be merely scholastic, pure gymnastic training, or an esthetic variation of it. In creating Biomechanics, I tried to shield the young actor from a passion for the saccharine barefoot dancing à la Duncan, or the plastic affectation in the spirit of Goleizovsky. *Cuckold* showed everyone that Biomechanics is not the "arithmetic" of actor training, but already the "algebra". I thought some day we would also reach "higher mathematics". A beginning was made in *Bubus* and *The Inspector General*.

* * *

Of my unborn productions, I often regret *Rienzi* with music by Wagner and set designs by Yakulov. I had already almost finished rehearsing it in 1921, but I didn't succeed in showing it to an audience because our theatre, the RSFSR Theatre No. 1, was closed by my enemies. Recently Eisenstein and I were reminiscing about it.

* * *

I love it when the audience is divided. Sarah Bernhardt also said that the worst thing of all was when everyone liked and accepted a production.

* * *

Child's play is always so convincing, because when they play, children imitate what they have seen instead of illustrating something abstractly understood.

* * *

Contemporary conductors know that music is made up not only of notes but also those almost imperceptible *luft-pauses* between the notes. In the theatre, this is called the sub-text, or one might also say, the between-text. Stiedry once told me that the poor conductor performs what is indicated in the score, whereas the good one performs what the score offers him for his free interpretation as an artist. That is, you can play: one, two–three, or also another way: one–two, three. The time segment is the same, but the structure is different: it gives a different rhythm to the meter. Rhythm is what overcomes the meter, what disputes meter. Rhythm is knowing how to leap off the meter and back again. The art of such a conductor allows for rhythmical freedom in a measured segment. The art of the conductor lies in mastering the empty moments between rhythmic beats. It is essential that the theatre director also be aware of this.

* * *

Take any episode where there is an alternation: dialogue 12 minutes, monologue 1 minute, trio 6 minutes, ensemble "tutti" 5 minutes, and so forth. You get a relationship: 12:1:6:5, and that defines the composition of the scene. One must watch that the relationship is strictly observed, but this doesn't limit the opportunity for improvisation in the work of the actor. It is precisely that stability in time which enables the good actor to enjoy what is fundamental to his art. Within the limits of those twelve minutes he has a chance to vary the interpretation and to put expressive nuances into the scene, to try new ways of acting, to look for new details. This relationship between composition and improvised play is the new production formula of our school.

* * *

I like *The Wild Duck* for the fact that it is the least talky of Ibsen's plays.

* * *

In the best movies there are always elements of genuine theatre.

* * *

When I think over a play for a long time, the staging of it goes more quickly.

* * *

I decided to abandon acting when during the production of *Pelléas and Mélisande* with Komissarzhevskaya, in which I played Arkel, I understood how difficult it was to act and direct simultaneously. That's one more reason why I consider Chaplin a genius. [Meyerhold's experiments with static Symbolist drama ultimately resulted in a showdown between Komissarzhevskaya and Meyerhold. *Pelléas and Mélisande* (première, October 10, 1907) proved to be the last straw and led to the final break between the two artists.]

* * *

Hamlet at the Vakhtangov represents a very poor understanding of Meyerhold. [Meyerhold has in mind the 1932 production directed and designed by Nikolai Akimov.]

* * *

The artist Yuri Bondi was the father of theatrical constructivism. Long before the word appeared, he staged Blok's *The Unknown Woman* with me at the Tenishev Academy [in 1914].

* * *

When an actor comes out on the stage he always feels within him a certain urge for symmetrical well-being; for locating an imagined air bubble in a carpenter's level; for the absolute center of the stage; that is, toward the place where he can be seen and heard equally well from both right and left. On the box stage of the old Renaissance theatres, that leads to a frontal structuring of the mise en scène. This also evokes in the audience a feeling of compositional equilibrium, or as I call it, a sense of compositional well-being. But this is not always what the play needs. Sometimes it is essential to turn the actor, to put him in a position of imbalance, as it were, to disturb the accustomed point of view, to shift the imaginary center of the play. Then the members of the audience won't lounge in their seats, feet spread out, but will begin to feel involved.

Marinetti, before the beginning of a performance in his theater, poured glue on some of the seats. Someone would sit down and find himself stuck to his seat. (Imagine what this meant to a lady in a new dress!) A ruckus would ensue, and in that atmosphere of excitement the show would begin. I want to achieve a condition of involvement in the audience, not with the help of glue, but by other means, that is, with compositional devices.

An actor standing full-face toward the audience always tends to pose a little, as if he were performing a solo number. Therefore, I look for expressive *raccourcis* for him which might put him off this position. If I don't keep my eye on a play that's been running for a long time, the actors always gradually change the *mise en scène*, striving toward the traditional full-face position. That's the reason I so like watching a production from the wings: everything is much more expressive.

* * *

The *mises en scène* are the notes by which the spectator reads the melody.

* * *

When I staged *The Lady of the Camellias*, I constantly recalled Ibsen's mastery of psychology. For example, he would have written the scene with Armand's father and Marguerite more subtly. He would have split it and inserted another scene with Marguerite and one of her women friends. There we could have learned all the doubts that Marguerite could not express to Armand's father. Then the other half of their scene would have been much sharper and more dramatic. More than once I raised my hand... But no, I said to myself, stop! Try to find that in the material given to you. There's nothing to be done. Precisely after working on *Camellias*, I began to dream again of staging *Ghosts* in order to enjoy in abundance Ibsen's great art.

* * *

The commanding position in the theatre is inevitably occupied by that member of a production who has the broadest cultural outlook, who knows what he wants, and can lead the way. Sometimes it is the author, sometimes the director, sometimes an actor, sometimes an artist.

* * *

I doubt that it's mere happenstance that rare geniuses like Shakespeare appear in one period, and in other periods, for some reason less fortunate, they don't appear. It seems to me that great dramatists arise when there are great spectators. When I call a spectator of a certain type "great", I do not have in mind the remarkable people of a given period, people of some relatively high general level. Who would argue that the

Russians of 1812–1915 were remarkable people, but they were not great spectators. They didn't need the theatre. The same was true during the French Revolution. Perhaps this is also the case now.

Let the social historians explain to us why in some periods people appear who desperately need the theatre, and then I will call them great spectators. They appeared in Shakespeare's time and pushed him ahead of his crowd. After him, other remarkable dramatists also followed, like mushrooms after a rain. Spectators such as that also appeared in Russia at the end of the last century and right after the Revolution. But in the latter instance, they created theatre directors instead of dramatists. Perhaps in historical terms they are one and the same. Then for some reason (Oh, why?!) that generation of great spectators disappeared.

I often look at the auditorium and see some laughing or sentimental types sitting there. Notice how everyone comes to the theatre in couples now. That's a sure sign of the decline in spectators. When we were young, we went to the theatre with a group of friends, or alone. But when only couples go to the theatre, it means it has become something on the order of horseback riding or going to a city park.

* * *

Turning to the public is traditional for vaudeville (farce or comedy with singing numbers), but you must obtain an endless variety of these turns and not make them direct. That means sometimes openly addressing the auditorium, sometimes just adding a barely noticed accentuation: a nod or a half-smile. You mustn't play vaudeville like a production with a "fourth wall" and then suddenly in the finale line up in front of the footlights for the singing number. You must prepare the audience in advance through various touches for this traditional finale, the musical number at the footlights.

* * *

Vaudeville is always constructed symmetrically. Therefore any imbalance in vaudeville is inadmissible. In [Chekhov's] *The Anniversary* we repeat the waltz twice. This gives the spectators a feeling of compositional balance, a musical perception of vaudeville's structure, so to speak.

* * *

I love the dramatic form of the old Spanish theatre with its false dénouement at the end of the second act and the accelerated pace of the third act, which is as full of action as the first two. It's astonishing the way this three-part formula takes into account the laws of a spectator's perception. I've learned a lot from it, although I'm not a dramatist.

* * *

The director's theatre is the actor's theatre plus the art of the compositional whole.

On Pushkin, Gogol, Lermontov, Dostoevsky

I shall ask that the following words of Pushkin's be carved on the pediment of the new building for our theatre: "The spirit of the age demands important changes on the dramatic stage as well".

* * *

The draft Pushkin wrote for a preface to his *Boris Godunov* is a programmatic document of genius for all time. How much more lofty and profound it is than the famous prologues to Victor Hugo's dramas! Pushkin demanded "the free and broad depiction of characters". Has this demand really become obsolete nowadays? I can reread it *ad infinitum* and always find new profundities!

* * *

Simplicity is the most precious thing in art. But each artist has his own concept of simplicity. There is the simplicity of Pushkin, and the simplicity of a primitive. There is no simplicity accessible or comprehensible to all, just as there is no "golden mean" in art. The artist must strive to attain his own particular simplicity, which will not at all resemble the simplicity of his fellow artist. The lofty simplicity of art is the final goal, and not the starting point. It is the pinnacle, not the foundation.

* * *

My credo is a simple and laconic theatre language leading to complex associations. That's the way I would like to stage *Boris Godunov* and *Hamlet*.

* * *

Pushkin strove to imitate Shakespeare, but he is better than Shakespeare. He is more transparent and atmospheric. The main thing in Pushkin is that he achieves everything through small means. This is in fact the height of artistry.

* * *

Pushkin's letter to Bestuzhev after reading *Woe from Wit* gave me the main idea for the production plan of my *Woe from Wit*. The letter is all but forgotten. Hence the surprise caused by the dramatic characterizations I gave to Sofiya, Molchalin, Chatsky, and the others. I realized there what Pushkin had said one hundred years ago, and I was accused of being overly original!

* * *

Have you ever noticed how similarly Pushkin's two dramatic masterpieces, *Boris Godunov* and *A Feast During the Plague* end? *With silence*: "The people are silent", (*Boris*) and "The Chairman remained immersed in deep thought". (*A Feast*) It's clear that this isn't simply a pause, but a musical notation *for the director's score*. In Pushkin's day, the art of the director didn't yet exist, but he brilliantly foresaw it. That's why I'm right when I say that Pushkin's dramas are the theatre of the future.

* * *

When I was in Wrangel's prison in Novorossiisk, I had with me a small volume of Pushkin with his dramas in the "Prosveshchenie" edition. I got so used to it that later when I began to work again on *Boris*, or *The Stone Guest*, or *Rusalka*, for some reason I felt I had to have for my work that very same compact and convenient edition. Or maybe for me this edition simply was associated with my fantasies. There in prison, following in Pushkin's footsteps, I invented a scenario for a play about a pretender. I had already begun to compose it in my mind, but the Red Army burst into town and I found myself free. Later I offered the plot I'd worked out to Sergei Esenin and Mariana Tsvetaeva, but poets have their pride and they like to dream up things for themselves.

* * *

Have you noticed that in the famous list of ideas for plays drawn up by Pushkin, *Anthony and Cleopatra* stands alongside *Dmitry and Marina*? Do you think that's a coincidence? No, in my opinion this is a brilliant associative relationship of Pushkin's, and we have to take it into account...

* * *

Pushkin was a student of Shakespeare and that was quite revolutionary for a theatre burdened with the legacy of neoclassicism. But the spirit of his *Boris Godunov* is even more revolutionary than the formal structure of the play. When, at the censor's demand, he changed the ending from the people's cry, "Hail Tsar Dmitry Ivanovich!" to the famous stage direction, "The people remain silent", he outfoxed the censor because he didn't diminish, but rather strengthened the theme of the people. There is a vast distance between a people shouting "Hail" first to one and then to another tsar, and a people expressing its opinion with silence. In addition, Pushkin gave the future Russian theatre a most interesting and extraordinarily difficult task: how to play the silence so that it comes across louder than a shout. I found a solution for this problem, and I thank the stupid censorship for forcing Pushkin into this astounding find.

* * *

Pushkin is the most astonishing playwright. In his plays nothing can be left out. For example, when you read *The Stone Guest*, everything is clear. But you begin to play it and it seems that there's not enough text. That's because Pushkin, when he wrote, anticipated the future theatre, not the "verbal" theatre, but one in which movement would supplement the word.

* * *

The latest studies of *Boris Godunov* state that Pushkin did not provide for intermissions during the performance of his tragedy, just as in Sophocles' *Oedipus Rex* where there mustn't be a single break lest the thread be lost. That's almost the same, to give an easier example, as in my favorite prélude of Scriabin's where the *legato* line, beginning on the first page, extends in an arc to the very end of the second page. That means that the striking of a given chord must be done in such a way that the continuity of its sound, with the help of either the pedal or another technical trick, will be sustained to the end. Of course, that does not at all mean that within the unity of the action there will be no fragmentation, segments, and so forth. But they will be of a different nature. Shifting and breaking up the action under the condition that the main action is integral – that's one thing, but simply the alternation of episodes – that's another. In the second case, it is a kind of suite, a division into small one-act numbers.

* * *

Pushkin was not only a remarkable dramatist, but also a dramatist-director and the initiator of a new dramatic system. If we were to collect together all the observations about the theatre of his day scattered throughout his letters and drafts of articles, then we would see the amazing consistency of his views. For a long time already I have been guided by them in the course of my work and in my plans.

* * *

Always start your day by reading some Pushkin, even if only two or three brief pages.

* * *

The most important thing we have to learn from Pushkin is that internal freedom which is essential in a creative act, and which he possessed. The worst things in art are timid primness, ridiculous stiffness, servility, the urge to pander to one particular taste and to please it, the fear of offending someone of high rank, the fear of insulting the high and mighty. If you haven't rejected all that, then it's better not to attempt Pushkin.

* * *

The history of the staging of *Boris Godunov* is a history of many failures. How do you explain this? If we trace the history of the Russian theatre during the nineteenth and the early twentieth centuries, we see that the failures of great and remarkable dramatic works on the stage resulted mainly from the fact that these plays were written, as we now say, innovatively. That is, they were not in conformity with the stage techniques of the time, but with a desire to change those techniques and to attempt to create a new form of theatrical performance. The Russian theatre quickly caught up with Chekhov's innovations, but so far it still hasn't been able to catch up with that most extraordinary innovator of the drama, Pushkin. Even today, our theatrical techniques stand much lower than Pushkin wanted them. His plays still seem puzzling to us: either too swift in their movement or too compressed in their text. We haven't yet learned how to act them. But if we approach them as a kind of musical score for a theatrical production, then we will uncover their secret.

* * *

The grotesque isn't something mysterious. It's simply a theatrical style that plays with sharp contradictions and produces a constant shift in the planes of perception. An example is Gogol's *The Nose*. In art, there can be no forbidden devices. There are only inappropriately or irrelevantly applied devices.

* * *

I've been criticized because there wasn't very much gaiety in our *Inspector General*. But then, Gogol himself reproached the first performer of Khlestakov, Nikolai Dyur [1836 at the Alexandrinsky Theatre], for trying too hard to make the audience laugh. Gogol loved to say that what was amusing would often turn into something sad if you examined it for a long time. The magic of Gogol's theatrical style lies in this transformation of the funny into the sad.

* * *

Gogol's brilliant *On Leaving the Theatre* is a tragic dialogue between an author and his audience. Several times I've wanted to stage it. But on one condition: the most minor roles must be played by the best actors. I could stage it, but only with the combined resources of all the theatrical troupes of Moscow and Leningrad.

* * *

My revision of *The Inspector General* about which there was so much talk was preceded by the most serious and extended meditation. In the first place, I ascertained that in Gogol's lifetime, *The Inspector General* took only two and one-half hours to perform. As we know, Gogol was not satisfied with the performance of his play. He found, to put it bluntly, that they were just fooling around. And indeed, when you think how such an avalanche of text could be played in two and one-half hours, you understand that the performance must have been perfunctory. Furthermore, reading the final version of *The Inspector General* (the one which was played in Gogol's time), I constantly feel what in it is Gogol and what are the simplifications Gogol made on someone's advice. I see that Gogol listened to everyone, as happens when a dramatist wants desperately to have his play produced without delay. For example, in one scene in the first version, he had three characters, but only two remained. On consideration, I see that with three it was much more interesting. This was clearly a concession on Gogol's part. Of course, in the theatre it's always more convenient to have fewer characters, and Gogol heeded this.

I didn't personally make up my own additions to *The Inspector General*, but took those texts which I considered stronger in the first variants than in the final one. It's impossible now to stage Gogol, Griboedov, or Lermontov without taking into account the pressure of censorship which tied their hands, or the backwardness of stagecraft at that time. We owe it to their memory to study all the variants and establish the very best one, guided by our taste which was formed by those very writers. But that's not as simple as the pseudo-academicians and guardians of the canonical texts think. For them it's easier. They can print in a volume of Gogol or Lermontov three variants at once: one in bold type and two others in fine print in the appendix. But we must make up one text, the best that can be acted without inflicting any damage on the author.

* * *

In the course of some two decades of Russian literature there were created three such completely remarkable and dissimilar theatres as those of Pushkin, Gogol, and Lermontov. No other theatrical culture has known anything like it. One can add a fourth theatre, Griboedov's. It, too, is completely different from the other three. In these three or four facets, I see the structural outline of the entire Russian theatre as it must be for centuries to come. This extraordinary phenomenon has nothing in common with the Shakespearean canon, for example. The saturation of Pushkin's, Gogol's, Lermontov's, and Griboedov's masterpieces is extraordinary in its content and stylistic intensity. What Ostrovsky expressed in a couple dozen plays, these great playwrights conveyed in one or two.

* * *

Of course, Dostoevsky was a born dramatist. In his novels one can sense fragments of unwritten tragedies. In spite of all the mistakes made by his adapters, we have the right to use the expression, "The Theatre of Dostoevsky", alongside "The Theatre of Gogol", "The Theatre of Pushkin", "The Theatre of Ostrovsky", "The Theatre of Lermontov". I regret that I haven't had the opportunity to work on Dostoevsky, because it seems to me that I understand the meaning of his "fantastic realism". [During his final two years in Penza, the atmosphere of family strife, concern for his brother Teodor, who was already showing signs of becoming an alcoholic, and his reading of Dostoevsky "from cover to cover", combined to fill the young Meyerhold's mind with despair to the point where he even contemplated suicide. Many years later he told Gladkov that he never considered staging Dostoevsky because the writer was too closely connected with one of the darkest periods of his life.]

On Tolstoy, Chekhov, Blok, and Mayakovsky

I saw Leo Tolstoy close-up for the first time when I was studying at Moscow University. Like all young people, my friends jumped from one doctrine to another. And since the government persecuted Tolstoyans, we instinctively sympathized with them without thinking too deeply about it. It was a time when in any group of three students one was sure to be a Tolstoyan. Then once with several friends I went to see Tolstoy at his home on Dolgo-Khamovnichesky Lane. We rang. We went in. We were invited to wait in the drawing room. We sat there in a state of excitement. Until then, I had never seen Tolstoy. My feeling about him was such... There, I wanted to say, as toward Gorky or Romain Rolland... No, greater...

We waited rather long. I remember even my palms broke out in a sweat. We watched the door through which Tolstoy would soon enter. And then the door opened. Tolstoy entered... And immediately I had to lower my gaze. For some reason I instinctively looked at the upper part of the door, but he turned out to be quite short. Like so... A half-meter lower. I remember my momentary disillusionment. Quite a little old man. Simple, like our porter at the university. No, even simpler! Then he began to speak and immediately everything changed. And again astonishment. A well-bred, self-assured voice, with French "r's", as today generals in the White Guard are portrayed. He spoke to us sternly, in an almost unfriendly manner. What was striking was the complete absence in him of that playing up to youth that had us all spoiled at the time. And in that I soon felt more respect for us than in the little jokes and smiles with which other "intellectual leaders" invariably conversed with students. Well, of course, those of us who were bolder began asking questions about the meaning of life, and so forth. I kept silent. All the while it seemed to me that he would tell us it was all rubbish, and he would call the servant to show us out. But he answered patiently, although not very willingly. When he was sitting it wasn't noticeable that he was short, but when he stood up to say good-bye, I again marvelled: quite a little old man ... Several years later I again visited Tolstoy. But the first impression is always the strongest ... [Meyerhold told this story at one of the rehearsals of *Boris Godunov* in the autumn of 1936. He used it to illustrate the kind of "anti-Chaliapin" interpretation of Pimen he wanted, that is, not a hero with a mighty beard, but a nervous, quick, animated "little" old man.]

* * *

Chekhov loved me. That is the pride of my life, one of my most precious memories. He liked my letters. Everyone advised me to begin writing myself and even sent notes of recommendation to the editorial office. I had a fair number of letters from Chekhov, about eight or nine, as I recall. But they all disappeared except one which I submitted to be printed. In the others there was more that was flattering to me, and I was embarrassed to show them. When I left for the Crimea in 1919, I gave them to one of the Petrograd museums for safekeeping. But when I returned, it turned out that the person to whom I had given them had died. I can't forgive myself for that. What I didn't take care of was preserved, while what I worried over was lost. This often happens in life.

* * *

The first time I visited Chekhov I was astonished by the completely bare table in his room: a few sheets of paper, an inkwell, and nothing more. I even thought perhaps the table was about to be set for dinner, and out of shyness hastened to announce that I'd already dined. But it turned out the Chekhovs had also dined already. To Anton Pavlovich, a bare table was essential for working: it focused his attention.

* * *

Chekhov had a habit, when listening to another person talk, of laughing quite unexpectedly, and in places that weren't at all funny. At first this stumped his companion. Only later did he understand that while listening to the story, Chekhov was at the same time already altering it in his mind, recasting, strengthening, adding to it, extracting the humorous possibilities and delighting in them. He listened, thought, and imagined more quickly than his companions. His brain, working in parallel, was fed by the conversation, but it was much swifter and more efficient. He listened attentively and at the same time creatively transformed what he was hearing. I met that astonishing characteristic again in Igor Ilinsky, who often startled me in a conversation with his unexpected laughter. I sometimes even stopped, until I got used to the fact that he, like Chekhov, wasn't laughing at my words, but at the simultaneous workings of his own imagination. This is a characteristic of spiritual well-being and highly intensive creative thought.

* * *

Do you know who first planted the seed of doubt in me that all the ways of the Art Theatre might not be right? Anton Pavlovich Chekhov... His friendship with Stanislavsky and Nemirovich-Danchenko was not at all idyllic and cloudless as they write in the popular journals. There was much in the theatre Chekhov didn't agree with, and he directly criticized many things. But Chekhov didn't approve of my leaving the Moscow Art Theatre. He wrote me saying that I should remain and fight against the things in the theatre I disagreed with.

* * *

I would rephrase Chekhov's famous expression about the rifle hanging on the wall in the first act thus: if in the first act there's a rifle hanging on the wall, then in the last act there must be a machine gun... [In *The Last, Decisive*, Meyerhold went even further by having the doomed sailors in the finale fire right into the audience.]

* * *

What can I tell you about my relationships with Blok? They were very complex. And they changed all the time, especially on his side. After *The Fairground Booth*, discord set in. Later, we again drew together several times to the extent of becoming intimate friends and then broke apart not so much on personal grounds as on matters of principle... When I read Blok's correspondence and diary, I was struck by the variety of nuances in his attitude toward me: respect and sarcasm, sympathy and coolness. I think the explanation for this is that in criticizing me for something, Blok was fighting certain traits in himself. We had a great deal in common. And, indeed, one's own defects are never so obnoxious as when seen in another. All the things Blok at times criticized in me existed in him, although he did wish to get rid of them. However, I didn't understand this at the time and was annoyed, because I loved him. We rarely quarreled. Blok didn't know how to quarrel. He would express his deeply-felt opinion and then fall silent. But he was a wonderful listener – a rare trait...

* * *

Right now I could stage *The Fairground Booth* as a Chaplinada *sui generis*. Reread *The Fairground Booth* and you'll see that it contains all the elements of the Chaplin scenarios. Only the environment is different. Heine is also akin to Chaplin and *The Fairground Booth*. In great art there are such complex kinships.

* * *

I loved Mayakovsky as a poet, as a person, as a fighter, and as the leader of a distinct school of poetry.

* * *

There is always a bit of Mayakovsky in the characters of his plays, just as in all of Shakespeare's heroes there's a little bit of Shakespeare. If we want to imagine the legendary personality of Shakespeare, we don't have to rummage in ancient church records or genealogies, but study his characters. I can even imagine his voice, just as I can always hear Mayakovsky's voice in the characters of his comedies.

* * *

I was the first to stage all three of Mayakovsky's plays, but I would like very much to work on them again. By some ill-fated coincidence, all three times I had to hurry, pressed by business conditions in the theatre. That's why I consider my productions as only director's first drafts, like *Woe to Wit – Opus* 1928. I think I was more successful with *The Bathhouse* than with the others. I dream of returning to them and this time working at leisure.

* * *

The life of every true artist is the life of a man constantly lacerated by dissatisfaction with himself. Only amateurs are always self-satisfied and tormented by nothing. A master artist, on the other hand, is always strict with himself. Self-satisfaction and conceit are not part of his makeup. Usually, when an artist seems satisfied and self-confident, it is only a pose of self-defense, an artificial armor against the contacts that wound him. Mayakovsky was like that. From the outside, he sometimes seemed self-confident. But I knew him well and understood that Mayakovsky's outward aplomb and a certain crudeness were only armor, and an armor that was infinitely fragile. The life of a real artist is the triumph of a single day, that day when the last touch is put to the canvas, plus the tremendous suffering of the many other days when the artist sees only his mistakes.

* * *

Mayakovsky was almost twenty years younger than me, but from our very first meeting there was no distance between us as between a "senior" and a "junior". From the first minute of acquaintance, he began to treat me without any deference, and that was natural because we immediately agreed on "politics". And in 1918, that was the most important thing. For both of us the October Revolution was a way out of the impasse the intelligentsia was in. And when we began to work on *Mystery-Bouffe*, there wasn't a single moment of misunderstanding between us. Even in his youth, Mayakovsky possessed an astonishing political maturity which I, "the senior", learned from him. Furthermore, he possessed amazing tact, in spite of his reputation as a boor. When we began to work on Selvinsky's *The Second Army Commander*, the literary hounds tried to make Mayakovsky and Selvinsky enemies. It was a very difficult situation. But although I sometimes felt Mayakovsky's silent, unexpressed jealousy, he behaved absolutely correctly, in spite of the fact that he didn't like *The Second Army Commander* very much.

* * *

One mustn't use the same methods in playing Mayakovsky and Chekhov. In art there are no universal skeleton keys to all locks such as burglars have. In art, one must look for a special key for each author.

* * *

Mayakovsky told me that while working on *The Bedbug* and *The Bathhouse*, he learned much from our productions of *The Inspector General*, *Woe to Wit*, and [Erdman's] *The Warrant*. This is how the collaboration between the theatre and the poet should be: both learn from each other. And in some ways Mayakovsky went further and gave us new challenges. In *The Bedbug* there are a number of extraordinary shifts from one episode to another in which we feel the best rhythmic modulations of Shakespeare.

On Stanislavsky

You ask, was there "naturalism" in the Art Theatre's *The Seagull*? and you think you have asked me a "perfidious" question because I reject naturalism, whereas in that production I played my favorite role with awe and trepidation. Probably some elements of naturalism did occur, but that was unimportant because the main thing was the poetic nerve, the hidden poetry of Chekhov's prose which became theatre thanks to the genius of Stanislavsky's stagecraft. Before Stanislavsky, they acted only the plot in Chekhov's plays. But they forgot that with Chekhov, the noise of rain outside the window, the clattering of a broken bucket, the early morning through the shutters, the mist over the lake, all these are indissolubly connected with people's behavior. These things were a discovery then. "Naturalism" appeared when they became clichés. All clichés are bad, both naturalistic and "Meyerholdian" ones.

* * *

You who knew Stanislavsky only in his old age can't possibly imagine what a powerful actor he was. If I have become somebody, it is only because of the years I spent alongside him. Mark this well.

* * *

If anyone thinks that I enjoy it when someone speaks disrespectfully of Stanislavsky, he is wrong. I differed with him, but always deeply respected and loved him. He was a remarkable actor with a striking technique. After all, his professional attributes, as we call them, were of little help to him. In stature he was rather too tall, his voice was rather toneless, and there were shortcomings in his diction. He didn't even want to shave off his moustache because of a naïve vanity. But all that was forgotten when he came out on the stage. Sometimes I would return to my little room after acting in a performance with him or after a rehearsal and I wouldn't be able to fall asleep all night. In order to achieve something in art, first you have to learn to admire and to be astonished.

* * *

The fact that Stanislavsky was ill during the last years of his life and rarely left his apartment in Leontyev Lane was at the same time a great good fortune (away from the hustle and bustle of theatrical life, he was able to concentrate on his pedagogic experiments as well as his research) and also a very great misfortune (he almost ceased his creative activities). I am certain that if it hadn't been for his illness, Stanislavsky would have given us more extraordinary productions. I know this from personal experience, having seen what marvelous sketches he did for *Rigoletto*. Too old? But, after all, when Tolstoy wrote his masterpiece, *Hadji-Murad*, he was certainly not any younger.

* * *

Stanislavsky especially tormented me when I was rehearsing Baron Tuzenbach in *Three Sisters* [1901]. For a long time I couldn't get it right. The task seemed so simple: to come out, go up to the piano, sit down, and begin to speak. But no sooner had I started when Stanislavsky would send me back again. In those moments I almost hated him. It must have been ten times that we began again with my entrance. At first I didn't understand what he wanted from me. Now it is clear. Each time I would come out, strike a pose and begin to recite the text. Finally Stanislavsky climbed up on the stage, threw a piece of paper on the floor and asked me to break up my text in the following way: after having said three lines, I would see the paper, pick it up, continue to speak, then unfold it and speak further. Everything immediately fell into place. The oratory disappeared as if by magic. The natural gesture of picking up and unfolding the paper helped me to saturate with life what had seemed to be a "soliloquy": "When I studied at the military school" ...

Another time Stanislavsky demanded tension and inner energy from me, but I was as cold as a dog's nose. Then he gave me a sealed bottle of wine, telling me to open it with the corkscrew and at the same time say my lines. The physical difficulty of opening the bottle and the energy needed for doing it immediately awoke me. That was a purely pedagogic, directorial technical device, which I often use now. You've probably noticed. Pavlov should have been told about that. He would have been interested. If just once you can get something right in rehearsal, then it will always go right because of conditioned reflex.

* * *

Once Zinaida Raikh and I went to see *Two Little Orphans* [d'Ennery play adapted by Vladimir Mass and renamed *The Sisters Gérard*] at the Moscow Art Theatre. Stanislavsky found out that we were in the audience and after the first intermission came and sat with us. Zinaida Nikolaevna, with her characteristic directness, asked K.S. why the Art Theatre put on such plays. Stanislavsky answered that he needed melodrama as a remedy for his weak actors. He pointed out one actor and said, "There, look, that actor always suffered from sloppy gestures, but now he will deliver a long monologue and not make a single superfluous movement". But the actor, after starting his monologue, didn't utter more than two sentences before he began wildly waving his hands. K.S. hung his head ... How well I understood him at that moment! [Meyerhold often attended performances at other theatres. He would always sit in the first row at premières. If he liked the performance very much he would applaud with his hands above his head so that all could see that it was Meyerhold. If he didn't like it he would leave silently, sometimes making negative comments on his way out.]

* * *

I was never so hurt in all my life as I was the one time Stanislavsky became angry with me. That was before my departure from the Art Theatre. It was all caused by the usual theatre gossip. Someone hissed during the première of Nemirovich-Danchenko's play, *Dreams*. And at about the same time, I wrote a letter to Chekhov in which I spoke critically about the play. This became known in the theatre (I have no idea how), my letter was connected to the hissing, and Stanislavsky was told that I had organized the protest. It's absurd, but for some reason K.S. believed it. He stopped speaking to me. I wanted to talk it over with him, but he wouldn't see me. Later everything was straightened out and he became friendlier than ever, as if he felt guilty. It was then that I understood what Stanislavsky's regard meant to me. [*Dreams* had its première on December 21, 1901. In his letter to Chekhov, Meyerhold wrote, "Nemirovich-Danchenko's play has aroused the public's indignation. The author takes an indifferent attitude toward the hated (especially by the young) bourgeoisie. Variegated, colorful, but neither significant nor sincere. They recognized in the author a pupil of Boborykin and are offended in the name of their favorites – Chekhov and Hauptmann... So much work, so much money, and to what purpose?!" Meyerhold wasn't alone in his opinion of *Dreams*. The critics also condemned it. And judging by his annotations in the director's copy of the play, even Stanislavsky was hard put to draw any inspiration from it. This is probably why so much money was spent on its external trappings.]

* * *

When I was in Kislovodsk and learned about Stanislavsky's death from Livanov, I wanted to run off alone, far from everyone, and cry like a child who has lost his father.

On Lensky, Komissarzhevskaya, Duse, Moissi and Others

I was rereading Lensky's *Memoirs* and thought: are they as understandable to those who didn't see Lensky on the stage as they are to me? I understand a lot between the lines. But I'm afraid if I get from them two hundred percent of the content, the majority understands only twenty percent. Alas! That's the fate of most theatrical memoirs!

* * *

You can't bracket Lensky and Yuzhin-Sumbatov and exclaim, "Oh, the Maly Theatre!" Lensky is one thing and Yuzhin-Sumbatov another. When Lensky played Famusov, I was delighted and I still remember the outlines of his depiction. But when Yuzhin-Sumbatov played the same role, I saw a cabinet with a phonograph record in it. Perhaps the record wasn't so bad, but the cabinet remained a cabinet.

* * *

In the twenties I fought with the Maly Theatre, but in my student years I spent almost every evening in the gallery there. No, I think that the Maly Theatre has changed more than I have, though I too, of course, am no longer the same. In the mid-nineties the ushers in the top balconies of the Maly Theatre knew my friends and me so well by sight that even when we met in the public baths [the popular Sanduny Baths near the Maly Theatre] they would greet us. We adored Ermolova and Fedotova, Lensky and Muzil, and the elder Sadovsky. Before taking the liberty to condemn, one has first of all to know. And I ask myself: do those who censure me and my productions know? In checking, it is almost always explained by the fact that they have seen only one or two of my productions, or they didn't sit through even one of them. There have always been such cases.

* * *

You ask, who was the best actor I've seen in my life? Yes, I've seen all the great actors for almost half a century. But I'm won't vacillate: from one point of view, from another... I'll answer immediately because I've thought about it. The best actor I have known was Alexander Pavlovich Lensky. He possessed all the qualities I value in an actor, and he was a genuine artist.

* * *

Alexander Pavlovich Lensky taught that one should always begin to speak a role at half-voice, almost completely inaudibly, as if reading to oneself. He directed that one read at a voice level equal to how clear the role was. This was a purely pedagogical device. I can't always recommend it, but sometimes it may be useful.

* * *

Lensky possessed the precious gift of a *light touch*, which is not at all the same as being lightweight or light-minded. He *lightly* played even such "heavy" roles as Famusov or Hamlet. He knew how to convey the most complex things, the most tragic situations, with striking lightness, without any apparent tension, yet conveying all the nuances, always in motion, lightly achieving striking profundity. Like no one else, he could be at one and the same time serious, tragic, profound – and light. Even Stanislavsky didn't approach him in the lightness with which he conveyed Famusov's lines. Whatever Lensky played (and I probably saw him in a couple dozen roles), I never saw traces of labor in his acting, and it even seemed blasphemous to assume that he skillfully concealed that labor. In tragedy, comedy, realistic plays, everywhere, there was lightness, a festive spirit. I think this can be explained by a broad schooling in vaudeville. This is a good school for comedy. No, it's a good school for tragedy too. Orlenev, Moskvin, Stanislavsky, and Komissarzhevskaya also went through this school.

* * *

Komissarzhevskaya was an astonishing actress. But they wanted her at the same time to be Joan of Arc. In fact, she didn't die of smallpox, but from the same thing Gogol died of, from anguish. The organism, tormented by anguish caused by an imbalance between strength of vocation and realizable artistic goals, absorbed the smallpox infection. You know,

Gogol also had some kind of sickness with a long name, but was that really the point?

* * *

Komissarzhevskaya is remembered more for her dramatic roles, but she was also an excellent Mirandolina [in Goldoni's *The Mistress of the Inn*] and she played vaudeville remarkably well. She had great artistic *joie de vivre*, but at the same time no one needed it. She possessed a wealth of expression, and was musical in the highest sense. That is, she not only sang well but also built her role musically. She had natural body co-ordination, a rare quality, generally speaking – with a lowering of tone, her hands drooped. Her technique as an actress wasn't craftsmanlike, but individual, and therefore it seemed that she had no technique. The young people of my generation considered Garshin their favorite writer. That seems almost incomprehensible now. I even changed my non-Russian name to Vsevolod in his honor. Garshin carried within himself the music of his own time... I don't know why I suddenly remembered Garshin when I was speaking of Komissarzhevskaya. It must not be a coincidence.

* * *

Komissarzhevskaya had a strange mannerism: she always pronounced the first lines of a role rather sharply, as if not in her own voice, and only later her voice seemed to soften, its tone growing warmer. And then not a single false note would jar you any more. She had a weak and fragile lower register, especially when speaking. But in singing it would suddenly open up. The variety of modulations and intonations was striking. She wasn't beautiful and never tried to make herself so with the help of makeup. But I never encountered a more feminine actress (not excluding even that woman of genius, Eleanora Duse). With this, there was a complete absence of affectation: a small, slightly asymmetrical face, a stooping carriage, rounded shoulders, and an extraordinary smile, which seemed to make the footlights grow bright. They say she utterly failed in the role of Ophelia (I didn't see her in this role), but it's not surprising. She wasn't a tragic actress. Still, she was a magnificent dramatic actress in her time. The period in which she lived didn't demand from her all the potential she possessed. She had no high romantic comedy in her repertory, but she had all the essential qualities for it: great resources for playful *joie de vivre*, an inner buoyancy.

* * *

You ask, was Ida Rubinstein talented? She wasn't completely without talent; it all depended on which director worked with her. She was very perceptive, quick, eager-minded. Of course, Ida Rubinstein was, after all, a very vivid, unique figure.

* * *

In recalling the acting of Eleanora Duse, I would like to tell about her extraordinary ability to economize her energy and "rest" on stage in the passive moments of a role. She so cleverly selected these moments that these empty segments themselves seemed full of expressiveness. This enabled her to save her strength and to play almost daily tremendous roles without fatigue or apparent tension. They say that someone once asked Duse after a performance of *The Lady of the Camellias* whether she was tired that evening, and she answered in an offended tone, "Signor, you forgot that I am an actress!..."

* * *

A gift of a fine voice can both help an actor and ruin him. Yes, yes, don't be surprised. The great actresses Komissarzhevskaya, Sarah Bernhardt, Duse, Ermolova all built on verbal performance and wonderfully controlled their voices. But it can happen that the voice starts to control the actor, and he begins to declaim. If Kachalov had not had such a beautiful voice, he would have been an even better actor. Ostuzhev, too. A voice is necessary, but it's not everything. The extraordinary actor, Mikhail Chekhov, had no voice at all.

* * *

In Duse's acting, the force of the steady development of dramatic tension was striking. No one could transmit the process of change in a person as she did. She began the role of Juliet in every way a child, but concluded it as an adult, broken woman. So that the contrast would be especially expressive, she even lowered Juliet's age in the beginning: she wasn't fourteen, but barely twelve. People love to talk about the seemingly complete intuitiveness of her creative work and the absence of any artistic calculation. But this is nonsense. In this exaggeration of Juliet's childlikeness in the first act, there is the subtle aim and the sharp eye of a master, just as in her famous monologues, which she always began barely audibly, enlarging with conscious intent the scale up which her voice was to soar. By nature, her voice was not very strong, but it seemed strong in contrast to the half-whisper of the first lines. In this skillful extension of her voice range, Duse knew only one rival – Sarah Bernhardt, who was, by the way, completely different from her in every other respect.

* * *

A favorite device of Eleanor Duse's was the repetition of one word in different intonations. If this didn't occur in the text of the dialogue, then she changed the text. You should have heard how she repeated "Armand" with infinite variety in the gambling-house scene in *The Lady of the Camellias*. Probably there wasn't a play in which Duse didn't use this device, which is so full of possibilities for a skilled actor and so flat for a poor one. Sometimes it was a simple, "Well", now with an exclamation point, now with a question mark, now contemptuous, now angry, now surprised, now tender, that she would throw in between her partner's lines. I wouldn't deny it if some one of the old timers in the theatre were to tell me that my stories about Duse's acting in the role of Marguerite Gautier influenced the execution of this role by Zinaida Raikh, just as, by the way, the remarkable tradition of Mikhail Sadovsky influenced Ilinsky's Arkashka [in Ostrovsky's *The Forest*].

* * *

Rossov is an amateur who has had a long theatrical life and yet has never become a professional. Strange, but I still remember his beginnings, although now he seems to belong to the world of Neschastlivtsev [the tragedian in *The Forest*], while I subscribe to *Pravda* and *Izvestia*. That shows how long I've already lived. Rossov was more cultured than Orlenev, but still he remained a dilettante, while Orlenev was an excellent actor. Of the actors of that type, I was most taken with Mamont Dalsky with his extraordinary temperament which he masterfully controlled (and not the other way around as happened with certain other touring actors).

* * *

I first became aware of many of the laws of Biomechanics when I watched the acting of the remarkable Sicilian tragedian, Grasso. He conveyed the impression on the stage of wild, unbridled emotion. But watching him carefully, I understood that this was his remarkable technique. If he hadn't had this technique, he would have gone mad at the end of each performance.

* * *

Speaking of an actor's easy manner [*myakost'*], you must remember first of all the amazing Sandro Moissi, that half-Jew, half-Italian who acted in German, a language that was foreign to him. In Russia, we consider Kachalov to be the standard of softness, but Moissi held his own in competition with him. And I even consider him the victor. His softness was never amorphous. He was always virile and sonorous. I remember Moissi's performance with the cast of our Maly Theatre – the tense, strident, forced voices of the actors and the indifferent and inattentive audience. But Moissi made his entrance and the performance, which was taking place in the huge auditorium of an opera house, was boldly lowered several registers. The auditorium suddenly became quiet, as if bewitched by the sounds of an unknown speech. His speech was extraordinarily musical, a kind of magical melodiousness that, however, had nothing in common with the declamatory singsong à la Ostuzhev. And in his striking diction every sound seemed a pearl. After the performance, I couldn't resist writing a hot-tempered article about Moissi's sorry partners. Later, when I met him, he magnanimously rebuked me about this and even elegantly (although rather ambiguously) joked about the advantage for him of such a contrast. [When asked to explain what Meyerhold meant by "an easy manner", Gladkov referred to Spencer Tracy as the epitome of what Meyerhold had in mind in using that term: a seemingly casual, relaxed manner that belied the fact that the person was acting.]

* * *

Sometimes Chronegk, in the interests of a production, would cast a leading actor in a minor role. Of course, the production would greatly benefit from this, but I think those actors also benefited. I consider it very useful sometimes for a "star" to play in a good episodic scene. The leading roles can themselves carry the actor along, but here everything must be worked out. I wonder. Maybe I should cast *Boris Godunov* so that the best actors in our troupe play the minor roles. For example, in the role of one of the two courtiers (in our production there will be three) who talk about Boris before his monologue, I need an actor like Kachalov. One line of text, but the actor must be outstanding. To whomever can play it the way I want, I will immediately give a big raise. Well, who wants to try?

* * *

When I first saw the Japanese actress Hanako, I raved about her for a long time, although of course she played in a rather Europeanized manner in comparison with the Kabuki masters. [Hanako performed in St. Petersburg in Autumn 1909. She made an enormous impression on Meyerhold. Meyerhold did not see any genuine Japanese theatre until 1927 when the Kabuki theatre toured Paris.]

On Opera and Chaliapin

I don't understand why our opera houses still retain such a senseless anachronism as placing of the orchestra in front of the stage. This obliges the singers to strain their voices and robs the singing of subtle nuances. It is terribly difficult for singers to break through the powerful musical curtain of the orchestra. In the Bayreuth Theatre, the orchestra pit is much deeper than in our theatres, and the effect of this is enormous. When Wagner indicated in his scores from four to six *forte* notations, he of course had in mind such a disposition of the orchestra. But our conductors, in other conditions, blindly follow these notations. Allowing the orchestra to boom, they create an intolerable muddle of sounds. I can't stand shouting in opera and therefore I've stopped going to Wagner here. In the Mariinsky Theatre, the singers shouted to the point of exhaustion and damaged their vocal chords because of this, and Ershov retired prematurely.

Opera cries out for many reforms. The architects must find another place for the orchestra, and·the singers must learn their parts so that they don't have to watch the conductor constantly. I've promised myself that if I ever put on another opera, come hell or high water, I'll seat the orchestra differently!... (This was written in 1936. At the beginning of 1939, I asked V.E., who had begun to work at the Stanislavsky Opera Theatre, whether he still intended to bring about this reform? V.E. answered, "Yes, absolutely. Just allow me time to strengthen my position there a little more." A.G.)

* * *

In my opinion, Tchaikovsky's opera, *Eugene Onegin*, should be called *Tatyana*. Listen carefully to the music and you'll see that the composer is almost indifferent to the inner world of his hero. But on the other hand, he's in love with the heroine.

* * *

My career as an opera director (I have staged about ten operas) is sharply divided into two parts. In my pre-Revolutionary productions at the Mariinsky Theatre, I set as my goal the subordination of the direction and the acting, not to the text of the libretto, but to the music. I sought a solution for the staging in the orchestral score. In this period of my career, I made certain gains, but there were losses as well. In my productions after the Revolution, while not rejecting a general subordination to the score, I began striving to liberate the actor-singer from being shackled too much by the music. The example for me was Chaliapin, about whom one might say regarding his relationship to the music: it wasn't the horse that carried him, but he who rode the horse, as they say in the cavalry. What I tried to achieve in *The Queen of Spades* will genuinely be realized in Mozart's *Don Giovanni*, on which I am beginning to work. (V.E. Meyerhold didn't live to complete work on the production of Mozart's opera *Don Giovanni* at the Stanislavsky Opera Theatre – A.G.)

* * *

If you had seen *Tristan and Isolde* in the Mariinsky Theatre, then you would understand what progress in the art of directing opera I've made

with *The Queen of Spades*. If in *Tristan* I insisted on an almost mathematically precise coincidence of the actors' movements and gestures with the
tempo of the music and the tonal design, then in *The Queen of Spades* I
strove for rhythmic freedom for the actor within the broad musical
phrase (like Chaliapin). I strove to allow the actor's interpretation,
growing out of the music, to be not metrically precise, but in a contra-
puntal relationship with it, sometimes even contrasting, varying, moving
ahead and falling behind, not following it in unison. The situation here
should be the same as the one I often refer to in rehearsing drama: the
director must know the play so well that he has the right to allow himself
to forget it.

* * *

You say that you don't like opera? It's simply that you lack the imagination to picture what opera might be. It was no accident that Stanislavsky
devoted the final years of his life to opera. I'm proud that I was fated to
inherit the musical theatre he created.

* * *

The possibility for improvisation is precisely what distinguishes drama
from opera where the conductor doesn't allow for expanding a time
segment and where one can only expand the tempo. Chaliapin, who was
a genuine actor and felt the need for improvisation, made up for it in the
tempo. That explains all his conflicts with conductors: he tried to expand
the tempo. I never give up the right to encourage actors to improvise. In
improvisation it's important only that the secondary doesn't detract from
what is paramount; that, plus the problem of time and the interrelation
of time segments on the stage.

* * *

I worked with Chaliapin only on the production of *Boris*. Of course we
immediately quarreled and never again sought to collaborate, although
Yurev tried to reconcile us. But I was always a grateful admirer of his performances. [Meyerhold produced Mussorgsky's opera at the Mariinsky
Theatre in Petersburg (première, January 6, 1911) using the settings
Golovin had designed for the 1908 Paris production organized by Serge
Diaghilev. Meyerhold's production was not a success. Chaliapin sang at
only the first two performances. In 1917, Meyerhold flatly refused to
work with Chaliapin on Dargomyzhsky's *The Stone Guest*.]

* * *

Chaliapin's strength lay not in the resources of his voice or in the beauty
of its timbre (there were others, stronger and more beautiful), but in the
fact that he was the first to begin singing not only the notes but the text

as well. He succeeded in this because he was so musical that he could allow himself not to think about the notes at all. Therefore he sang more naturally than many people speak.

* * *

Chaliapin's hot temper, scandals, and explosions at rehearsals and performances, and his quarrels with conductors and partners could be explained very simply: he was so extremely musical that a barely noticeable false note wounded his ear, as the scratching of a brick on glass grates on you. Try to sit quietly when a mischievous youngster begins to move a piece of brick on glass. Chaliapin heard everything in the orchestra, and the very smallest "off-sound", which we don't even notice, pained him like torture. This vulnerable sensibility is not only a psychological trait, but also psycho-physical, just like the vulnerability of the lyrical poets whom we must protect from suicide as we protect a worker in a dangerous industry. Mayakovsky's death was a violation of safety rules in that most hazardous industry, poetry.

* * *

Few people know how willfully Chaliapin manipulated the score of *Boris Godunov*. In the "mad" scene he needed time for his extraordinary improvised acting: there he played an entire segment without singing. But the orchestral part was too short. Then he asked the conductor to repeat in this place the so-called "chimes" music. Those who heard and saw Chaliapin in that role must admit that the result was extraordinary. I don't think that Mussorgsky himself would have argued with it.

But it goes without saying, even here some connoisseurs of the score turned up who were indignant. After our experience with the classics, we were well acquainted with this particular species of bookworm who could have been so aptly described by Anatole France. Once I heard *Boris* on the radio and I caught in the "mad" scene those same "chimes". That means they had become a tradition. This is what always happens. At first you are an arbitrary innovator, and then, a silver-haired founder of tradition.

* * *

When I was in France, I saw Chaliapin in the movie *Don Quixote*. It was quite bad, but I blame the director [George Pabst], not Chaliapin. In the theatre Chaliapin was always his own director. (That's why he liked "directors" of Sanin's type so much.) But in this case, obviously his lack of knowledge of cinema technique hampered him. I didn't recognize him. He was timid, inexpressive, sugary. And that from Chaliapin! If this film reaches us, I don't advise seeing it – you'll understand nothing of what the great actor and singer Chaliapin stood for in the theatre.

On Self-restriction, Improvisation, Rhythm, Associations

Self-restriction and improvisation – these are the two main working requirements for the actor on the stage. The more complex their combination, the higher the actor's art.

* * *

Balzac said that the ultimate in art is to build a palace on the point of a needle. In essence, both *The Magnanimous Cuckold*, with its very deliberate external asceticism, and *The Inspector General*, performed on a small platform, were motivated by such an aspiration. I call this the self-restriction of the artist.

* * *

The skilled actor must know how to play in a large expanse, on a broad area (as in my *Don Giovanni*), as well as (Varlamov and Davydov) sitting for a long time on a sofa (as I aimed for in *The Inspector General*). In one production (I forget the name of the play), for *almost* twenty minutes Varlamov played alone, lying motionless in bed, and that was brilliant. It was according to the play, but it was also a virtuoso example of an actor's self-restriction. Without self-restriction there is no craftsmanship.

* * *

Speaking about the actor's art of self-restriction, I remember a still more brilliant example: the remarkable French actress Réjane played an entire first act lying on a couch. At the end of the act she had to get up and approach the door, and she got up... But how she got up!... At that point the curtain fell.

* * *

By self-restriction within the given temporal and spatial composition, or within the ensemble of partners, the actor makes a sacrifice to the whole of the production. The director makes a similar sacrifice in allowing improvisation. But these sacrifices are fruitful if they are mutual.

* * *

Have you ever thought about why there's always music during acrobatic numbers in the circus? You might say, for the mood, for the sake of festivity, but that would be a superficial answer. Circus people need music as rhythmic support, as an aid in keeping time. Their work is built on the most exact calculation, and the least deviation from it can lead to a break and a catastrophe. Against a background of very familiar music, the timing is usually flawless. Without music it's already difficult, but still possible. But if the orchestra suddenly plays music other than what an acrobat is used to, it may lead to his death.

To some degree. the same thing is true in the theatre. Supported by the rhythmical background of music, the actor's playing acquires precision. In the Eastern theatre, the stage assistant strikes a board during moments of climax. This is also done to help the actor play precisely. The actor needs a background of music in order to train himself to pay attention to the flow of time on the stage. If an actor is used to playing with a musical background, then without it he will sense time completely differently. Along with developing the ability to improvise, our school demands that the actor develop the gift of self-restriction. And nothing helps acting to be self-restrained better than a musical background.

* * *

It was my concern for managing the huge amount of text in *The Inspector General* that led me to use a small acting platform in order to avoid losing time on long transitions. And having constructed such an acting platform, I was able to understand the beauty of what I call "self-restriction". In varying degrees this principle lies at the heart of any art. This seeming "lack of freedom" becomes a source of greater skill in techniques of expressiveness: it reveals true mastery.

* * *

An acting pause is very alluring for the good actor who is skilled at mime play. But with actors who don't have a feel for time, it can be unbearable. That's where a developed ability for self-restriction is needed. From production to production I have experimented in the director's score with finding devices for self-restriction. In [Faiko's] *Bubus, The Teacher* the musical background helped the performers achieve self-restriction in time. In *The Inspector General*, the small forward platform served to achieve self-restriction in space. For the actors, these two productions were a major school in self-restriction. I observed that those who went through it immediately and noticeably grew in professional stature.

* * *

Good actors always improvise, even within the limits of the most exact director's plan. Even before I saw Mikhail Chekhov in the role of Khlestakov, I'd already heard that at one point in the performance he parodied the portrait of Nicholas I hanging on the stage. When I went to see the production, I anticipated that clever detail. But I didn't see it, although Chekhov was in good form and played excellently. What's more, during the performance I completely forgot about that anticipated segment. On that evening Chekhov played that bit differently, and this was his right, which no one could take away from him. He didn't "forget". He replaced it with something else. Only those who saw the performance several times in a row noticed the absence of this clever detail. Later, when people said to me, "And what about Chekhov's little game with the portrait!" I answered, "Yes, yes", but I didn't at all feel robbed...

* * *

An actor can improvise only when he feels internal joy. Without an atmosphere of creative joy, of artistic *élan*, an actor never completely opens up. That's why during my rehearsals I so often shout "Good!" to the actors. They're still playing badly, very badly. But an actor hears your "Good!" and lo, he will in fact play well. One must work happily and joyfully! When I am irritable and nasty at rehearsal (I'm only human), then afterwards at home I reproach myself severely and repent. A director's irritability instantly fetters an actor. It's inadmissible, just as is scornful silence. If you don't sense a look of expectation in the actor's eyes, then you're no director!

* * *

Afinogenov, in his lecture at a theatrical meeting of RAPP, said some nonsense to the effect that the significance I gave to rhythm made me a mystic and even almost an anthroposophist. But I would like to see a genuine director who disregards the importance of rhythm. Say that to Stanislavsky and he would throw you right out the door. An understanding of rhythm in a production is one of the fundamental principles, as the Greeks would say. Here, everything is turned around. We not only don't overvalue the meaning of rhythm, we undervalue it. We still haven't sufficiently studied its nature, the entire sphere of its influence on the work of the actor. But we already do it, whatever name you give it. [Meyerhold has in mind a directive, "On the Goals of RAPP on the Theatrical Front", (*Rabis*, Nos. 35-36 [1931], pp. 24–25) which attacked Meyerhold's use of "mechanical rhythm" as part of his biomechanical system, and the "idealistic, anthroposophical devices of Mikhail Chekhov and Andrei Bely" ("rhythm as dialectics"). The directive concluded that Meyerhold's theoretical concepts, which it linked to the artistic methodology of Theosophy, could not serve as the basis for Soviet theatre.]

* * *

The absence of improvisation in an actor's performance is evidence that he has ceased growing.

* * *

Mochalov played the same scene in different ways, but he never changed the motif of the acting. Instead he found new variants depending on his mood on a particular day, the makeup of the audience, even the weather.

* * *

I think it was Scriabin who called rhythm "time bewitched". Brilliantly put!

* * *

Once in Constantinople I happened into a Moslem school attached to a mosque. I was struck by the fact that while memorizing the Koran, the pupil held the teacher's hand and they both swayed rhythmically. And then I understood that the strict rhythm focused the pupil's attention and facilitated memorization. Rhythm is a great helper!

* * *

Just how much more powerful associative images are than the text of a play can be proved by two examples from the repertory of the Moscow Art Theatre. According to the author's conception, *An Enemy of the People* [*Doctor Stockman* at the Moscow Art Theatre] is an extremely conservative and anti-social play, preaching social isolation, but emotionally conceal-ing the motif of the struggle of a lone person against the majority. In the revolutionary situation in Russia on the eve of 1905, before an audience brimming with revolutionary excitement, the play was a great success. Audience associations completely transformed the story of the play. The same thing happened with *At the Gate of the Kingdom* by Knut Hamsun. The audience didn't want to listen to the text of Kareno's monologues preaching Nietzscheanism. But through the power of its associations, audiences linked the active minority's (*menshevist*) battle with the major-ity (*bolshevist*) to the beginning of the Revolution. And coloring Kareno's struggle with their own leftist ideas, they perceived his battle with the liberals, which for the author was a struggle with a more "rightist" position, as a revolutionary struggle. I remember that very well because I played the role of Kareno many times.

* * *

My favorite associations... Look for associative parallels! Use associative parallels in your work! So far I've only approached an understanding of the enormous power of imagery in the theatre. There are a wealth of possibilities here.

* * *

You need not think that my thesis about "associations" leads to some kind of subjectivism in the perception of art. Some day physiologists, psychologists, and philosophers will show that the realm of associations is connected with certain general (and even social – after all, in the final analysis everything is social) phenomena for the majority of people. The sound of a factory whistle means one thing to me and something else for those who their entire life have gotten out of bed at the sound of that whistle. Sounding in the background of a scene, it will say one thing to one person, and something else to another. That isn't subjectivism, but is in the realm of social associations. Without a communality of associations, no art would be possible: then the only audience would be the artist himself, as is the case in the most extreme surrealist trends in painting.

* * *

You are listening to *The Queen of Spades* and suddenly remember some episode from Stendhal. Or not even exactly remember, but a momentary half-memory passes in parallel through your mind. The image of Herman and Stendhal's characters – this is a correct association. Correct associations strengthen a production, infinitely broaden the power of its effect, while wrong ones ruin it. In a production everything may be according to the letter of the play – wigs in place, noses stuck on, the text correctly spoken; but the associations evoked in the spectators are alien to the author's intention and to the spirit of the work. The only way to read the classics is to take them not singly, but together with the whole library shelf on which they stand. Pushkin could almost not have known Stendhal. And, it seems Byron, who was personally well-acquainted with Stendhal, did not even suspect what a great writer he was. But for modern man, Herman, Lermontov's prose heroes, Stendhal's heroes, and Byron's heroes stand side by side. And associative memories of the entire row will involuntarily flash through the mind, if we ourselves don't close off the path to these associations. In using associations, we don't have to spell everything out. The spectator himself will do it for us.

* * *

Imagine the usual disordered and unorganized noise of the street, the diversity and bustling movement in a crowd. And then along the street a company of soldiers passes, singing. They may only be on their way to the bathhouse, but see how everyone turns to look at them, how many still continue about their business, going wherever they were going, talking about their own affairs, but already doing it differently. The marching music has organized everyone, and suddenly the street lives differently: subjected to the rhythm of the marching song and to the measured tramp of boots...

On Miscellaneous Subjects

I don't like it when someone says, "I work in the theatre". One works in a vegetable garden, but in the theatre, one serves, as in the army or the navy.

* * *

If all the scenes in a play are written with the same force, then its failure is guaranteed: the audience can't sustain such tension. The beginning must captivate and promise something. In the middle there must be one stunning effect. Before the finale a slightly lesser effect is needed, without tension. All the rest can be however you like. Extracts don't go over in the theatre.

* * *

I often demonstrate to my actors for three different reasons: first, to explain to the cast more quickly and simply what I want from them; second, in order to see whether it can be played that way, to test it out, so to speak, on my own self as an actor; and third, sometimes also because I simply want to do a little acting... But please don't tell anyone that! Okay?

* * *

The current style in the theatre is a combination of the very boldest stylization and the most extreme naturalism. But of course the important thing is the proportions. And that is already a matter of taste, talent, intelligence.

* * *

I am the purest realist, only in its most pungent form, understand?

* * *

If everyone praises your production, almost certainly it is rubbish. If everyone abuses it, then perhaps there is something in it. But if some praise and others abuse, if you can split the audience in half, then for sure it is a good production. Sarah Bernhardt also maintained that the worst thing of all was a production accepted by everyone. It is often a polite form of indifference.

* * *

What is music? A fistful of notes, thrown by the hand of a genius onto five staff-lines, onto five of the most ordinary lines, which can set into motion an avalanche of imagination and feelings.

* * *

Electra was a mistake of mine and Golovin's. We were too carried away by the visual aspects and disregarded the music. We were overcome by archeology, which became an end in itself. I never repeated that mistake again.

* * *

Do you want to hear a strange confession? When I read the murder scene in *Crime and Punishment*, I always want Raskolnikov to succeed in escaping, not to get caught. You too? Therein lies the great gift of the novelist. Reading about the same happening in the paper, you of course want the criminal to be caught quickly. No, art is not at all a simple matter. It's a very ambiguous thing.

* * *

There are facial features and there are facial expressions. The bad portrait artist paints only the first, but the good one paints the second...

* * *

The main theme in *Othello* isn't love or jealousy, but evil, intrigue, and slander. And the main character is the sinister machine of perfidious intrigue in whose wheels Othello and Desdemona perish. Hence, the main hero is the vile operator of this machine, Iago.

* * *

To fear mistakes to the point of panic means that you will never know achievement.

* * *

Look at good pictures more often and you'll never have to think about what to do with your hands and feet. They will find the right position by themselves. Look, look at pictures! [Meyerhold always brought back many art reproductions when he returned from abroad. His students also brought him art monographs and reproductions because they knew that Meyerhold valued them. Many of his mises en scène were based on works of art. The famous banquet scene in *Woe to Wit* (Episode 14), for example, was inspired by Michelangelo's *The Last Supper* and Diego Rivera's *The Feast of the Millionaires*.]

* * *

Always seek asymmetrical movements. Don't hold your arms hanging at your sides, but at different levels.

* * *

Don't be afraid of small interruptions in your work: only don't put it completely out of your mind during that time. Don't labor at it, but just let your work come into your mind now and then. I've noticed that after a break one often comes to rehearsal with something more than what one stopped with before the break. Work properly begun continues by itself within you, and wisdom consists in not hampering it.

* * *

There is no limit to the search for perfection by a genuine master. As you know, during his final year the famous Japanese artist, Hokusai, painted only birds. When his friends came to congratulate him on his ninetieth birthday, one of them, looking at his most recent pictures, said that Hokusai's birds seemed just about to fly away. "When I reach one hundred, they will fly away!" Hokusai said. And he was right. They would fly away if the artist lived to be one hundred. The perfection of his art had already become almost magical.

* * *

The basic problem of the contemporary theatre is that of preserving the element of improvisation in the actor's art within the complex and exact form the director has found for a production. Usually the same thing happens as in the fable: you pull the animal out by the tail and its muzzle gets stuck in the mud. I recently spoke with Konstantin Sergeevich. He also thinks about that. We are approaching the solution of the same problem like builders of a tunnel under the Alps. He is moving from one side, and I from the other. And inevitably, somewhere in the middle we must meet.

* * *

A static mise en scène demands that the dialogue be delivered as quickly as possible.

* * *

Theatrical traditions live a complex life through the centuries. They decay and seem to have died, and then suddenly they come to life and are resurrected in a new way. Every theatre is stylized. But there is stylization and stylization. It seems to me that the stylization of Mei Lan-fang or Carl Gozzi is closer to our age than the stylization of Ozerov's tragedies or the Maly Theatre "in the period of its decline".

* * *

Artistic skill is achieved when the "what" and the "how" come simultaneously.

* * *

Mayakovsky once said, "In order to laugh you have to have a face". Well said! Very well, indeed!

* * *

When I worked with Vishnevsky, I was very pleased that he seemed to be cautious with words. He gave us a magnificent scenario in *The Last, Decisive*, and then he came to rehearsals and sparingly doled out words. We would ask, "Vsevolod, give us more words", and jealously guarding them, he would carefully dole them out. That was by no means because he had so few – he had a vast reserve – but because he was economical out of a sense of good taste and a feeling for genuine theatre. In my opinion, it is better to have to beg a dramatist for needed words than to have to cross out whole pages by writers for whom these words are cheap.

* * *

More and more frequently it seems to me that the difference between Stanislavsky and me is mainly a matter of terminology. What he calls "the task" I call "the motif". But we are speaking of one and the same thing.

* * *

The most beautiful thing in art is that at each new stage you again feel yourself to be a pupil.

* * *

Observation! Curiosity! Attention! Yesterday I asked several of my young actors in succession what was the shape of the streetlight standing in front of the theatre and no one answered correctly. That's terrible, indeed! And of the classics, most of all read those from which you can learn how to observe. The champion observer is Gogol in *Dead Souls*!

* * *

I don't remember who said, "Art is to reality as wine is to the grapes". Superbly said! [These are Franz Grillparzer's words.]

* * *

In life, charlatans usually feign illness, but in art they most often feign well-being.

* * *

I never liked Persimfans [a symphonic orchestra in the 1920s that played without a conductor]. The conductor's gestures help me to understand the rhythmic subtleties of the score.

* * *

Vrubel has a drawing titled "Insomnia". It's simply a rumpled eider-down, a crumpled pillow. There's no person in the picture, but everything is clear from the way it's drawn. No person is there, and yet there is...

* * *

Read Bernard Shaw's essay on Eleanora Duse and Sarah Bernhardt! There's theatrical criticism for you!

* * *

The visible process of the hero making a decision is far more dramatically effective than eavesdropping, a slap on the face, or duels. That is why *Hamlet* is the most popular play of all times and peoples. This is more powerful than "recognition", although in *Hamlet* there is also "recognition". In *Hamlet* there is everything. And for the most inexperienced and naïve, it's an excellent melodrama to boot. *Ghosts* is a good play, but compare it to *Hamlet* and you'll see how much richer *Hamlet* is.

* * *

The dramatic plot is a system of inevitable surprises.

* * *

Carlo Gozzi was victorious in his struggle with Goldoni not because he revived (though not for long) the folk comedy of masks, which was dying under pressure from the literary theatre, but because he made these masks speak the language of his day. Restoration and stylization as objectives are alien to genuine art.

* * *

Vaudeville doesn't tolerate unpleasant characters. In vaudeville, even the villains are pleasant. This is a law of the genre.

* * *

Rereading Belinsky, here's what he writes in his article, "Russian Literature in 1843": "The art of evoking laughter is more difficult than the art of evoking tears" ... What do you think, is that true? Very likely, with reservations, but all the same it's true! And comedy lives longer than drama. Fonvizin is still alive, as are Griboedov and Gogol. Even Shakovskoi is still played on our stages, while dramas contemporary to them are dead. Who needs Ozerov's, Polevoi's, Kukolnik's plays, or "Poor Liza"? Comedy absorbs the truth of its time more fully. A paradox? Think about it!...

* * *

Leconte de Lisle said, "In a strictly etymological sense the concept of form doesn't exist. Form is the most natural expression of thought". I agree with this completely!

* * *

I love Oscar Wilde, but I can't stand those for whom he is their favorite author.

* * *

Read more! Read tirelessly! Read! Read with a pencil in your hand! Make notes! Leave slips of paper in your books with notes of all the passages that have caught your attention! This is essential. I have such slips and notes in all the books in my library. For example, I read all of Wagner in German. Everyone knows him as a composer and librettist. But he also wrote ten volumes of the most interesting articles. I have thoroughly studied all of them. You can take from these volumes the slips of paper scribbled over by me and you will at once understand what interested me. Don't spare book margins! Scribble all over them. A book I've made notes in is ten times more valuable to me than a new one.

* * *

The modern airplane, light, streamlined, seemingly made out of a single piece, appears at first glance to be a less complicated machine than the earlier "Farmans" and "Blériots". The same is true of art. The beautiful creation of a master seems simple and elementary in comparison with the unwieldy work of a striving amateur.

* * *

Here's a seeming paradox: for the interpretation of minor roles, I sometimes need actors with higher qualifications than for the leading roles. *The Queen of Spades* was such a success because I insisted that the role of the Countess, who has only one song to sing, and the role of Yeletsky be sung by the best artists and singers who in other productions could fill the major roles. I was deeply hurt recently when someone in our theatre said to me that Luka's role [in Chekhov's *The Bear*] isn't even a role, but just a vehicle serving the plot. If I hadn't stopped acting long ago, I myself would have loved playing Luka, and then I would have shown all of you whether this is a role or not! The secret of performing *Boris Godunov* lies in the distribution of the so-called minor roles.

* * *

I'll take the liberty of telling you, my comrades-in-arms and students, that the thesis of the director's theatre is absolute nonsense, not to be believed. There is no director – if he is a real director – who would put his art above the interests of the actor as the main figure in the theatre. The art of directing, the art of constructing the mise en scène, of the alternations in the lighting and music – all this must be subservient to outstanding, highly-qualified actors!

* * *

He who hasn't given everything to art, has given it nothing.

* * *

A bitter admission: we theatre people live in Moscow in such an isolated fashion, in such separate monastic communities, that in our information about each other we often nourish ourselves with legends. It's easier for me to communicate with Gordon Craig, who's in Italy, than with Stanislavsky, who lives on the next street... (Written in 1935 – A.G.)

* * *

A certain Greek dramatist, Phrynichus, a friend and rival of Aeschylus, was exiled from his native land because his tragedy, in depicting the destruction of Miletus, gave such a naturalistic portrayal of national disaster that the spectators could not refrain from groans and tears. He was punished because his art was not a purification but a sentimental exploitation of the spectator's compassion. If I had taken part in the voting, I would also have voted for Phrynichus' exile.

* * *

The greatest enemy of beauty is prettiness.

* * *

In his piano concerto, Tchaikovsky used the melody from a French music hall song that his brother told me his uncle often hummed. An artist has the right to take his material from anywhere. What matters is what he does with it.

* * *

I recently read that Emperor Ferdinand, having been exposed as Wallenstein's murderer, ordered three thousand requiems to be celebrated for him. Now there's a character more complex than Macbeth!

* * *

In art it's more important to seek than to know.

* * *

Don't confuse the concepts of "tradition" and "cliché". A cliché is a tradition made meaningless.

* * *

Did you know that Conan Doyle's son married Hans Christian Anderson's granddaughter? How amusing! If the eugenicists are right, then we may expect from that marriage the birth of the most brilliant storyteller of all times. But nature doesn't like to be mocked, and no doubt they will give birth to some boring type.

* * *

Salvini had two sons and they both became actors. They were as alike as twins, but one inherited his father's talent while the other didn't. The same upbringing, almost the same physical qualities – and nothing in common. I often think about the mystery of talent, and it sometimes strikes me that the story of Salvini's children could be an excellent subject for a novel.

* * *

The ability to sense keenly the dramatic climaxes of a play is one of the most essential qualities of a director. I've sometimes had to correct and rework productions staged by other directors when there was already little time left for this and the theatre administration was calling for the première. I've always done the following: I define for myself one or two climactic scenes (how often they are incorrectly identified – the greatest mistake!), work on them, and lo and behold, the production succeeds, everything having fallen into place at once.

* * *

MEYERHOLD REHEARSES

Meyerhold's talent was such that tedious analysis during rehearsals was alien to it. He was a genius at improvisation, a genius at artistic synthesis, a genius of instantaneous inspiration. Those who were present at his rehearsals can testify to this. A cascade of devices, a waterfall of improvisations, a wealth of brilliant sketches tossed off quickly and passionately.

But this is only half the truth. This is what we saw at rehearsals: always festive, always resembling a performance, the performance of a solo actor. But there was also another stage of work, work in the study. There, the calculating Salieri precedes the inspired Mozart. This is the stage of the project's maturation, the stage of consideration from every angle, the stage of dreams. There we see the bespectacled Meyerhold sitting with a book (always with a pencil), or going through the thick folders of art reproductions he has been collecting throughout his entire life. In preparing to stage *The Lady of the Camellias*, for example, Meyerhold looked through hundreds of engravings by Gavarni and other masters of the mid-nineteenth century. The ones he marked were photographed and sent to the scenic designer. There are albums of these photographs preserved in his archives. From them, one can reconstruct how the visual image of the play was born.

As an actor, Meyerhold performed for the last time during the 1916–1917 season. At the Alexandrinsky Theatre, he played the Prince of Aragon in *The Merchant of Venice*, a role he had already prepared with Stanislavsky in the young Art Theatre. That same year he played two roles in the movies. At the end of the twenties, he again performed, also in the movies, the role of a high official in *The White Eagle* (based on *The Governor*, a story by Leonid Andreev), directed by Yakov Protazanov. Meyerhold didn't perform again in the last twenty years of his life.

There was, it's true, in the mid-twenties also a half-joking incident when huge announcements were pasted all over Moscow of a performance of *D.E.* in honor of someone "with Meyerhold's participation". But that participation was purely an advertising stunt. In the course of the action a motorcyclist was supposed to rush across the stage. That motorcyclist was Meyerhold. He put on huge glasses so it was difficult to recognize him. And although this passage was rehearsed for a long time

Meyerhold rehearsing *The Last, Decisive* in the lobby of the theatre (1930–1931).

in advance, witnesses say that before it, Meyerhold was very nervous and upset.

While Meyerhold gave up appearing as an actor before an audience, he continued to remain an actor at his rehearsals. In essence, Meyerhold played all the roles in all the plays he staged.

* * *

Meyerhold often removed his jacket in the heat of rehearsal. But sometimes he took it off even before the beginning of the rehearsal, while the workers were still setting up the panels on the stage, someone was sweeping, someone laying out the wiring and trailing a lamp over to the director's table.

The performers had not yet gathered, the assistant director's bell had not yet rung. But Meyerhold, his jacket off, was already standing on the right side of the stage, silently peering at the markings for the panels. Then he would move over to the left and watch from there. This meant that today there would be not merely a skirmish, but a decisive battle. What was he thinking about as he gazed into the dusty twilight of the stage? At this moment, one could not approach him with a question – he

Meyerhold, pen in hand, working on the text of *Woe to Wit* (1927).

wouldn't answer anyway. His head lowered, and hunching over, he would run along the inclined ramp into the auditorium still meditating about something for several seconds. Then he would lift his head, notice those who were already sitting in the auditorium, greet them, and ask something entirely unexpected, something that had nothing to do with the present rehearsal.

Meyerhold demonstrates

Meyerhold was not one of those directors who begin work on a play knowing about it only as much as the performers sitting around the table for the first reading. He always came to the very first rehearsal with a clear vision of the future production. He burned with a passionate, impatient desire to realize this vision. He infected, enthused the actors with it. He interfered in the scenic designer's work, he prompted the composer. He rarely remained at the director's table with its lamp under a green shade. He jumped up, paced around the auditorium, looked at the stage from every possible angle. I remember many rehearsals when he never sat down at all. Such was the nature of his temperament. He encouraged the actors with his unchanging, characteristic, sharp, and abrupt "Good!" or he ran up onto the stage and demonstrated, demonstrated, demonstrated...

Yes, and I never once saw in Meyerhold's *The Forest* a Neschastlivtsev like Neschastlivtsev–Meyerhold at the rehearsals for updating the production. I also never saw a Lidochka Muromsky in *Krechinsky's Wedding* like Lidochka-Meyerhold, a gray-haired old man with a long nose and a hoarse voice – but even in those roles where actors weren't on a par with Bogolyubov, Garin, Ilinsky, and Babanova, there was the flaming reflection of his talent, his internal stature, his strength.

Meyerhold himself never recommended the demonstration as a basic methodological device in a director's work with actors. He always distinguished between the "technique of the demonstration" and the technique of the actor in performance. At one of the rehearsals for a revival of his production of *The Inspector General*, he shouted from the auditorium to Nikolai Mologin, the actor playing Dobchinsky, "You aren't acting, you're demonstrating to me how to play Dobchinsky! This isn't an actor's performance, but a director's demonstration!"

But Meyerhold himself brilliantly "demonstrated". It was a facet of his character which was endowed with an extraordinary imagination, of his passionate, impatient temperament, of his ability to see simultaneously the "what" and the "how". It was not a method, not a rule, but an inimitable peculiarity of his talent, just as personal as Chaliapin's sense of rhythm.

It is simply impossible to imagine Meyerhold sitting for weeks at his table, patiently awaiting the awakening of creative initiative in his actors. At the beginning of work on *Boris Godunov*, he tried to increase the "period around the table" but soon after the fine points of Pushkin's versification had been analyzed with the help of the poet Vladimir Pyast, Meyerhold quickly dragged everyone away from the table over to the sets. Activity, a passion for work in all its stages, clarity of purpose, ease of imagination, a wealth of invention – all this is Meyerhold.

* * *

I wasn't yet working in the theatre when, helped by an actor friend, I quietly sneaked into the back of the uncomfortable auditorium of the former Zon Theatre, very much afraid that I would be noticed and asked to leave. It was when Meyerhold was directing the final scene of Vishnevsky's *The Last, Decisive* and was showing Bogolyubov how a sailor wounded in battle dies.

Bogolyubov later played this scene excellently (it was the starting point of the upward swing in his acting career), but Meyerhold's demonstration was unforgettable. Any discussion of whether or not the actor had encompassed the remarkable directorial demonstration seems absolutely petty. Actually, the audience saw Meyerhold only through Bogolyubov; what's more, in showing the actor *how* to perform, in his mind's eye the director could already see it in the text and in Bogolyubov's individuality, as a sculptor sees a statue in a piece of bronze or marble.

Probably, if Garin had been playing the sailor, Meyerhold would have demonstrated this action to him differently.

* * *

In 1925, Meyerhold was working on Aleksei Faiko's *Bubus, The Teacher*. Only a few days remained before the première when Igor Ilinsky, who was rehearsing the leading role, left the theatre (he subsequently returned and walked out again twice). The role of Bubus was given to Boris Belsky. The assistants began to "introduce" him into it. One time Meyerhold came to a rehearsal, watched this "introduction", and himself took over, rearranging everything to fit the personality of the new performer. In eight days he constructed anew the already finished production. Ilinsky's personality demanded one kind of stage approach, Belsky's another.

In his book *A Wind from the Caucasus*, Andrei Bely introduces a page from his diary on which he had noted an observation typical of Meyerhold. "Tiflis. 21 June. Evening – a warm, lively conversation with V.E. He told us in detail how he tries by scrutinizing an actor (morally and physiologically) to understand him clearly, and having understood, to put him in a role where his shortcomings could serve as advantages. It's nothing to cultivate talent, one must make an actor's shortcomings the source of an irreplaceable strength. For me that explained for once and all – he's a director–teacher."

Meyerhold willingly worked with actors who had not been trained by him (in contrast to Stanislavsky who never staged a single production outside the walls of his own theatre), and he often achieved brilliant results in a very short time with a troupe completely new to him.

His production of *The Queen of Spades*, which he staged at the Maly Opera Theatre in Leningrad in 1935, could serve as an example. And in 1935, he realized a new director's version of *Masquerade* at the Pushkin Dramatic Theatre in Leningrad. While remaining himself in his creative work, Meyerhold easily found a common language with actors of the most varying schools and tendencies.

I remember how in the spring of 1938, on returning from an examination at the Stanislavsky Opera-Studio where at Stanislavsky's invitation he was to begin working, he excitedly told me about the drama student-singer Vera G. Solovyeva. "Even her hands sing", he said.

* * *

I loved to observe Meyerhold after his demonstrations. I noticed that after running down the gangway into the auditorium, V.E. seemed to be absent for several seconds. Why? I wondered. Evidently, after finishing the demonstration and leaving the stage, he still internally lived what he had just performed. As a consequence, he often missed the beginning of the actor's repetition of what had been demonstrated. Only after coming to and shrugging off, as it were, the state he was in during the demonstration, would V.E. lift his head and again look at the stage. Often he would then run or walk quickly up the gangway to demonstrate or explain again. Those seconds of "absence" always seemed mysterious to me.

With the exception of perhaps Kiligin and Samoilov, the old-time Meyerhold actors – his pupils from GVTM and GEKTEMAS – more quickly and easily understood Meyerhold's instructions than did the actors who joined the troupe in the final years, despite their qualifications and experience. When Meyerhold rehearsed with Bogolyubov, Zaichikov, Ilinsky and others, less time was lost on explaining how to carry out the tasks set by the director. Sometimes it was sufficient merely to point out *what* had to be done.

At times, Meyerhold was gloomy, at times angry, at times frenzied, at times infectiously cheerful, at times enthusiastic. But he was never indifferent, even when rehearsing a play he didn't much care for.

It seems unbelievable to me now, although I witnessed it, that once during an ordinary daytime rehearsal (April 8, 1937), Meyerhold climbed up on the stage sixty-one times in order to demonstrate something to the actors. He made the usual remarks from the auditorium, but he went up on the stage eighteen times before the break, and forty-three times after a ten-minute interval. During this entire time, he did not once sit down. In front of me now lies my notebook in which I marked with a stroke each time he ran up the ramp.

It was one of those rehearsals when he had already taken off his jacket before it began. The mass scene, "The Procession of the Cross" from Lidiya Seifulina's play, *Natasha*, was being rehearsed. Meyerhold was sixty-three years old. That was the kind of phenomenal energy this man possessed. He didn't get up on the stage to say something. Each time he *demonstrated*, that is, he performed an entire segment for one of the thirty participants in the mass scene.

* * *

By the end of a rehearsal, everyone would be exhausted except V.E. When he finished, he still felt a need to speak with someone about the rehearsal, or, as he said himself, "to savor what had been done". Generally during the work, and especially during rehearsals onstage, Meyerhold had a

Meyerhold at a rehearsal of Bezymensky's *The Shot* (1929).

habit, which he enjoyed, of asking the opinion of those present, not always, however, paying attention to the answer. And what sort of answers could there be when everyone was as carried away as he was?

Onstage, an episode that had just been worked out was being repeated and V.E. was wandering around the auditorium watching, of course, from various points (I rarely remember his sitting behind the director's table). From time to time he would approach one person, then another, and ask, "Well, how is it? Interesting, right? Well?"

"Well?" with a question mark was his favorite expression. It even turned up in the scene of Khlestakov's lies [in *The Inspector General*].

Meyerhold at a rehearsal of *Prélude* (1933). Sergei Eisenstein is seated at the far left. Author Yuri German is seated at the far right with his back to the camera.

Meyerhold improvises

Meyerhold defined improvisation in his own way. In one of his earlier writings, he characterized the term "improvisation" as follows: "the free combination of previously prepared elements". Meyerhold believed that an actor's available reserve – what Stanislavsky's system called "adaptations" – had to be larger in number than the elements any given performance might necessitate putting into actual use. He gave the actor the right within certain compositional limits to select freely out of this reserve some "adaptations" for today, and others for tomorrow, or to vary them in a novel way.

Moreover, Meyerhold considered essential an actor's improvisation arising in the process of the actor's development in a role. He often spoke of this. In his opinion, the absence of improvisation demonstrated an absence of creative growth in a dramatic actor.

Meyerhold could describe in detail entire acts from his productions that had not yet been staged. Thus he talked about *Hamlet*, which he didn't realize. Thus he talked about *Boris Godunov*, which he staged in rough form in 1936–37.

I remember one evening in Kiev in the summer of 1936, during a tour of the theatre, when in the director's office of the Ivan Franko Theatre, Meyerhold told in detail, down to the finest point, about his staging of the scene in *Boris* with the monologue – "I have achieved the highest power." He then went on to play all the characters in the entire scene. (According to Meyerhold, Boris isn't alone when he delivers this famous monologue.)

And I remember the rehearsal of this scene in Moscow during the winter when Meyerhold worked with Nikolai Bogolyubov, the actor playing Boris. I remembered what he had said in Kiev about the scene, but it seemed to me that I was seeing it for the first time as so much that was new had appeared in it, inspired by Bogolyubov's individuality as an actor. That wasn't a copy made from an idea thought up in a director's study. It was genuine, direct creation, something being born right in front of our eyes.

* * *

During the 1935–36 season, Meyerhold assigned one of his assistants to watch the performance every evening and afterwards post a notice of how it went. He trusted his assistant and for a while didn't check on him. The eager assistant with all the zeal of youth began to note not only the deficiencies but also all of the actors' digressions from the form fixed during the dress rehearsal. One of the actors called Meyerhold's attention to this. He immediately forbade the further issuing of notices and arranged a general showdown with the eager assistant. Before me now lies the minutes of the meeting in the theatre at which Meyerhold came out as a passionate defender of the actor's right to improvise. I must admit, we were surprised. After all, everyone thought that Meyerhold allowed no digressions from the form once it was found. But that wasn't the only time he surprised us with his "inconsistencies".

The assistant made the mistake of engaging in a discussion with Meyerhold, not noticing that he was in the position usually called, "being holier than the Pope". One would have had to be present to see how patiently, but with what deeply hidden irony Meyerhold attacked the stubborn defender of Meyerholdian "orthodoxy".

Meyerhold rehearses Mayakovsky

For a while in 1936, Meyerhold had the idea of staging a production dedicated to Mayakovsky. By this time, Mayakovsky's plays had already long since stopped being performed. Many people considered them entirely out-of-date and unnecessary. V.E. asked me to find in the theatre archives all the directorial and prompt scripts of Mayakovsky's plays and to obtain the texts of the movie scenarios he had written.

Before the start of work on the production, Meyerhold arranged a meeting in the theatre of Mayakovsky's friends and comrades-in-arms (February 10, 1936). I remember that Nikolai Aseev, Osip and Lily Brik, Aleksandr Fevralsky, and others were present. After long arguments about which play would be best to revive, a suggestion was accepted to create a free composition, which would include scenes from *The Bedbug* and *The Bathhouse*, with several poems, and a prologue and epilogue written by one of Mayakovsky's poet friends, Semyon Kirsanov. The

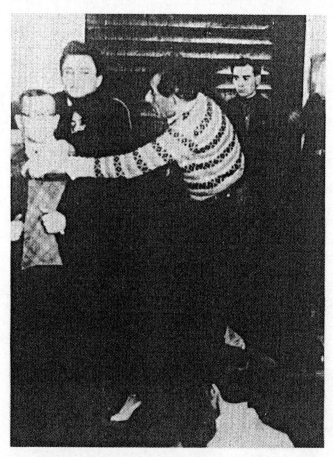

Meyerhold directing Igor Ilinsky, Nikolai Bogolyubov, and Varvara Remizova during a rehearsal of *The Bedbug* (1929).

production was to be called *A Fantastic Comedy*. This is the way that Mayakovsky himself defined the dramatic genre of *The Bedbug*. V.E. was immediately enthusiastic and started eagerly picturing the future production. That same evening he started distributing the roles.

Before the final text was determined, work was started on the scenes from *The Bedbug*. Rehearsals soon began.

At first, the scene "In the Hostel" from *The Bedbug* was rehearsed. The role of Prisypkin was played by Nikolai Bogolyubov, the role of the Inventor by Evgeny Samoilov, Oleg Bard by Aleksei Temerin. Then they moved on to "The Wedding".

Meyerhold was staging this scene entirely from scratch. In the director's plan of 1936, it became more deeply realistic. He proposed radical changes in the second, "Utopian" part of the play, toning down the "elements of decadent abstraction" (V.E.'s words). V.E. gave special attention to the stage sound of the text, striving to preserve in its intonations the uniqueness of Mayakovsky's living speech. Thus, for example, V.E. spent an entire day's rehearsal working over a short monologue by the Inventor (February 8, 1936).

In every line of every character, Meyerhold looked for the uniqueness of Mayakovsky's stage style.

"Suppose our Inventor is a mechanic or locksmith. In our production he won't wait passively for his lines. Why shouldn't he climb up on the cupboard? Perhaps he has invented a new doorbell system and is

Meyerhold, jacket off and sleeves rolled up, at a rehearsal of the wedding banquet from scene 3 of *The Bedbug* (1929).

adjusting it, or he is busy with the clock, or is simply hammering something on... (To Samoilov) Do you understand? Then your lines will come alive. He bangs and speaks. An almost musical rhythm arises. A bang. Then he turns and speaks. Another bang. Again he speaks. These bangs and turns of yours break up the text rhythmically and will make it seem an improvisation. Look – a bang, a turn, a line, a turn, a bang, again a turn, a line... (V.E. demonstrates.) Because the others are distant from you, and you are higher than they are, you can speak louder than usual, and all your lines will sound Mayakovskian, as though from a podium.

"Now the locksmith goes quickly to his cot and begins to put on his shirt. Yes, this is everyday life, a detail from everyday life, but again we'll do it à la Mayakovsky. This segment must be perceived by the audience as a reminiscence of a particular ROSTA poster: 'We are many'... Well, of course, it was a verse poster, and here is how Mayakovsky himself would have read it... (V.E. reads the script, imitating Mayakovsky's manner.) You see, it's almost poetry... But word characterization isn't enough for us. We'll further strengthen it by a gesture, since we're in the theatre. The right hand is slipped into the shirt and... tra-ta-ta, tra-ta-ta, tra-ta... Then he pulls the shirt over his head and from there shouts, tra-ta-ta, tra-ta... The movements are powerful and the pose is paradoxical, poster-like, but entirely justified by the process of putting on the shirt. Suddenly the other hand shoots up, again a poster, it slips into the sleeve, and again tra-ta-ta, tra-ta... And he waves his hands. In the washing scene, we can speak the script intimately, but here it's wrong; here we have the ideological programming of the character, a character in a Mayakovsky play.

"In the characters of Mayakovsky's plays there is always a bit of Mayakovsky himself, as in all of Shakespeare's heroes there is a bit of Shakespeare. I have always thought that if we want to imagine the legendary personality of Shakespeare, we don't have to delve into old church books with their family records, but must study his characters. After all, he's preserved alive in them. I can even imagine his voice, as I always hear Mayakovsky's voice in the heroes of his plays. So let's work so that we hear his voice now.

(To Samoilov) "You must write out this script for yourself as Mayakovsky wrote his poems, with the same rhythmic breaking up of the lines. In acting in this scene, you are still thinking in prose, but you should be thinking in verse. (V.E. reads the Inventor's lines in his own way.) And toward the end of the monologue, after you get into the shirt, I would like you to pull out a comb from somewhere in your pants and calmly comb your hair. Period!"...

Meyerhold made the same demands of the other participants in the scene. At the following rehearsal he said to Temerin:

"You mustn't hurry! You don't feel comfortable with this text because you're forcing the tempo. But Mayakovsky's manner here doesn't suggest a rapid tempo. Can you ever remember when Mayakovsky hurried? I can't. All this must be spoken slowly, monumentally, even heavily... All Mayakovsky's words must be as if served up on a platter, in italics. He liked that. You mustn't jumble it up! 'In fashionable society...' Here Mayakovsky's exact turn is needed, a turn with the whole body, as at public debates when Mayakovsky tossed out his famous remarks, heavy as stones... 'Yes, it turns out that you have talent...' This again is given with Mayakovsky's juiciness. Listen to his living voice!"...

Meyerhold worked on the scene where Prisypkin's visiting card is read...

"The text of the card is read, and at once there is a burst of general laughter. Then the laughter falls off. At this point comes the line: 'What good is Prisypkin?' Laughter again. 'What's the point of Prisypkin?'

Meyerhold at a rehearsal of *The Bathhouse* (1930). Meyerhold often removed his jacket in the heat of rehearsal. But sometimes he took it off even before the beginning of the rehearsal, while the workers were still setting up the panels on the stage.

Laughter. If we stage this scene in this way, then we'll obtain the result I'm always looking for, that is, where Mayakovsky's method of constructing a line is preserved by the actor with almost an author's care. (To the actor Donskoi) You must say this more flashily. (V.E. demonstrates.) Here Mayakovsky's voice must be heard. After all, these lines are like those with which he frightened the bourgeoisie at public debates.

"Let's imagine a debate with Mayakovsky participating. The chairman announces, 'Comrade Prisypkin has the floor!'... And here Mayakovsky turns to the auditorium and says, 'What good is Prisypkin?' 'What's the point of Prisypkin?'... It's precisely from here, from his personal mannerisms, that this verbal twist and this unique speech construction come from! Let the spectator at our production imagine that he has suddenly been transported to the Polytechnical Museum, to a debate with Mayakovsky taking part... No giggles under any circumstances! Absolutely not! That only weakens the text. You yourself laugh at what you're saying, and Mayakovsky immediately disappears. He rarely laughed. That was his style. He would throw out a wisecrack and the auditorium would burst with laughter, but he was almost gloomy. Everyone would be exploding with laughter, and he would silently chew on his cigarette"...

All these remarks by Meyerhold are characteristic of his directorial methods. One of the critics wrote about him that he always staged not so much a particular play as an entire author. V.E. himself very precisely defined this basic principle of his directing, advising that the play be approached not with a universal pass key, but with a special key. In this magnificent formulation lies the *key*, to use his words, of Meyerhold's art as a director.

Having staged anew the scenes "In the Hostel" and "The Wedding" (scenes two and three), Meyerhold proposed radical changes in the second, "Utopian" part of the play as well, removing the "elements of decadent abstraction" (V.E.'s words) inherent in its first version.

In the course of rehearsal, however, it became clear that a montage of basically different excerpts along with verses could not yield a firm dramatic basis for the production, and the work was discontinued. The fact that this attempt came to nought was perhaps one of the reasons for the artistic crisis of the Meyerhold Theatre during the final years of its existence. I recall Meyerhold saying that the Committee for Arts Affairs also greeted this initiative without any enthusiasm. There were many in those years who considered Mayakovsky too abrupt, coarse, awkward, and blunt.

In the stage history of Mayakovsky's plays, this episode is usually not mentioned, but it is interesting as an attempt in the middle of the thirties to find a new approach to Mayakovsky's dramatic art.

At the rehearsals that did take place, V.E. told a lot about Mayakovsky. At his request, I wrote down his recollections and they were printed in the newspaper, *Soviet Art* (April 11, 1936). Then I sent the editors my own notes of the rehearsals of the scenes from *The Bedbug*, but they weren't published and subsequently they turned out to have been lost. In those notes there were a great many interesting observations by Meyerhold about the stage devices of Mayakovsky the dramatist.

"I don't like to spend a long time reading a play around the table, and I always hurry as quickly as possible to get the actors onto the stage", Meyerhold said. "But with Mayakovsky's plays it always happened just the other way around. Here I tried to keep the actors at the table as long as possible so that Mayakovsky himself could teach the actors how to relate to the words of the text. Therefore on the posters it always said: the production of so-and-so plus Mayakovsky working on the text... Mayakovsky was knowledgeable in the very subtle technological things of the theatre, which we as directors know. Mayakovsky always figured out all kinds of correct and incorrect stage interpretations precisely like a director. He was brilliant when it came to composition and knew superbly the laws of the fine arts. He was always correct in pointing out any of my mistakes."

Meyerhold admitted that he hadn't managed to find the appropriate theatrical form for Mayakovsky's plays, and in returning to them, he dreamed of realizing a new director's version of them as he had done with Griboedov's *Woe from Wit*. He was especially critical of the first production of *The Bedbug* (1929). He regarded the production of *The Bathhouse* (1930) as more successful.

"In all of Mayakovsky's plays, beginning with *Mystery-Bouffe*, there is an vital demand to look into the great future about which all men can't fail to dream, a future in which a genuinely new life will be built. They want as quickly as possible to fling open the doors leading to this beautiful world of the future. Mayakovsky always thirsted to gaze into the future. In all his plays, not only does the pulse of the contemporary world beat, but a fresh wind is felt, blowing from the world of the future."

Meyerhold rehearses Chekhov

At one of the rehearsals of Chekhov's vaudeville, *The Proposal*, Meyerhold worked long and enthusiastically with Igor Ilinsky who was playing Lomov. As was usual in our theatre, many spectators were present.

It was a pleasure watching Meyerhold and Ilinsky work together. The director's boundless artistic imagination was caught by the actor, who possessed a virtuoso's improvisational technique and receptivity.

Ilinsky was not one of those actors who says, after hearing the director's instructions, "Good, I'll do it tomorrow". He did it immediately. The brilliance of Meyerhold's demonstrations is well-known. In repeating them, Ilinsky lost nothing. On the contrary, they were enriched. This spurred the director on anew. There would be general laughter. Ilinsky would laugh, and even Meyerhold himself laughed a little.

In one of the demonstrations pointing out the next "swoon" (the production was called *33 Swoons*, and music by Tchaikovsky or Grieg accompanied each swoon) Meyerhold unexpectedly grabbed a pitcher full of water and dumped it on his own head.

A general "Oh!" Laughter. Applause.

In general, Meyerhold never spared himself at rehearsals. The sixty-year-old man climbed up on the highest mountings, tumbled down all the stairs, leapt, danced, sprawled on the dusty (alas!) floor. He possessed a magical ability to keep his clothes from getting rumpled and dirty. After the riskiest demonstration, he would return to his place looking every bit as elegant as when he had arrived at rehearsal. By the way, I never saw Meyerhold come to a rehearsal carelessly dressed.

But back to the rehearsal of *The Proposal*...

Having demonstrated the "trick" with the pitcher, Meyerhold, as always a little hunched over, returned to his little table. He removed his wet jacket and remained in his vest. I should point out that the rehearsal was taking place in an unheated lobby where it was quite cold.

Meyerhold invited Ilinsky to repeat what he had done.

Ilinsky put the empty pitcher in its place and prepared to repeat the segment.

"But what are you doing with an empty pitcher? Prop man!" Meyerhold shouted.

The prop man brought out an absolutely identical pitcher filled with water. Ilinsky touched the pitcher and winced.

They began to rehearse. Meyerhold was distracted, explaining the scene to the actress Antonina Atyasova. He showed her something and happened to turn his back to Ilinsky. Ilinsky put his finger to his lips, indicating that we should not give him away, and quickly carried the full pitcher behind the screen, replacing it with the empty one.

The rehearsal continued.

Meyerhold returned to his place.

In the course of the action in that scene, Ilinsky-Lomov turned his back.

And then, to everyone's surprise, Meyerhold, in a flash and with devilish agility, again switched the pitchers, also putting his finger to his lips, and returned to his place. It turned out that he had not missed Ilinsky's trick.

But Ilinsky noticed nothing. The fatal moment approached. He took the pitcher and boldly poured the cold water on his head...

His surprise was indescribable. I won't convey our ecstasy.

Narrow-minded people may consider inappropriate such jokes at a rehearsal, but then, how easy it is to rehearse a vaudeville in such a "creative atmosphere". It is, in fact, a vaudeville atmosphere.

Another time, before a rehearsal Meyerhold dragged out onstage a stuffed bear which had been prepared beforehand, and announced a "contest". Whoever could guess the reason for the presence of the bear in the production would receive fifteen rubles. Everyone began guessing. Meyerhold listened with a smile. Someone guessed. Meyerhold handed over the fifteen rubles. And then he said, "Yes, that's what I wanted to do. But since you guessed, we'll do something else instead". And the bear played a completely different role.

Meyerhold rehearses Shakespeare

Several times during his life, Meyerhold planned to stage *Hamlet*, but in the end, he never did. He once said in jest, "Write on my tombstone: here lies an actor and director who never played and never staged *Hamlet*". (December 1936)

In 1915, at his "Studio on Borodinskaya", Meyerhold worked on *Hamlet* as an experimental production. At that time under the influence of traditional theories, Meyerhold attempted mainly to achieve the spirit and form of the theatre at the time of Shakespeare.

Meyerhold turned to *Hamlet* again at the beginning of the twenties, during the stormy period of the breakup and overthrow of the old theatre. He conceived the staging of *Hamlet* in the RSFSR Theatre No. 1 as a protest against the decrepit "traditions" of the bourgeois theatre in the name of a revival of the healthy traditions of folk theatre (which he partially achieved later on in *The Forest*.) For that, a new translation of Shakespeare's tragedy was needed, and he ordered one from Mayakovsky and Pasternak; (at one time Marina Tsvetaeva's participation was also proposed). Mayakovsky was commissioned not so much to translate as to rewrite the prose text of the gravedigger scene in order to introduce jokes and witticisms about contemporary politics.

According to Meyerhold, he intended to give the role of *Hamlet* to Igor Ilinsky. This was before Ilinsky had played a whole series of comic mediocrities (in the theatre and in the movies). In the public's imagination, Ilinsky's *emploi* had not yet been defined as purely comic. In his speech at Ilinsky's "special" evening at the Theatre Club in January 1922, Meyerhold maintained that Ilinsky's "healthy and sunny" personality was cramped within the limits of the role of the "funny man". In those years, when Ilinsky created the tragi-comical image of the lovesick poet, Bruno, in *The Magnanimous Cuckold*, and in another theatre [The Moscow Dramatic Theatre], Tikhon in *The Storm*, as well as Arkashka Schastlivtsev in *The Forest*, Prisypkin in *The Bathhouse*, Aleksei Samushkin in *The Last, Decisive*, and all his grotesque roles in the movies, choosing him to play *Hamlet* couldn't help but seem a strange whim.

In 1931, a fragment from *Hamlet* was performed on the stage of the Meyerhold Theatre as part of Yuri Olesha's play, *A List of Benefits*, whose plot has the role of *Hamlet* played by the actress Elena Goncharova. Zinaida Raikh performed that role.

After this, it seemed that a staging of *Hamlet* was not actually planned for Meyerhold's theatre, but this didn't mean that Meyerhold himself was not dreaming of it and preparing for it. On the contrary, in his creative imagination, the project for the production grew and matured. By the mid-thirties, Meyerhold was describing separate scenes from this unborn production with such brilliance and precision of detail that later it seemed as if one had already seen the play on the stage...

In telling about his interpretations of *Hamlet*, V.E. again recalled the dramatic art of Mayakovsky:

"*Hamlet* is constructed so that you feel that this figure stands on the shores of a new life, while the King, Queen, and Polonius are on the other side: they are in the past... This is the greatest theme of art: the confrontation of the past with the future."

After returning from Paris in the autumn of 1936, Meyerhold told us that he had conferred with Picasso about a stage design for *Hamlet*. This was the last good, peaceful working period in his life, the autumn of 1936. Rehearsals of *Boris Godunov* were taking place and again on some not very remote horizon, dreams of *Hamlet* arose...

Meyerhold sometimes dreamed of creating a special theatre in whose repertory there would be only one play, *Hamlet*, produced by various directors: Stanislavsky, Reinhardt, Craig, and himself... Sometimes half in jest, he told us that the fragments of his future *Hamlet* were contained in all his productions of the last twenty years. "But I have hidden them so cleverly that you won't find them", he said. "My *Hamlet* will be the summation of my directing. There you will find the guiding lines for everything."

Meyerhold didn't like the two recent translations then in use. He considered Mikhail Lozinsky's translation "too dry and barrenly precise", and he called Anna Radlova's translation "tasteless".

He regarded Nikolai Akimov's production of *Hamlet* at the Vakhtangov Theatre (première, 1932) very negatively. He always used this production as an example of Meyerholditis, as he called all modernistic affectations and formal experimentation not possessing great ideas.

Of course, one ought to question all those to whom Meyerhold described individual scenes from the *Hamlet* maturing in his imagination, in order to reconstruct the production, if only in a literary form. Especially since Meyerhold, when left without his theatre in 1938, no longer dreamed of producing *Hamlet*, but of writing a book about this production: *Hamlet: The Novel of a Director*. In it, he wanted to recreate his imagined and unrealized production, in order, as he said, that "sometime, someone on some nth anniversary of mine would produce the play according to this plan. Perhaps some kind of draft of it is preserved in his archive. I heard a great deal about it from him. This was already after the closing of the theatre. At this same meeting, he told me that he was preparing to write an opera libretto for Lermontov's *A Hero of Our Times* for Shostakovich. In general, this was a period of "literary fantasy".

This conversation took place under strange circumstances. V.E. had called me and suggested we go for a walk. It was a hot summer day. We walked along the boulevards, then for some reason we wandered into the Hermitage Garden and sat down there. A rehearsal was taking place in the Music Hall Theatre. One could hear the music to which jugglers were practicing. Somewhere billiard balls were knocking. V.E. discussed his literary plans, praised Belinsky's articles on Lermontov which he had just reread, told me of the plan for organizing a Lermontov circle at the Actors' Club and talked about his book, *Hamlet*. As I recall, it was on that day Meyerhold described the scene of Hamlet's encounter with the ghost of his father from his imaginary production.

A leaden gray sea. A dull northern sun behind a thin haze of clouds. Hamlet is walking along the shore wrapped in a black cape. He sits on a rock near the water's edge and gazes into the distance of the sea. And now out of this distance appears the figure of his father. A bearded warrior in silver armor, he walks along the sea toward the shore. He comes nearer and nearer. Hamlet rises. His father steps onto the shore and his son embraces him. He seats his father on the rock, and so that he won't be cold, Hamlet takes off his cape and wraps it around him. Under Hamlet's cape there is the same silver armor as his father's. Now they sit next to each other – the black figure of the father and the silver one of Hamlet...

On this hot day, sitting with V.E. on the garden bench in the Hermitage, I keenly sensed, as never before, the frenzied force of his director's vision.

Hamlet covers the ghost of his father with his cape so that he won't feel the cold... In this one magical stroke there is both the tenderness of poetry and the reality of life.

Meyerhold rehearses Pushkin

It was in Kiev, the summer of 1936, during the Fascist uprising in Spain. After a day of work, there was a meeting at Dynamo Stadium. Meyerhold gave a fiery speech, and then directly after the meeting he went to the theatre. We had a business meeting scheduled during the performance. Meyerhold sat with an absent-minded look, although the meeting had been scheduled at his request, and then suddenly, interrupting someone, he said, "No, I can't. I'm too upset... Let's talk about Pushkin instead. I was planning to make a rough timing of *Boris Godunov*... Who has a copy?"

A copy was found. Meyerhold took his watch from his vest pocket, put it in front of him and began to read the play aloud in order to calculate the time for each scene. He got carried away and his voice climbed upward. Soon he was acting out the play for us. We listened in ecstasy, forgetting about time and timing...

Meyerhold could get carried away forgetting about time. Once during the winter of 1936, a review of work by students from the Technicum was scheduled after a performance at the theatre. V.E. arrived tired – during the day there had been a difficult rehearsal of *Godunov* and in the evening some kind of meeting. Among the various excerpts, Pushkin's *A Feast During the Plague* was shown in full. I don't remember who directed it, but it was done very badly. V.E., who had yawned indifferently through everything else, suddenly became animated. As the last lines of Pushkin's verse were heard, V.E. was already on his feet. He began to speak about how this piece should be performed. After a few minutes he was already onstage. He asked someone to prompt him and began to demonstrate some point. A few minutes more, and he was already restaging the whole play. Sitting in the auditorium were several students, Kseniya Goltseva, director of the Technicum, and I. V.E. "demonstrated", watched, repeated, descended to the auditorium, again ran up onto the stage. He rehearsed at full tilt, giving attention to each actor. He spoke about Pushkin, Wilson, Shakespeare, about "old England", about what tragedy is, about how to recite verse in a drama. He recited. An hour passed, two, until the woman on duty ran in to say that they had telephoned from home and were worried about what had happened to him.

Meyerhold was astonished that it was already late at night.

"Yes, it's time to finish up. It seems we got a little carried away...
But do you know what? Let's try it again just once more, from the
beginning. Gladkov, watch the clock and stop me after forty minutes if I
get carried away again!"

I confess that I did not stop him after forty minutes. It was difficult
to resist the temptation of being the only viewer of a Meyerhold
production unknown to anyone else.

"Yes, Pushkin", he said when we went out onto the deserted
Gorky Street. "One could devote the rest of one's life to him alone, and
even then not succeed in doing anything"...

Meyerhold divided all his productions into two groups: those
which he worked on for many years (*Masquerade*, *The Inspector General*,
Woe to Wit, *Boris Godunov*, the unstaged *Hamlet*), and those which he had
to stage quickly, and which he staged by developing and varying the
devices he had found in other work (almost all the rest of his productions). Thus even those "quickly-staged productions" turned out to be
created on the basis of many years of reworking and preparation.

"How strange it is that almost all of Pushkin has been staged over
and over again, but *A Feast During the Plague* – this most perfect masterpiece – has never been staged. That's probably why I fell on it so hungrily
tonight"...

"No, V.E., you have already staged *A Feast During the Plague*."

"Oh, no, never"...

"You've staged it in almost every production of yours"...

At first he looked at me in bewilderment. Then catching my drift,
he frowned.

"Well, and so?"

That had already occurred to me several hours earlier during that
improvised rehearsal and I triumphantly presented my hypothesis to
him.

"The third act of *The Warrant*, the fourth act of *The Lady*, the final
act of *The Inspector General*, the restaurant scene in *Prélude*, the third act
of *Krechinsky's Wedding*."

"And *Masquerade*", Meyerhold added, smiling. "And also"...

Recalling all his other productions, we both began to enumerate individual acts and scenes from his productions which were complex variations of essentially one theme: the theme of *A Feast During the
Plague*.

"There, you should write about that work," he said to me on
parting at his door.

Later, he half-jokingly reminded me several times, "For your
dissertation, '*A Feast During the Plague* in Meyerhold's Productions'!"

The return to certain constant themes running through many productions was characteristic of Meyerhold's work as a director. It seems to me that the theme of *A Feast During the Plague* was for Meyerhold one of those leitmotif themes.

* * *

With the same hallucinatory brilliance and precision of detail, Meyerhold described scene after scene from his *Boris Godunov*, but in contrast to *Hamlet*, there his director's imagination had already begun to be transformed into reality: the play had been sketchily rehearsed during the second half of 1936.

When rehearsals of *Boris* were discontinued at the beginning of 1937, V.E. didn't plan to abandon completely the continuation of that work which had begun so interestingly. He said at the time that he was only postponing it, but he was fated never to return to it...

Like *Hamlet*, and even more than *Hamlet*, the staging of Pushkin's tragedy was a lifelong dream of Meyerhold's.

The approaches to it were also made long before.

In January 1911, at the Mariinsky Theatre in Petersburg, the première of Meyerhold's production of Mussorgsky's *Boris Godunov* took place with Chaliapin in the title role. V.E. didn't consider it one of his successful works. In the first place, he didn't like the opera. He considered Mussorgsky's music "saccharine" (except for the scene, "In the Forest near Kromy"). The production also didn't turn out well because of his complex relationship with Chaliapin. The bass didn't wish to rethink the image of Godunov he had created long before, which Meyerhold did not accept in toto. There had to be a compromise. Furthermore there was too little time for preparing the production (barely three weeks!)

Meyerhold nevertheless very interestingly staged the mass scenes in a novel way.

During the 1925–26 season, Meyerhold began to stage *Boris Godunov* in the 3rd Studio of the Moscow Art Theatre [the present Vakhtangov Theatre], with Boris Shchukin as Boris. The more important scenes were rehearsed and a maquette was built, but work had to be discontinued when it became clear that the young theatre could not afford to mount this complex production. "Each rehearsal was a major holiday for all of us. The troupe was again granted an opportunity to study," Boris Zakhava recalled later.

However, Meyerhold's production plan for 1936 wasn't a repetition of the 1924 plan. In 1936, the production was worked out by him anew. By his own admission, the production of Mussorgsky's opera in

1911 and the rehearsals in the 3rd Studio were for Meyerhold stages in realizing the production of his most-beloved play in all of world literature.

"I have retraced all my productions since 1910, and have realized that all this time I was fully the captive of Pushkin the director and dramatist," Meyerhold stated in a talk with the troupe at the beginning of work. I still have the directing copy of *Rusalka* that he gave me, with many very interesting notes. From this copy one can judge how painstakingly and with what care he worked on Pushkin's text.

But it wasn't only Pushkin the poet and dramatist who attracted Meyerhold. To an equal if not greater degree, he prized Pushkin's analytical and critical statements about drama and theatre. Meyerhold often referred to them in his speeches and lectures and in the course of rehearsals, always citing from memory the longest quotations from Pushkin's so-called "Notes on Drama" and from various letters. Once V.E. said that he would like to carve on the pediment of his new theatre Pushkin's words, "The spirit of the age demands great changes even on the dramatic stage".

But while thoroughly and closely studying all of Pushkin for the staging of his tragedy, Meyerhold flatly rejected any study of the multi-tomed commentaries to Pushkin that have piled up for a hundred years. On the contrary, before the start of rehearsals, he advanced the slogan: "Pushkin without intermediaries".

"We must perform Pushkin, and not Klyuchevsky", he constantly repeated. "Poetry and not archeology." The immediate and pure perception of Pushkin, unencumbered by discourse about the period.

"In Pushkin's text, there is everything the actor must know about the period. Pushkin, morning-fresh; Pushkin, taken out from under the pillow and read with a clear head."

Meyerhold came to rehearsals of *Boris* as though he were in love... with Pushkin; he came in a festive mood, cheerful and dandified.

"You know, I come to every rehearsal as to a tryst with Pushkin," he said to me once when in greeting him before a rehearsal I asked why he looked so happy.

"We haven't had such interesting work for many years, isn't that true?" he asked in a whisper close to my ear during one of the rehearsals...

All these weeks he was in a good mood. He joked, played tricks, laughed, recalled funny episodes from his life, and used every occasion to take up the little volume of Pushkin and begin reading to himself, now one, then another scene. And always, as he became enthusiastic, his voice soared upward and vibrated strangely. By this one sign alone, one could judge the degree of his enthusiasm.

While rehearsing the scene, "A Cell in the Chudov Monastery", he talked about Tolstoy for one whole hour. The Pimen he imagined wasn't a majestic patriarchal elder, but a small, spare, and almost fussy old man, such as V.E. remembered the living Tolstoy from a visit he made as a student to the writer's home in Khamovnichesky Lane.

"Remember, Pimen is a professional man of letters. He has no business other than to write. He's in the monastery because during that stormy time only monks in their isolation could write peacefully. Back then, the technique of writing was difficult since there weren't any typewriters or fountain pens. Only goose quills, and with them there is always a lot of trouble. They must be sharpened all the time. So here he sits, all surrounded by 'the means of production', and fussing with them. He loves this fussing. The pen gets dull, it must be sharpened again, and this allows time to think a little."

"I used to smoke a pipe. It would go out all the time – the moment I wasn't watching it – but it was pleasant, because during those pauses as I lit up again, I couldn't help looking back at my work. So it is with Pimen and his quills and little bottles. What did they write with? Well, whatever it was, there were no stationery stores then, you know. In those times, they made everything. There were many technical problems with a manuscript. It wasn't so simple: just sit down and write."

"Do you think that Pimen in fact finishes his chronicle on that day? Nothing of the sort! He has this pet expression: 'One more last story'... Everyday he says the same thing to himself before work. The most difficult thing in a great undertaking is when there is still much ahead, when the shore, the end is not visible. So he deceives himself – the end is near. After all, he's old. He must believe he'll have time to finish before he dies. Such a nice, spry little old man"...

"At first, this puts us off. We are so used to Chaliapin's magnificent Pimen. But it's interesting. The actor's dozing imagination is awakened. This fussing with the goose quills and little bottles helps, this living, unstilted concreteness of the stage situation. On getting the role of Pimen, the actor at first thought, 'Well, what's the use, even Chaliapin'... But now everything has changed, and the most difficult thing – to be new, innovative – seems simpler and easier than imitation"...

The rehearsal continues. Now Grigory has awakened...

"Do you remember the famous engraving of Pushkin as a young man, his chin resting on his hand? That's how Grigory observes Pimen. Let's have something of Pushkin here too. All right? And if the association does arise, that's good too; after all, there it is in Pushkin... When I look at that engraving, I always think the young Pushkin has fallen into a reverie just after waking up. You know what good, genuine thoughts come to you when you are young, when you think about something just after waking up"...

"Now it's different. You wake up and spit out phlegm. That's Pimen. But Grigory is young. He dreams when he wakes up. (To the actor.) Now, you try. That's it! It's good, right? You ready?" (When he got excited, Meyerhold, often without noticing, would use the familiar form even with people he usually addressed formally.)

"Stop!" V.E. shouts. " 'Bless me, honorable father' should not be said like that. More simply, without profound significance! Those are ritual words. You don't think about my health, do you, every time you ask 'How are you?' This must be done with no theatrical emphasis, in passing"... (V.E. demonstrates from the beginning, parodying the conventional theatrical emphasis, then as it should be, modestly and simply.)

"Again, Pimen is not right. The *raisonneur* is popping up again. He's not a *raisonneur*. He's tense and nervous, an impetuous old man."

"Both must have something childlike about them. They are friends precisely because they resemble each other through this childlike quality."

"Your Pimen would be wearing a long silken cassock. There won't be any cassock. He'll wear a shirt—under it his bare bones. Only when he goes to matins does he put on a cassock. But the rest of the time, he's in his shirt"...

"We must find signs of Grigory's childlike love for the old man."

"Rhythmically, the scene goes this way: the old man sets the pace and Grigory does the braking. Usually when dialogue takes place onstage, of necessity someone must drive it on and someone else must apply the brakes. Even in life that's how it is. In earlier productions of *Boris*, it was the reverse: Grigory was vital, and the old man slow. That's not right. Grigory dreams, he has the rhythm of a dreamer, while the old man hurries. He has the *idée fixe* that he will die before he finishes all he has to write, so he's in a hurry ...

"Now it's good! That feels right, doesn't it? You know, although Pushkin tried to imitate Shakespeare, he's better than Shakespeare. He's more transparent and savory. The main thing in Pushkin is that he achieves everything with small means. This is in fact the summit of craftsmanship. And Pushkin must be performed modestly, also with small means, otherwise it will be stilted"...

The rehearsal continues. Meyerhold suddenly laughs.

"See, see what pleasant humor is revealed. 'My old man's sleep is not peaceful and sinless.' If he were a heavier, more powerful man in a silk cassock, it wouldn't be surprising: a healthy fellow. But if this is our

Pimen, it's another story. He's practically all skin and bones, and to have such dreams... This is also like Lev Tolstoy. You remember how he said to Gorky, 'I'll be lying in my coffin, but if a woman beckons, I'll lift the lid and jump out'... Pimen is like that too – small, sparse, but nervous, and vital... This touch of color about dreams is a revelation!"

When we came to Pimen's story about the murder in Uglich, V.E. slapped his hand on the table and shouted, "Dostoyevsky! The roots of all our literature actually lie in Pushkin. And here are the roots of Dostoyevsky!"

V.E. related how in 1919, when he was detained by the Whites in Novorosiisk prison, he obtained a small volume of Pushkin with Polivanov's notes and studied *Boris*, and how he composed there the scenario of a play about Grigory which he later proposed to Sergei Esenin for a drama in verse...

"We'll have it almost dark in the cell with only two sources of light: one yellowish from Pimen's lamp, the other bluish from the window under which Grigory sleeps ...

"The sleeping Grigory moans. Pimen looks around at him solicitously. No fewer than three moans, different in coloration. Then when Grigory tells about his dream, the audience will perceive it as something already familiar. Let's try it!"

Mikhail Tsarev was rehearsing the role of Grigory that day. (The following actors were assigned the role: Erast Garin, Evgeny Samoilov, Mikhail Tsarev.) Tsarev tried a light moan. The result was very expressive. Meyerhold himself applauded. He was very pleased with this unexpectedly discovered detail.

"Revelation number two," he shouted. "Pay me 1,000 rubles for it! You understand how these soft moans of a sleeping man will make the audience wait for his awakening. What tension arises! Very good! No, I get too small a salary, I'll declare straight out, too small ...

"And Pimen, gazing at the moaning Grigory, should make the sign of the cross over him ... That's it! Good!...

"I'll surprise you now by saying whom our Pimen should resemble... Plyushkin [a character in Gogol's *Dead Souls*]! Yes, yes... Only a very likeable Plyushkin, a Plyushkin who is not Plyushkin at all... But there is something of that sort. His world is here, in this cell, on this table with the manuscripts, little jars, goose quills. They are his wealth... This coloration will help you right now at this stage. Use it more boldly...

"There is wisdom in his eyes, but not cold reasoning"...

The scene was repeated. V.E. carefully worked out all the newly found details with the moans, with the sign of the cross, with the lamp. And when it came to Grigory's waking up, he found an expressive segment with the washing. He left the towel in Grigory's hands during his story of the dream and very precisely demonstrated all the acting possibilities which could arise from a towel in one's hands. The towel was needed here, according to Meyerhold, because "when one holds something in one's hands, the gesture becomes larger" ...

He illustrates by demonstrating.

After the rehearsal, as always when he was satisfied with himself, V.E. could not move on at once to other matters, although the chief accountant had been waiting a long time for him in the director's office. Taking me by the arm, he walked around the lobby with me, commenting on and recalling everything that had been done that day ...

"In *Boris Godunov* there are scenes which are usually not printed in the basic text, but among the variants, under the title, 'Scenes omitted from the published version.' These are 'The Monastery Wall' and 'The Castle in Sambor; The Dressing Room of Marina Mnishek.' Both scenes are very necessary to the action, but are written in a completely different verse style than the tragedy as a whole. The former is in rhymed trochee (like Spanish dramas), the latter in free iambics (like the verse in *Woe from Wit*). Apparently in these scenes Pushkin was trying various methods of versifying. In one of his letters he complained that the unrhymed iambic pentameter he had selected "gives insufficient variety necessary for the work". Taking into consideration Pushkin's remark, Meyerhold planned to introduce Grigory's scene with the wicked monk ("The Monastery Wall") into the production. But how could this be done so that its verse construction wouldn't destroy the musical sound of the play to which the audience had become accustomed?

"Let us imagine a scene traditional for folklore: a road and a stone. Grigory is a vagrant. It's autumn. He's poorly clad and sick. He's feverish and he shivers. Trying to warm himself, he falls asleep and has a dream. This dream is, in fact, the scene with the wicked monk. And if it's a dream, then the verse might well be different; it would be natural. We'll do this entire scene to music, almost operatically. Prokofiev will write the music for us on the boat, on his way to America, as he once wrote *Love for Three Oranges*."

Returning to the figure of Pimen, V.E. named Mikhail Chekhov as the ideal performer for this role: "In his old men there was always artistry, humor, and a childlike quality. Only in the story about the event in Uglich must there be something different. It's almost like the account by the messenger in a Greek tragedy. Here his anxiety becomes tragic. He's not a raisonneur! Nowhere a raisonneur!"

The actor Sergei Kiligin, who rehearsed the role of Pimen, rapidly caught onto V.E.'s instructions. Already by the third rehearsal of this scene, V.E. often interrupted him with his approving "Good!" It was a new, completely unusual, unaccustomed Pimen, but V.E.'s interpretation was so convincing and well-motivated that it soon seemed to be the only one possible.

A fierce battle against declamation, against phony emotionality developed during the rehearsals of the scene "The Lithuanian Border".

V.E. mercilessly parodied the actors who did not master at once the simplicity and modesty which he demanded from all the performers in *Godunov*. When V.E. parodied some theatrical cliché, he did it with such professional brilliance that at first it didn't even seem at all bad. Only with the overdoing of the mannerisms would one see how false it was. V.E. would then conclude his "parody-demonstration" with such hyperbolic exaggeration that it was impossible to keep from laughing. And as everyone knows, laughter is the best medicine for any phoniness.

"No, this is not Pushkin! It's Aleksei Konstantinovich Tolstoy, it's Ostrovsky's chronicle plays, whatever you like, but not Pushkin! It's *Prince Serebryany*, a novel I hate; it's caramelized sugar dipped in port wine" ...

The actor playing Kurbsky [five different actors rehearsed the role] had an especially difficult time.

"The shop, 'Oriental Candies', " V.E. shouted at him.

"You're playing a page in tights, not a warrior. What do you have in your hands?"

"Gloves, probably, V.E."

"No, not gloves, no, not gloves! Mittens, dammit! Do you understand? Mittens!"

"You're getting saccharine again! Is that the way to say, 'The dust of foreign lands'? He spits on the ground here, do you understand? He spits. Do it! Don't be afraid! Let it be naturalism. This will help you right now. We'll take it out later if Kerzhentsev is shocked, but for now you need it" ...

"The Pretender isn't talking to himself here. He speaks his monologue to an orderly who is nearby. Let's abandon pseudo-theatre, otherwise we'll not perform Pushkin!"

"Two more silent figures will be in this scene: an orderly and a peasant guide who shows the way. Before his first monologue, Kurbsky shields his eyes from the sun and peers into the distance where the guide is pointing... (V.E. demonstrates.) That's how! With dogs, this is called pointing. It immediately produces tension... We'll make it a quiet scene anyway; the clatter of hooves, frogs croaking, and low voices" ...

"Kurbsky's tale needs Bogolyubov's temperament. Externally he's reserved, but internally he's emotional. One always senses this in Bogolyubov's voice. It's a pity that he can't play two roles."

"Fight against any kind of prettifying. Out with it, out, out!"

"Again, *Vasilisa Melenteva* [a melodrama about Ivan the Terrible by Aleksandr Ostrovsky, also set in the Kremlin] is popping up!"

"What are you pleased about? Some senseless rejoicing! What is this?"

The actors explain to V.E. that joy is the natural feeling that seized the exiles on touching their native soil.

"Not true! It's superficial! Here I am, dreaming of a new theatre. Well, now after so many years it will finally be built. What do you think? That I'm going to sing and dance? No. I'll dully walk along its corridors, then I'll go up to a window somewhere and pick at the caulking with my finger nail... When one's wishes are fulfilled, it's always a little sad because you immediately recall all the years when you waited and dreamed. And where are those years? They are no more"...

Meyerhold had his pet expressions. Often they were musical terms: *crescendo, staccato, andante,* etc. In our theatre, not only the musicians, but the actors also knew them very well. Not to know them meant not to understand the director's instructions. V.E. had still another favorite word: *"exigeration"*. He loved strange verbs: "to contact with", "to seismograph".

For the most part, the rehearsals of *Boris Godunov* proceeded without breaks. V.E. would get carried away and forget about the need for rest, and no one dared remind him of it. One hated to interrupt his unrestrained creative outbursts. Meyerhold had many such rehearsals, but I remember especially the rehearsal of one of his favorite scenes in *Boris Godunov*, scene 9, "Shuisky's House" (May 17, 1936).

It seemed no one predicted the storm that would burst. V.E. didn't take off his jacket before beginning; he was even a few minutes late, something which very rarely happened with him.

The chairs were placed in a half-circle on the stage. It was dark in the auditorium. The rehearsal was planned for "around the table". Everyone was seated. There were still no sets as yet.

His assistants and the poet Vladimir Pyast were seated next to Meyerhold. At first they quietly read the scene. Pyast painstakingly analyzed the technique of iambic pentameter and Meyerhold, putting on his glasses, followed the text from the book. Among the participants in the scene was Lev Sverdlin, who was rehearsing the role of the boyar Pushkin. It wasn't completely clear why this role had been given precisely to him. He was one of the leading actors of the theatre. He had brilliantly played Arkashka in *The Forest* and Hugo Nunbakh in *Prélude*, and had appeared frequently and successfully in the movies, while the Pushkin role was quite minor. It's true, there was a monologue, but not a very big one.

The rehearsal was proceeding peacefully. The actors read through the scene once. Pyast analyzed all the mistakes. They read through it again. Meyerhold took the floor. He said that he hated "boyar plays", and spoke about the "psychological thickets" in which the performers felt themselves to be right from the first reading: "You're already seeing yourselves in brocade and with beards".

Meyerhold said it was necessary to make all the characters younger, to look candidly at the living people of that period. He spoke of "Pushkin without intermediaries", without the Pushkin scholars, Pushkin as if read for the first time.

"All the people in this play are warriors, not clerks with beards and fur coats. Everyone is just off his horse." Suddenly turning to his assistant, Meyerhold ordered him to write down: "Arrange with a riding school for the whole troupe to ride horseback every day! Otherwise we won't be able to perform *Boris*!"

The assistant pretended to write it down. He thought that this was the usual hyperbole of the maestro, but who knows? There was excitement among the actors. Horseback riding! What will he think of next?

If in fact this was hyperbole, then it must be admitted that it was very vivid. We heard this right from the first rehearsal: "Not boyars in fur coats, but soldiers! Just off their horses! All young!" He often repeated this, but for the present, he didn't demand live horses...

With precise, vivid, picturesque details, Meyerhold enthusiastically "opened up the stage directions", as he loved to express it; that is, he related this entire scene to us, the very same one we had just read. But was it really that same scene?

The boyars who hated and opposed Boris have assembled in Shuisky's house. They are drinking because it is safer that way. Boris' spies don't watch carousers as carefully. The drinking cups clink, the dipper goes around the circle. A general hum of voices, noise, altercations. The low chamber is in semidarkness. In the corner, curled up on a bench, a golden-haired boy is sleeping. He is suddenly poked in the side. He must recite the prayer for the Tsar's health. Without this, Boris doesn't permit a single gathering. The crafty Shuisky allows his guests to say anything they like about the Tsar, but the boy with the prayer is always at the ready. In a breaking alto voice, unsteady from sleep, but pure as a spring, the boy begins to recite the prayer amidst the general hubbub. At first the boyars don't listen to him. They are all drunk and excited. But gradually the noise dies down. It is the magic of a pure, adolescent voice. Now it is completely quiet, except for this crystal voice pouring forth like a brook. Someone crosses himself. The effect of drunkenness immobilizes everyone. The guests disperse, one after the other. Shuisky and Pushkin remain, the latter gloomy, excited, embittered...

This entire scene must be performed during thirty-four of Pushkin's lines. Is it possible? It will be, if Meyerhold sees it that way.

The scene between Shuisky and Pushkin is complex, difficult. Here every sentence is a turn in the action. So this is what actually happens. And to us it had all seemed rhetorical.

Finally Pushkin's monologue... Sverdlin begins to read it, but Meyerhold soon interrupts. "No, no, no! This is pure Mamont Dalsky!"

Sverdlin looks confused.

"You see, all the roles have been distributed among the members of our troupe, Boris and all the others, but for this role we need Mamont Dalsky, his temperament, his flights, his frenzy! This is a role for a guest star! People must come to see the production several times especially for this scene. They must come from other cities! Do you understand, Sverdlin?

Sverdlin is nonplused. "Mamont Dalsky" is a new hyperbole of V.E.'s, but where could he get in one shot such incandescent temperament and passion as Meyerhold wanted.

Meyerhold doesn't insist that it be all at once... Like everyone else, he knows that Sverdlin doesn't catch fire quickly, but once he does, he burns with power and heat. It's for good reason that the scene with Hugo Nunbakh always ends with an ovation. At that time it had also seemed impossibly difficult to carry out Meyerhold's objective, to repeat his brilliant demonstration.

Meyerhold explains precisely the inner idea of the monologue, how it flows, over what boulders it rushes and falls. He begins to read it himself, at first from the book, with his glasses on. Then the glasses fall off. He is no longer looking at the book, and someone is prompting him. When the entire text is finished, Meyerhold, now improvising lines in unerring iambic pentameter, shows us how Mamont Dalsky would have played this scene.

But he doesn't stop there. He continues to perform, improvising iambs. He knocks a glass off the table and no one dares pick it up...

Holding our breath, we follow this brilliant improvisation... And it continues. He is already standing on the table. We hadn't even noticed him jumping up there.

Is this Meyerhold? Is this Mamont Dalsky?

No, it is a frenzied, drunk, wild Afanasi Mikhailovich Pushkin, a living man of the seventeenth century with his hurt, his pain, his uncontrollable anger... at Tsar Boris, no at Borka Godunov, the usurper and villain...

I look at Sverdlin. He is pale. I look at Zinaida Raikh. Our eyes meet. In her eyes is fear for someone dear to her. This is impossible! After all, he is over sixty. What a glow of temperament! What a fury of passions! What a frenzy! And still he goes on and on... It is almost terrifying...

Suddenly he stops. He jumps lightly from the table and turns to Sverdlin: "Is it clear?"

Sverdlin wordlessly spreads his hands.

Everyone is silent. What we have just seen could be seen once in a lifetime. Everyone is afraid to move. Only after a long pause does applause ring out.

Meyerhold takes his briefcase from the table and coolly announces, "A ten-minute break!" and leaves to change his shirt. The one he has on is absolutely soaked.

In ten minutes the rehearsal continues.

Could Sverdlin repeat this "demonstration", and in fact did it have to be repeated? Pushkin's monologue contains thirty-four lines, whereas Meyerhold improvised a good one hundred and fifty lines. He gave us the sense of the character, its emotional horizons. Only a quarter of all this could go into the performance, and maybe even that would be too much.

Bogolyubov rehearsed Boris brilliantly. He could execute the most difficult director's tasks almost immediately. Not only did his talent help him, but so did the fact that in his imagination Meyerhold already saw Godunov in Bogolyubov's own acting potential.

Once at a rehearsal of one of the scenes in which Boris appears, V.E., satisfied with the actor's work, recalled the story about Michelangelo who, in answer to the question of how he created his sculptures, replied, "I take a piece of marble and cut away everything unnecessary"... This really was very similar to Meyerhold's work. From rehearsal to rehearsal, the "superfluous" was somehow subtly cut away, and relatively soon for such a complicated work we already saw on the stage not the Bogolyubov we knew well, but a suffering, intrepid, wise Tsar Boris.

I especially remember the rehearsals of the scenes, "The Tsar's Chambers" (both of them) and "The Tsar's Duma". The scene of Boris' death was hardly rehearsed at all. V.E. once said that this scene demands immense emotional tension and must "pour out" spontaneously. He put it off until the end of our work. "I don't want to keep picking at it in my imagination. The later we take it up, the fresher it will be"...

V.E. resorted more than once to this method of work, especially for the climactic scenes. The famous scene of the lies in *The Inspector General* he staged in one inspired nighttime rehearsal six days before the première. In forty minutes he staged the stunning suicide scene of the little Chinese "Boy" (performed by Maria Babanova) in *Roar China!*

While painstakingly trimming and polishing what would sometimes seem the most secondary scenes in his productions, Meyerhold consciously left unstaged the climactic, high-point segments. Erast Garin tells how during work on the first version of *Woe to Wit*, V.E., as usual, left for last Chatsky's monologue in the fourth act: "I can't come to reason, I confess." Finally a rehearsal was announced very shortly before the première. V.E. sat silently for a long time, then stood up and said, "No, I don't know how this should be played! (To Garin) Play it the way you feel it"

At one of the first rehearsals of *Godunov*, in the scene "The Tsar's Duma", Bogolyubov began his long monologue on a high note. V.E. stopped him at once:

"No, wait, you are already giving the flame, but there are only sparks here."

And then again:

"No, no! You want to convey a great emotion technically, and technically it can't come out now. It will come out technically when you store up in yourself the genuine, albeit small emotions... Don't anticipate your emotional soaring, don't profane it, even with fine craftsmanship...

"Remember that intonation as such doesn't exist in nature. It's always the result of either a fleeting thought or a nervous shiver. For correct intonation you need the right irritant. Now let's do some more searching.

"You can't overhear a good intonation somewhere and bring it onto the stage. You must look for the right action and the correct circumstances. Then the proper intonation will come ...

"No, no, stop! You have a barren sound, and no spark"...

And further, a very typical remark for V.E.:

"It must be all *staccato*, separate jolts. Here, there is no *legato*"...

"In this monologue, Boris borrows the external form from Ivan the Terrible, whose speeches Boris often had occasion to hear. He does not at all resemble the Dread Tsar, but sometimes he imitates him ...

"He is trying to shake loose from the madman in himself.

"You must gradually prepare everything internally so that one time it will come out right. And then the conditioned reflex, if only from a cigarette butt, will be enough for you to repeat it. But for now, you won't get anything and it's not necessary... Now we are only blocking everything properly.

"Don't try to memorize the intonations. All the intonations here should come *ex improvisio*. Look for the correct action, keep your inner trembling"...

At one of the rehearsals of the scene "The Tsar's Chambers", Meyerhold nonplused the actors who had brought to it everything already acquired in other scenes (Boris and Shuisky).

"No, no, you are both different here! Boris is different and Shuisky too. They are complex people, aren't they? They turn toward each other in different ways. I don't like this dull theatre where the actor finds something in the first act and drags this one thing through the whole play. And don't be afraid to lose the "kernel". Your "kernel" lies in your physical and internal makeup. Search, search ...

"Our Shuisky will be grander, more imposing in comparison with previous interpretations of him. He's usually played as a kind of sly fox. But he isn't simply foxy. After all, he will be the Tsar. Watching Shuisky in the theatre, I never believed that this conniver could become Tsar. But we have to believe this. He's very talented and clever. He's cleverer than Talleyrand. That one got no further than the ministry, did he? Shchukin put on a fine show playing Polonius as a fool, but this is wrong. Polonius is no fool. He's very cunning, and Shuisky is Polonius ten times over. Our Shuisky has a different temperament than the usual one"...

V.E. demonstrated to Bogolyubov how Boris begins to rock back and forth mechanically when he is confused or worried. "This is how the Tatars sway when they are troubled. And this is where the Tatar heredity in him sings out... And after the 'Hat of Monomakh', let him also sway a bit. In this way, we will eliminate the pseudo-theatrical end effect of this too well-known phrase. Let him sway once, twice, three, four, five times and only then will we put out the light... Here, Boris is a shaken oak"...

Bogolyubov repeats it. It's an amazing touch. V.E. can't resist and applauds him. "Oh, that's good!" he says, rubbing his hands...

On December 18, 1936, I noted in my diary: "Yesterday there was a remarkable rehearsal of the Boris and Shuisky scene. Already staged. Bogolyubov and Zaichikov rehearsed with great finesse. V.E. demonstrated magnificently. Inimitable hours. There was excitement, almost to the point of tears."

I remember this rehearsal well, and who of those present could forget it? From the very beginning, we were all so caught up in it that I couldn't even force myself to take notes, which as a rule I had learned to do almost automatically during my years of work with V.E.

"For moments of synthesis, one must pay with weeks of analysis", V.E. once said. And now these moments of synthesis had arrived. It was already one of those rehearsals from which even an outsider could judge what the future production would be like.

Meyerhold was rehearsing in a sort of ecstasy.

During the monologue about the murder in Uglich, on the words, "But the childish face of the Tsarevich was clear", Meyerhold asked Vasily Zaichikov (who was playing Shuisky) to outline a circle in the air with a gesture of his hand – a light, barely noticeable movement. Then Shuisky takes several steps to the side. Boris continues to look at this imaginary circle and not at Shuisky.

After Shuisky's departure, during the monologue beginning, "Oh, my heart is oppressed! Let me catch my breath"..., Boris still stares insistently, as though he were seeing something in empty space. V.E. told us that in this way he was preparing for the hallucination in the last scene.

"It is a device from old-time melodrama", V.E. said, "but you see how it works?"

It made a tremendous impression indeed.

Right then V.E. again quoted his favorite statement of Pushkin's: "True taste lies not in the arbitrary rejection of some word or phrase, but in a feeling for proportion and relatedness."

Also, on that day V.E. talked a lot, he spoke movingly and somehow touchingly about the fact that the actor must preserve and protect the emotional state he has found, and about the need to know how to "concentrate feelings."

Before beginning the rehearsals of *Boris*, Meyerhold announced that he was tired of reproaches that he was rewriting the classics, and that he would stage Pushkin's tragedy with no cuts or insertions whatsoever.

"The only liberty I'll take will be to introduce silent characters here and there. The techniques of our theatre and the theatre of Pushkin's time are different, and we can no longer accept without some strain those frequent monologues when the hero is all alone. Only here will I allow myself to add a bit to Pushkin. This is necessary so we can respond to Pushkin the dramatist, not as someone archaic or obsolete, but as a living, vitally contemporary author"... (Note of August 1, 1936)

V.E.'s proposal for staging Boris' famous monologue, "I have reached the highest power..." struck us as totally unusual and stunningly unexpected. It was one of the most impressive scenes in the production. In this scene (*scene 7*), Pushkin begins with the dialogue of the courtiers:

> *First:*   Where is the sovereign?
> *Second:* In his bedchamber.
>   He is closeted with some magician.
> *First:*   Yes, these are his favorite people: soothsayers,
>   fortunetellers, witches.
>   He ever asks the future,
>   like a pretty bride. I would like to know
>   what are the questions he asks.

Next follows Boris' monologue.

We all know how this scene is usually staged. Either Boris comes out the door, stops at the lintel, and begins to speak (as Chaliapin did), or he slowly comes down the stairs (as in the production at the Pushkin Dramatic Theatre in Leningrad), or something else along that line.

Meyerhold did it differently. The brief scene with the courtiers takes place on the forestage. When they exit, the action is transferred to Boris' bedchamber.

The small, low-ceilinged bedchamber almost overflows with strange folk. They are "sooth-sayers, fortunetellers, witches" brought from all over Russia by the Tsar's order. There are among them an old man with a rooster in a cage; an Asian with a snake in a sack; holy fools wailing something or other; and blind, old women fortunetellers. Boris is seated in an armchair, his face covered with a thin silk kerchief. From either side two women fortunetellers are chanting some exorcism over him. The stifling heat, the dissonant hubbub of this gang of charlatans, the stink of unwashed bodies, the cry of the rooster, and in the corner, at a small mica window, a Kalmyk is swaying as he plays a mournful Eastern melody on a pipe.

Next to Boris stands a large wooden jug of kvas. Suddenly pushing off the kerchief, he raises the jug and drinks avidly.

He is exhausted. He doesn't believe in these exorcisms and sorcery, yet he seeks in them consolation for his spiritual anxiety. He has lost the courage necessary to fight, but he still preserves it in order to look truth in the eye; a great, passionate, weary man among this gang of charlatans...

He feels stifled under the kerchief. He scratches. It seems to him that these people's lice have already crawled onto him. He's repelled by the dirty hands of the women keening over him and trying to touch his lips. He pushes off these hands, throws off the kerchief and again drinks avidly, but they again throw the silk over him. The Kalmyk at the window continues to play on his pipe. "A noise like at the bathhouse, a jazz band of the seventeenth century", says V.E.

And through all this, Boris' tragic monologue.

When V.E. first described his idea for the resolution of this scene, we, his assistants and helpers, immediately felt the reality of times long lost drifting over us, but it seemed to us terribly difficult to realize.

"Surprised?" V.E. asked. "That's precisely how it will be!"

And so it was. When this scene began to be rehearsed, when this most vivid musical painting of a directorial vision was clothed in theatrical form, when V.E. himself brilliantly demonstrated the acting goals to the performer playing Boris, when Bogolyubov began to master the complex design suggested to him, enriching it with his own discoveries, when V.E. hummed the melody of the Kalmyk's song which had been written by Prokofiev ("This song is the inner melody of Boris", said V.E.), then it became clear that such an interpretation would make the monologue resound with stunning freshness and truth...

"But I invented nothing here", said V.E. "All this is written in Pushkin; I only dramatized the hidden stage directions."

The novelty of the overall compositional resolution of Meyerhold's staging of *Boris Godunov*, not to mention the beauty of the resolution of individual scenes and characters, consisted in the fact that V.E., after a rigorous, truly scholarly analysis of Pushkin's text and the structure of the tragedy, categorically rejected the form of the so-called monumental production with realistically presented huge mass scenes, crowds of boyars, and architecturally realistic sets.

Meyerhold maintained that stylistically, *Boris Godunov* is close to Pushkin's "Little Tragedies". The extraordinary laconism and the psychological tension of the twenty-four scenes of the play can be conveyed in the theatre only if one rejects what he called "the spectacular display of a historically authentic production". Meyerhold defined the genre of the play as "a tragic suite in twenty-four parts", and interpreted each scene as a part of that suite. "The battle of human passions against the background of a violent popular storm", is another definition he made. And he sharply distinguished the background of the storm from the action within the scenes, resolved by Pushkin in an intimate manner.

"If we study the construction of the scenes in *Boris Godunov*, we will see that the dramatic technique is more perfect than in Shakespeare's plays. In *Boris Godunov*, each scene represents not only a step up the ladder of the narrative; it is also an independent entity, like a part in a musical composition. It not only narratively, but also musically prepares for the inevitable coming of the following part of the suite...

"Take the third scene in *Godunov*, 'The Maiden Field'. One mustn't load the stage with hieroglyphs intended to represent the disposition of the various social classes, as in the production at the Pushkin Dramatic Theatre, because in this laconic scene no one will have time to read these hieroglyphs. In this scene one must not use a large, badly organized crowd, but only a sufficient number of characters to get by. And one must mentally divide the stage into two parts, where one fulfills the function of the close-up, and the other that of the background. Only then will Pushkin's remarkable text not get lost. It won't be cluttered up with the din of the usual mass scene, which works well only at the première.

"Call a composer, commission him to construct this multiplicity of words in the style of an oratorio and create a grandiose sound so that we don't need words, but only the music of the popular storm... This chorus must be hidden by complicated curtains, as is done in a radio studio, so that the sound will be remote, while not losing its nuances. And then one must arrange on the stage simple figures, as in the canvases of Pieter Bruegel. Find a good composition for them, free the stage of any heavy construction, give light only to the foreground of the composition. This will be our resolution of the mass scenes in Pushkin's tragedy...

"We'll hide the crowd from the eyes of the audience and transmit its sound, the swelling of its will, only musically. And against this background we'll present Pushkin's twenty-four 'Little Tragedies' in all their tension, like a complex suite...

"We'll have on stage only the spokesman for the crowd. Any other presentation of the people would be mere props, pseudo-theatre.

"In this play the performance of every role is important. Here there are no minor roles. I maintain that in order to perform *Boris Godunov* we need good actors, not only for the roles of Boris, Shuisky, Grigory, and Marina. Much more important is a fine ensemble for the other roles because in quantity they fill up the whole play...

"Down with icon-like elders in brocade, down with pot-bellied boyars in fur coats and hats two feet tall. We'll make all the characters young; we'll make them all warriors, all fresh from their horses...

"We'll also interpret the battle musically. We'll have two orchestras: one European, so to speak, the other Asiatic, in single combat. The audience must be both against Boris and against the Pretender...

"Only in a musical interpretation of the popular storm is it possible finally to realize Pushkin's famous stage direction: 'The people are silent'.

"Complete set changes will take ten seconds...

"In the play, there isn't one raisonneur, not one second of declamation"... (Notes of August 1 and 4, 1936)

V.E. dreamed that the production would run without inter-mission.

Much of what was planned was realized. Almost all of the scenes were fully rehearsed.

Sergei Prokofiev wrote remarkable music, including the striking oratorio (without words) for the chorus: "The Sound of the People".

The music for the Polish scenes was very good.

Even now, Kseniya's tender, plaintive song resounds in my ears. When on November 16, 1936, after one of the rehearsals, Prokofiev played several of the already prepared musical numbers for the actors in the production, V.E., very moved, embraced and kissed him.

The rehearsals were discontinued at the beginning of 1937, but not all at once; they petered out gradually.

After this, I never again saw V.E. so enthusiastic, so inspired, so full of *joie de vivre.*

SELECTED BIBLIOGRAPHY

Alpers, Boris. *Teatr sotsial'noi maski* [The Theatre of the Social Mask]. Moscow-Leningrad: GIXI, 1931.

Benedetti, Jean. *Stanislavsky: A Life*. New York: Routledge, Chapman and Hall, 1990.

Braun, Edward. *Meyerhold on Theatre*. New York: Hill and Wang, 1969.

Braun, Edward. *The Theatre of Meyerhold. Revolution on the Modern Stage*. New York: Drama Book Specialists, 1979.

Braun, Edward. *Meyerhold. A Revolution in Theatre*. Iowa City: University of Iowa Press, 1995.

Carter, Huntly. *The New Theatre and Cinema of Soviet Russia*. London: Chapman & Dodd, Ltd., 1924.

Fevralsky, Aleksandr. *Desyat' let teatra Meierkhol'da* [Ten Years of Meyerhold's Theatre]. Moscow: Federatsiya, 1931.

Fevralsky, Aleksandr. *Puti k sintezy: Meierkho'ld i kino* [Paths to a Synthesis: Meyerhold and the Cinema]. Moscow: Iskusstvo, 1978.

Garin, E. P. *S Meierkhol'dom* [With Meyerhold]. Moscow: Iskusstvo, 1974.

Gladkov, Aleksandr. *Godi ucheniya Vsevoloda Meierkhol'da* [Meyerhold's Years of Apprenticeship]. Saratov: Privolzhskoe knizhnoe izd., 1979.

Gladkov, Aleksandr. *Teatr. Vospominaniya i razmyshleniya* [Theatre. Recollections and Reflections]. Moscow: Iskusstvo, 1980.

Gladkov, Aleksandr. *Meierkhol'd* [Meyerhold]. 2 vols. Moscow: STD/RSFSR, 1990.

Hoover, M. L. *Meyerhold. The Art of Conscious Theatre*. Amherst: University of Massachusetts Press, 1974.

Ilinsky, Igor. *Sam o sebe* [About Myself]. Moscow: VTO, 1961.

Lawton, Lancelot. *The Russian Revolution (1917–1926)*. London: Macmillan and Co., 1927.

Meyerhold, V. E. *Perepiska. 1896–1939*. [Correspondence. 1896–1939]. Comp. V. P. Korshunova and M. M. Sitkovetskaya. Moscow: Iskusstvo, 1976.

Meyerhold, V. E. *V. E. Meierkhol'd: stat'i, pis'ma, rechi, besedy* [V. E. Meyerhold: Articles, Letters, Speeches, Conversations]. Ed. Aleksandr V. Fevralsky. 2 vols. Moscow: Iskusstvo, 1968.

Picon-Vallin, Béatrice. *Meyerhold. Les voies de la création théâtrale*, No. 17. Paris: CNRS, 1990.

Rudnitsky, Konstantin. *Meyerhol'd* [Meyerhold]. Moscow: Iskusstvo, 1981.

Rudnitsky, Konstantin. *Meyerhold the Director*. Trans. George Petrov. Ann Arbor: Ardis, 1981.

Schmidt, Paul, ed. *Meyerhold at Work*. Austin: University of Texas Press, 1980.

Volkov, N. D. *Meierkhol'd*. 2 vols. Moscow and Leningrad: Academia, 1929.

Vstrechi s Meierkhol'dom: Sbornik vospominanii [Encounters with Meyerhold. A Collection of Recollections]. Ed. Lyubov D. Vendrovskaya. Moscow: VTO, 1967.

GLOSSARY OF NAMES AND PLACES

Afinogenov, Aleksandr Nikolaevich (1904–1940). Russian-Soviet playwright.

Aeschylus (525–456 B.C.). Greek tragic dramatist.

Agitprop. Acronym for the Department of Agitation and Propaganda (*Otdel agitatsii propagandy*) created in 1920 to oversee all Soviet institutions involved in political education, including communist-oriented propaganda disseminated through drama, music, and the other arts.

Akimov, Nikolai Pavlovich (1901–1968). Russian-Soviet theatre director and scenic designer.

Alberti, Rafael (1901–). Post-modernist poet and playwright. After joining the Communist Party in the early 1930s, he and his wife spent the next several years visiting different European countries, including the Soviet Union.

Alexandrinsky Theatre. Russia's first permanent public theatre, it was established in the middle of the nineteenth century. The present building was constructed between 1828 and 1832 by the architect Carlo Rossi and was named after Empress Alexandra, wife of Nicholas I. In 1920 the name of the theatre was changed to the Petrograd Academic Theatre of Drama (*Petrogradskii akademicheskii teatr dramy*); in 1937 it was renamed the Pushkin Theatre of Drama.

Andersen, Hans Christian (1805–1875). Danish poet, novelist, and writer of fairy tales.

Andreev-Burlak, Vasily Nikolaevich (real name Andreev, 1843–1888). Russian actor famous on the provincial theatre circuit in the second half of the eighteenth century. He began as a riverboat captain on the Volga, entertaining passengers with improvisations of humorous stories. In 1868 he made his acting debut in Rostov-on-the-Don.

Andreev, Leonid Nikolaevich (1871–1919). Russian prose writer, dramatist, and publicist. His plays were extremely popular at the beginning of the century.

    The Governor (*Gubernator*, 1906).

    The Life of Man (*Zhizn' cheloveka*, 1906/1908).

Antonov, Fyodor Vasilevich (1904–). Soviet artist best known for his paintings of collective farm life in the 1930s.

Anthroposophist. Follower of anthroposophy, a philosophy based on the teachings of Rudolph Steiner.

Apollinaire, Guillaume (Wilhelm de Kostrowitzky, 1880–1918). French poet and art critic. By 1912 he had gained wide notoriety as a vigorous advocate of the avant-garde.

Apollonsky, Roman Borisovich (1865–1928). Russian actor who spent his entire career at the Alexandrinsky Theatre.

Aragon, Louis (1897–1982). French poet, novelist, and journalist, considered one of the founders of Surrealism. After a visit to Moscow in 1931, he abandoned Surrealism to become a leading spokesman in the West for Communism.

Architectural Newspaper (*Arkhitekturnaya gazeta*). An organ of the Union of Soviet Architects, it began publication in 1934. In 1939, it was merged with the newspaper, *Construction Worker* (*Stroitel'nyi rabochii*).

Aristophanes (448?–380? B.C.). Athenian comic poet and playwright.

The Atheist (*Ateist*). A non-party anti-religious newspaper, later a magazine, published from 1922 to 1930.

Atyasova, Antonina Yakovlevna (1903–197?). Dramatic actress who played minor roles in Meyerhold's theatre.

Babanova, Maria Ivanovna (1904–1984). Dramatic actress. She worked in Meyerhold's theatre from 1920 to 1927. The rest of her career was spent at the Theatre of the Revolution, now the Mayakovsky Theatre.

Babel, Isaak Emmanuilovich (1894–1940). Russian-Soviet short-story writer and dramatist. He is best known for his *Odessa Tales* and *Red Cavalry* stories. In the 1930s he fell out of favor with the Communist regime. Arrested in 1938, he was executed the following year.

Bachilis, Israel (?). Russian-Soviet theatre critic.

Bagdasaryan, Stepan Khachaturovich (1888–1938). Armenian-Soviet playwright and physician.
     The Bloody Desert (*Morocco*) (*V krovavoi pustyne* [*Marokko*, 1927]).

Bakhrushin, Yuri Alekseevich (1896–1973). Theatre specialist and teacher, from 1924–1939 he was production and literary manager of the Stanislavsky Opera Theatre.

Bakst, Léon (real name Lev Samoilovich Rozenberg, 1866–1924). Russian artist, a member of the World of Art group, best known for his exotic designs for the Ballets Russes.

Balagan (from the Persian word *bālāhānā* or balcony). Originally a portable structure for dramatic presentations at a fair, it was later used to characterize popular theatre in general. Meyerhold wrote two articles entitled "Balagan", one included in *On The Theatre* and another in *Love for Three Oranges*.

Balmont, Konstantin Dmitrievich (1867–1942). Russian poet and translator.

Balzac, Honoré de (1799–1850). French novelist.

> *Splendors and Miseries of Courtesans* (1843–1847).

Baratynsky, Evgeny Abramovich (1800–1844). Nineteenth-century Russian poet, the most talented member of the Pushkin Pleiad.

Barkhin, Mikhail Grigorevich (1906–1986). Russian architect who with Sergei Vakhtangov designed the new Meyerhold Theatre in the 1930s.

Bayreuth Theatre. The Festspielhaus in the Bavarian town of Bayreuth. Planned by Wagner as an amphitheatre with many innovative features, it is the site of the annual Bayreuth Festival dedicated to Wagner's operas.

Bazhenov, Vasily Ivanovich (1737–1799). Russian artist and architect. After studying in Paris and in Rome, he returned to Russia where he was the author of numerous architectural projects in Petersburg and Moscow.

Beaumarchais, Pierre-Augustin Caron de (1732–1799). French dramatist and publicist.

> *The Barber of Seville* (1775).
> *The Marriage of Figaro* (1778).

Belinsky, Vissarion Grigorevich (1811–1848). Russian writer and critic.

> "Russian literature in 1843." (*Russkaya literatura v 1843 godu*).

Belsky, Boris Vasilevich (?). Actor at the Meyerhold Theatre; he replaced Igor Ilinsky in the title role of *Bubus, the Teacher* when the latter departed from the theatre in the middle of rehearsals.

Bely, Andrei (pseud. of Bugaev, Boris Nikolaevich, 1880–1934). Russian symbolist poet, novelist, and critic.

> *Moscow* (*Moskva*, 1926).
> *A Wind from the Caucasus* (*Veter s kavkaza*, 1928).

Bendersky, Aleksei Nikolaevich (1902–1981). Russian-Soviet theatre director, he worked at the Meyerhold Theatre from 1934 to 1938.

Bengis, Evgeniya Bentsianovna (1902–). Born in Kharkov where she began her career at the kharkhov State Children's Theatre; she came to Moscow in 1921 to enter Meyerhold's Directors' workshop. She performed in virtually all of Meyerhold's productions in the 1920s.

Beria, Lavrenty (1899–1953). A Georgian follower of Stalin, member of the party from 1917, he served as Stalin's agent in Transcaucasia from 1932 to 1938 when he replaced Nikolai Yezhov as head of the NKVD. He was arrested and executed in 1953.

Bernhardt, Sarah (stage name of Henrietta Rosine Bernard, 1844–1923). French actress, she was considered the queen of French romantic and classical tragedy. She toured Russia three times: 1881, 1892, 1908.

Bestuzhev (pseud. of Marlinsky), Aleksandr Aleksandrovich (1797–1837). Writer, poet, and Decembrist revolutionary.

Bezymensky, Aleksandr Ilyich (1898–1973). Russian-Soviet poet; activist in the organization of proletarian literature after the Revolution. *The Shot (Vystrel*, 1929).

Bill-Belotserkovsky, Vladimir Naumovich (1884/85–1970). Russian-Soviet Playwright. From 1911 to 1917, he lived and worked in the United States, returning in time to take part in the October Revolution. He is best known for his 1925 play, *The Storm*.

Biomechanics. Program of exercises and études developed by Meyerhold for training actors in the essentials of scenic movement.

Birman, Serafima Germanovna (1890–1976). Russian-Soviet actress and director at the Second Moscow Art Theatre from 1924 to 1936 and at the Lenin Komsomol Theatre from 1938 to 1958.

Blok, Aleksandr Aleksandrovich (1880–1921). Russian poet, considered the greatest of the Russian Symbolists.
The Fairground Booth (Balaganchik, 1906).
The Unknown Woman (Neznakomka, 1906).
Dances of Death (Plyaski smerti, 1912–1914).

Blériot, Louis (1872–1936). French aviator and inventor. He was the first to cross (July 25, 1909) the English Channel in a heavier-than-air machine.

Boborykin, Pyotr Dmitrievich (1836–1921). Russian novelist at the end of the nineteenth and the early years of the twentieth centuries. He is credited with coining the term "intelligentsia".

Boccioni, Umberto (1882–1916). Italian painter and sculptor, one of the leading Futurist artists. His *Unique forms of continuity in space* (1913) is considered one of the masterpieces of 20th-century sculpture.

Bogolyubov, Nikolai Ivanovich (1899–1980). Russian-Soviet actor, a pupil in the Meyerhold Workshop, and an actor in the Meyerhold Theatre.

Bondi, Yuri Mikhailovich (1889–1926). Russian-Soviet theatre artist and director. From 1912–1915 he worked as a theatre artist at Meyerhold's Studio, and later at GVRM. One of the founders of Soviet children's theatre, in 1923 he became head of the First State Children's Theatre in Moscow.

Brecht, Bertolt (1898–1956). German poet and playwright, best known for his creation of "epic" theatre. In 1932 he was invited to première his film *Kuhle Wampe* in Moscow.

Brik (née Kagan), Lili Yurevna (1891–1978). Wife of Osip, mistress of Vladimir Mayakovsky.

Brik, Osip Maksimovich (1888–1945). Literary theorist and playwright.

Bruegel, Pieter (1525–1569). Flemish painter best known for his depictions of sturdy peasants at work and at play.

Bryusov, Valery Yakovlevich (1873–1924). Russian poet, novelist, and critic.

Bubnov, Andrei Sergeevich (1884–1940). Soviet political activist, member of the Communist Party since 1903, he replaced Anatoly Lunacharsky as head of Narkompros in 1929, a position he retained until his arrest in 1939. He was executed in 1940.

Burian, Emil František (1904–1959). Initially an actor, he became the leading avant-garde director in the Czech theatre of the 1930s. From 1933 to 1938, Burian's D Theatre achieved international recognition.

Busoni, Ferruccio Benvenuto (1866–1924). German-Italian pianist, conductor, and composer.

Butyrka Prison. Located in northeast Moscow, it is by far the largest of the five main Moscow prisons. In the eighteenth century it housed the captured rebels of the Pugachev insurrection. During the Stalinist purge it was used for "political" prisoners.

Byron, George Gordon, Lord (1788–1824). English poet, leading figure of the Romantic movement.
> *Cain* (1821).

Chaliapin, Fedor Ivanovich (1873–1938). Russian operatic bass. His most famous role was Boris in Mussorgsky's *Boris Godunov*.

Chamberlain, (Arthur) Neville (1869–1940). British statesman; prime minister from 1937–1940.

Chaplin, Charlie (Sir Charles Spencer Chaplin, 1889–1977). British-born actor, director, and producer.
> *City Lights* (1931).

Chekhov, Anton Pavlovich (1860–1904). Russian short-story writer, dramatist, and physician.
> *The Bear* (*Medved'*, 1888).
> *The Proposal* (*Predlozhenie*, 1888–1889).
> *The Anniversary* (*Yubilei*, 1891).
> *The Seagull* (*Chaika*, 1895–1896).
> *Three Sisters* (*Tri sestry*, 1900).

Chekhov, Mikhail Aleksandrovich (1891–1955). The nephew of Anton Chekhov; actor at the Maly and Moscow Art Theatres, later head of the Second Moscow Art Theatre. In 1928 he emigrated to the West where in addition to acting and directing he continued the work in actor training he had begun in Moscow.

Chekrygin, Aleksandr Ivanovich (1884–1942). Russian-Soviet dancer, teacher, and balletmaster, he joined the Mariinsky Theatre immediately on his graduation from the Petersburg Theatre School in 1902. Best known for his character roles, he continued to perform on the ballet stage until 1928.

Chénier, André-Marie (1762–1794). French poet of mixed French-Greek parentage; his work is considered the peak of French poetic achievement in the 18th century.

Cherny, Sasha (pseud. of Aleksandr M. Glinkberg, 1880–1932). Russian poet and political satirist whose synthesis of the lyrical and satirical and harsh, anti-esthetic style influenced Vladimir Mayakovsky.

Chevalier, Maurice (1888–1972). French actor and music hall artist.

Chopin, Frédéric François (1810–1849). Polish-born French romantic composer and pianist.

Chronegk, Ludwig (1837–1891). Actor, later director with the Meiningen Theatre. Responsible for taking the Meiningen troupe on tour throughout Europe. The troupe performed in Russia in 1885 and again in 1890.

Chushkin, Nikolai Nikolaevich (1906–1977). Russian-Soviet theatre specialist. He is best known for his book, *Hamlet-Kachalov*, about Gordon Craig's 1912 production of *Hamlet* at the Moscow Art Theatre.

Cocteau, Jean Maurice (Clément Eugène, 1889–1963). French poet, novelist, playwright, film director, and critic.

Commedia del'arte. A popular form of theatre performance by troupes of masked actors using stock comic situations and characters that flourished in Italy from the 16th to 18th century; it had an enormous influence on European drama, including the works of Molière and Shakespeare.

Committee for Arts Affairs (*Komitet po delam iskusstv*). The U.S.S.R. state organ in charge of all aspects of art (except cinematography after 1938). From 1936 to 1946 it was under the Council of Peoples' Commissars; from 1946 to 1953, under the U.S.S.R. Council of Ministers.

Craig, Edward Gordon (1872–1966). British theatre director, producer, and designer. In 1912, Stanislavsky invited him to direct a production of *Hamlet* at the Moscow Art Theatre. After a hiatus of twenty-three years, Craig returned to Moscow in 1935 to attend a theatre festival.

Crocodile (*Krokodil*). A popular satirical magazine which began publication in 1922.

Crommelynck, Fernand (1885/1888–1970). Belgian playwright.
   The Magnanimous Cuckold (1921).

Cui, César (1835–1918). Russian composer and critic of French descent, a military engineer by profession.

Dalcroze, Émile Jaques. See: Jaques-Dalcroze.

Dalmatov (pseud. of Luchich), Vasily Pantelemonovich (1852–1912). Russian actor and playwright.

Dalsky (pseud. of Neelov), Mamont Viktorovich (1865–1918). Russian actor best known for his dramatic performances on the stage of the Alexandrinsky Theatre.

D'Annunzio, Gabriele (1863–1938). Italian poet, dramatist, and novelist.
Pisanelle (1913).

Dargomyzhsky, Aleksandr Sergeevich (1813–1869). Russian composer who with Glinka established a tradition of national opera based on folksong.
The Stone Guest (*Kammenyi gost'*, 1866–1869; completed by César Cui and Rimsky-Korsakov).

Davydov, Vladimir Nikolaevich (pseud. of Ivan Nilolaevich Gorelov, 1849–1925). A Russian actor, he spent most of his career at the Alexandrinsky Theatre.

Degas, Hilaire Germain Edgar (1834–1917). French painter and sculptor primarily interested in depicting movement in his works of art. He is most famous for his paintings and sculptures of ballet dancers.

d'Ennery, Adolphe Philippe (1811–1899). French playwright, one of the most popular authors of melodramas in the second half of the nineteenth century.
Two Little Orphans (1874).

Diaghilev, Sergei Pavlovich (1872–1929). Russian ballet impresario, founder of Les Ballets Russes, a troupe that was to revolutionize the dance world.

Dmitriev, Vladimir Vladimirovich (1900–1948). Russian-Soviet theatre artist. During the 1920s and 1930s he designed sets for a wide variety of theatres in Moscow and Leningrad, including the Meyerhold Theatre.

Doctor Stockman (*Doktor Stokman*). Russian title of Ibsen's *An Enemy of the People*.

Donato, Donat Vasilevich (1885–1964). Trained by his parents as an acrobat and clown, he also became famous as a comic juggler; at the beginning of the century he was the first to introduce into the Russian circus the emploi of the equestrian acrobat–clown.

Donskoi Cemetery. Moscow cemetery adjacent to Donskoi Monastery in southeast Moscow.

Donskoi, Yuri Fedorovich (?). Actor in Meyerhold's theatre.

Dostoevsky, Fyodor Mikhailovich (1821–1881). Russian writer.
Crime and Punishment (*Prestuplenie i nakazanie*, 1866).

Dovzhenko, Aleksandr Petrovich (1894–1956). Soviet film director, writer and scenarist.
The Earth (*Zemlya*, 1930).
Shchors (1939).

Doyle, Sir Arthur Conan (1859–1930). English author and creator of Sherlock Holmes.

Dumas, fils, Alexandre (1824–1895). French playwright.
> *The Lady of the Camellias* (1852).

Dunaevsky, Isaak Osipovich (Iosifovich, 1900–1955). Russian-Soviet composer and conductor, best known for his operettas and musical film comedies on Soviet themes.

Duncan, Isadora (1878–1927). American dancer. Her barefoot dancing caused a sensation when she visited Russia in 1905, 1908, and 1912. In 1921 she opened a school in Moscow. She was married to Sergei Esenin from 1922 to 1923.

Duse, Eleanora (1859?–1924). Italian dramatic actress. In 1891–1892 and 1908, she performed in Russia.

Dyur, Nikolai Osipovich (1807–1839). Russian actor at the Alexandrinsky Theatre famous as the first Molchalin (in *Woe from Wit*, 1830); and the first Khlestakov (in *The Inspector General*, 1836). He was also well-known as the author of music for vaudeville ditties.

Ehrenburg, Ilya Grigorievich (1891–1967). Russian-Soviet journalist, prose writer, memoirist, poet, and translator.

Eisenstein, Sergei Mikhailovich (1898–1948). Russian-Soviet film director, artist, and theoretician. A student in Meyerhold's Workshop, he left in 1922 to join the Proletkult Theatre before turning to film-making in 1924.

Elanskaya, Klavdiya Nikolaevna (1898–1972). Russian-Soviet actress who spent her entire career at the Moscow Art Theatre.

Erdman, Nikolai Robertovich (1902–1970). Russian author of several comedies and numerous comic skits.
> *The Warrant* (*Mandat*, 1925).
> *The Suicide* (*Samoubiitsa*, 1928–1932).

Ermolova, Maria Nikolaevna (1853–1928). Russian tragedienne who spent her entire career on the stage of the Maly Theatre.

Ermolova Theatre. Established in 1937 with the merger of two drama studios, it took over the site of the Meyerhold Theatre following the latter's closing in 1938.

Ershov, Ivan Vasilevich (1867–1943). Russian dramatic tenor.

Esenin, Konstantin Sergeevich (1920–1986). Journalist and authority on soccer, son of Sergei Esenin and Zinaida Raikh.

Esenin, Sergei Aleksandrovich (1895–1925). Russian poet famous for his simple lyrics about peasant life and the Russian landscape. Husband of Zinaida Raikh from 1917 to 1921, father of her two children, Tatyana and Konstantin.

Esenina, Tatyana Sergeevna (1918–1992). Journalist, daughter of Sergei Esenin and Zinaida Raikh.

Euripides (480?–406 B.C.). Greek dramatist, ranking along with
   Aeschylus and Sophocles as one of the three greatest classical
   tragedians.

Evreinov, Nikolai Nikolaevich (1879–1953). Russian playwright, director,
   theoretician, composer, and theatrical innovator. A self-proclaimed
   "aristocrat of the theatre", he emigrated to Paris in 1925.

Fadeev, Aleksandr Aleksandrovich (1901–1956). Russian-Soviet author,
   an active Communist who fought on the side of the Reds in the Civil
   War. One of the theoreticians of Socialist Realism, he headed the
   Union of Writers from 1946 to 1954. Following his removal from the
   top position of the Union, and tormented by memories of his role in
   the political persecution of other writers during the 1930s, in 1956 he
   committed suicide.

Faiko, Aleksei Mikhailovich (1893–1978). Russian-Soviet playwright.
   The Teacher Bubus (*Uchitel' Bubus*, 1925).

Farman, Henri (1874–1958). One of the pioneers of aviation.

Fedorov, Vasily Fedorovich (1891–1971). Director at the Meyerhold Theatre.

Fedotov, Aleksandr Filippovich (1841–1895). Russian actor, director,
   teacher, and playwright.

Fedotov, Pavel Aleksandrovich (1815–1852). A disillusioned army officer
   whose paintings expressed the grim realities of contemporary life.

Fedotova, Glikeriya Nikolaevna (1846–1925). Russian actress who spent
   her career at the Maly Theatre; she was best known for her interpretation of Ostrovsky's heroines.

The Fellowship of New Drama. The name Meyerhold gave to the "Troupe
   of Russian dramatic artists under the direction of A. S. Kosherov and
   V. E. Meyerhold", when he became the sole director of it in the
   summer of 1903.

Ferdinand II (1578–1637). Holy Roman Emperor from 1619 to 1637, he
   waged constant war against Protestant forces.

Fevralsky, Aleksandr Vilyamovich (1901–1984). Russian-Soviet specialist
   in literature and theatre. From 1923 to 1930, he was an academic
   secretary at the Meyerhold Theatre. He is the author of several books
   on Meyerhold and Mayakovsky.

Flaubert, Gustave (1821–1880). French novelist.

Fokin, Mikhail Mikhailovich (1880–1942). Russian dancer, choreographer,
   and teacher.

Fokine, Michel (See: Fokin, Mikhail Mikhailovich).

Fonvizin, Denis Ivanovich (1745–1792). Russian playwright, best known
   for his satirical comedy, *The Minor* (*Nedorosl'*).

FOSP Club. Club belonging to the Federation of Soviet Writers' Associations (*Federatsiia ob'edinenii sovetskikh pisatelei*), 1926–1932.

France, Anatole (pseud. of Jacques Anatole François Thibault, 1844–1924). French writer and social critic.

  The Life of Joan of Arc (1908).

Fučik, Julius (1903–1943). Writer, critic, and journalist; from 1921, member of the Communist Party in Czechoslovakia. He spent the years 1934–1936 in Moscow as a reporter. Arrested by the Gestapo in 1942, he died in prison the following year. His book, *Reportage by a Man with a Noose Around the Neck*, published in 1945, was awarded the first International Peace Prize in 1950.

Fuchs, Georg (1868–1949). German playwright, director, and theoretician.

  The Stage of the Future (1904).

Fuller, Löie (real name Maria Louisa, 1862–1928). American dancer who became internationally famous as the "Fairy of Light" because of her pioneering use of color, light, and fabric to create a fantasy world of dazzling movement.

Gabrilovich, Evgeny Iosifovich (1899–1993). Soviet writer and film scenarist.

Garin, Erast Pavlovich (1902–1980). Soviet actor and director. A graduate of the Meyerhold workshops, actor in the Meyerhold Theatre from 1926 to 1936 where he played leading roles in several of Meyerhold's productions.

Garshin, Vsevolod Mikhailovich (1855–1888). Russian short-story writer.

Gastev, Aleksei Kapitonovich (1882–1941). Russian-Soviet worker-poet and scholar. Founder in 1920 of TsIT (*Tsentral'nyi institut truda*), the Central Institute of Labor, and a leading proponent of the "scientific organization of labor", or NOT (nauchnaya organizatsiya truda).

Gavarni (pseud. of Sulpice Guillaume Chevalier, 1804–1866). French caricaturist and lithographer. He produced over 8,000 drawings, watercolors and lithographs.

GEKTEMAS (*Gosudarstvennyie eksperimental'nyie teatral'nyie masterskie imeni Meierhkhol'da*). The Meyerhold State Experimental Workshops (1923–1931). In 1932, it became *GEKTETIM*.

GEKTETIM (*Gosudarstvennyi eksperimental'nyi teatral'nyi teknikum imeni Vs. Meierkhol'da*). The Meyerhold State Experimental Theatre Technicum. In 1934, *GEKTETIM* became the Meyerhold State Theatre Technicum. It was also known simply as the Technicum. It closed when the Meyerhold Theatre was closed in 1938.

German, Yuri Pavlovich (1910–1967). Russian-Soviet writer and playwright.

  Prélude (*Vstuplenie*, 1931).

Giacomino (real name Cireni), Giacomo (1884–1956). Italian clown, acrobat, juggler, musical eccentric who performed in Russia from

1902–1917. In St. Petersburg he was friends with Chaliapin and Aleksandr Kuprin, who included him in his story, "The Nightingale." After 1917, he performed in Paris and in movies in the United States. He spent his final years in Italy working as a cashier and translator at a casino.

Gippius, Zinaida Nikolaevna (1869–1945). Poet, fiction writer, playwright, essayist, and critic.

    The Green Ring (*Zelyonoe kol'tso*, 1915).

Gladkov, Aleksandr Konstantinovich (1913–1976). Russian-Soviet playwright, poet, critic, and essayist. His 1941 heroic comedy in verse, *Long, Long Ago*, about the War of 1812, proved extremely popular. Gladkov is best known for his essays and articles on Meyerhold, Mayakovsky, and Pasternak.

Glaviskusstvo. Acronym for the "Main Administration of Artistic Literature and Art" (*Glavnoe upravlenie po delam khudozhestvennoi literatury i iskusstva*). The central Soviet state organ for control of all forms of art (theatre, music, film, applied arts, circus, variety performances, and amateur activities), it was formed in 1928 as part of Narkompros. In 1936, it was absorbed by the Committee for Arts Affairs under the U.S.S.R. Council of People's Commissars.

Glavrepertkom. Acronym for the "Main Repertory Committee" (*Glavnyi repertuarnyi komitet*), or later, "Main Committee for Control of Entertainment and Repertories" (*Glavnyi komitet po kontrolyu za zrelishchami i repertuarom*). It was formed as part of Narkompros R.S.F.S.R. in 1923. In addition to publishing lists of allowed and banned dramatic, musical, and cinematic works, it also worked with playwrights and film organizations and organized discussions of plays, productions, films. In 1928 it became part of Glaviskusstvo; in 1933 it was made an independent agency.

Gluck, Christoph Willibald Ritter von (1714–1787). Bohemian-German operatic composer. With his *Orpheus and Eurydice* (1762), he introduced a new kind of opera in which musical and dramatic elements were fused into a single unity.

    Orpheus (1774). A French revision of *Orpheus and Eurydice*, written for the Paris Opera.

Gnesin, Mikhail Fabianovich (1883–1957). Russian-Soviet composer and teacher.

Goethe, Johann Wolfgang von (1749–1832). German poet, dramatist, novelist, and philosopher.

Gogol, Nikolai Vasilevich (1809–1852). Russian short-story writer, novelist, and playwright.

    The Inspector General (*Revizor*, 1835).

The Nose (*Nos*, 1836).

Dead Souls (*Mertvye dushi*, 1841).

On Leaving the Theatre (*Teatral'nyi raz"ezd*, 1842).

Goldoni, Carlo (1707–1793). Italian dramatist.

Goleizovsky, Kasyan Yaroslavich (Karlovich) (1892–1970). Russian dancer and choreographer. He was strongly influenced by the Russian dancers and choreographers, Mikhail Fokin and Aleksandr Gorsky (1871–1924).

Golovin, Aleksandr Yakovlevich (1863–1930). Russian artist and scenic designer.

Goltseva, Kseniya Ivanovna (1898–1943). Dramatic actress, director at the Meyerhold Theatre, a niece of Meyerhold's.

Goncharov, Ivan Aleksandrovich (1812–1891). Russian novelist.

Oblomov (*Oblomov*, 1859).

Gorky, Maksim or Maxim (pseud. of Aleksei Maksimovich Peshkov, 1868–1936). Russian writer, considered the father of Soviet literature and the founder of the doctrine of Socialist Realism.

Malva (*Malva*, 1897).

The Lower Depths (*Na dne*, 1902).

Children of the Sun (*Deti solntsa*, 1905).

Gorsky, Aleksei Stepanovich (?). Actor at the Meyerhold Theatre.

GOSET. The State Jewish Theatre (*Gosudarstvennyi evreiskii teatr*). Founded in Petrograd in 1919 as a theatre studio, on moving to Moscow in 1922, it became the State Jewish Chamber Theatre, (after 1925, the State Jewish Theatre). It was closed in 1949, a year after the murder of its leader, Solomon Mikhoels.

GosTIM. The Meyerhold State Theatre (*Gosudarstvennyi teatr imeni Meierkhol'da*), 1926–1938. Formerly TIM.

Gozzi, Carlo (1720–1806). Italian dramatist.

Granovsky, Aleksandr (Abraham Azarkh; 1890–1937). Theatre director who studied and worked in theatres in St. Petersburg and Munich until war broke out between Germany and Russia. Founder of the Jewish Theatre Studio in 1919 (later the Moscow State Jewish Theatre [GOSET]), Granovsky emigrated in 1927.

Griboedov, Aleksandr Sergeevich (1795–1829). Russian playwright and diplomat.

Woe from Wit (*Gore ot uma*, 1824); see also, *Woe to Wit*.

Grigoriev, Apollon Aleksandrovich (1822–1864). Russian poet and critic.

Grillparzer, Franz (1791–1872). Austrian dramatist, a leading figure of the Romantic movement.

Grotesque. Literary style characterized by comic distortion or exaggeration.

Guglielmo (Guglielmo Ebreo of Pesaro, c. 1400–1475). Italian dancing master famous for his treatise on the dance, *De Pratica seu Arte Tripudii* (*The Practice or Art of the Dance*) in which he outlined six essential qualifications for a dancer. One of them, "partire di terreno" (apportionment of the terrain) has to do with the dancer's ability to adjust his steps to the area in which he is performing.

GVRM–GVTM. (*Gosudarstvennye vyshie rezhisserskie/teatral'nye masterskie*). State Higher Directing (later Theatre) Workshops. Also known as the Meyerhold Workshop (*Masterskoe Meierkhol'da*). Organized by Meyerhold in 1921, its subjects included training in Biomechanics. In 1923 it was reorganized as GEKTEMAS.

Hamp, Pierre (pseud. of Henri Bourillon, 1876–1962). French author, a self-made and self-taught man whose novels of industrial life were based on firsthand experience.

Hamsun (pseud. of Pederson), Knut (1859–1952). Norwegian playwright, novelist, and poet.
> *At the Gate of the Kingdom* (1895).

Hanako (real name Ōta Hisa; 1868–1945). One of many Japanese entertainers who flooded Europe at the beginning of the century. Under Löie Fuller's guidance, she became famous as the "Bernhardt of the Flowery Empire".

Hardt, Ernst (1876–1947). German writer and playwright.
> *Tantris the Fool* (1908).

Hauptmann, Gerhart (1862–1946). German novelist, dramatist, and poet. His play *Before Dawn* (1898) inaugurated the naturalistic movement in German theatre.
> *Lonely People* (1891).
> *Schluck and Jau* (1901).

Hegel, Georg Wilhelm Friedrich (1770–1831). German philosopher who believed that truth could be reached by a continuing dialectic.

Heine, Heinrich (1797–1856). German poet and prose writer.

Hemingway, Ernest (1899–1961). American novelist.
> *The Sun Also Rises* (*Fiesta*, 1926).

Herzen, Aleksandr Ivanovich (1812–1870). Russian revolutionary leader and writer.

Hippolytus. In Greek mythology the son of Hippolyta and Theseus who was falsely accused by his stepmother Phaedra of raping her after he had rejected her advances and who was killed by Poseidon.

Hofmannsthal, Hugo von (1874–1929). Austrian poet, dramatist, and essayist.
> *Electra* (1903), libretto for the opera by Richard Strauss, adapted from the Greek drama.

Hokusai, Katsushika (1760–1849). Japanese painter, draftsman, and wood engraver.

Hugo, Victor Marie (1802–1885). French romantic poet, novelist, and playwright.

Ibsen, Henrik (1828–1906). Norwegian playwright and poet.

    The Pretenders (1863).

    A Doll's House (1879).

    Ghosts (1881).

    An Enemy of the People (1883).

    The Wild Duck (1884).

Ignatov, Sergei Sergeevich (1887–1959). Russian-Soviet critic, theatre historian, and teacher.

Ilf, Ilya and Petrov, Evgeny (pseud. of Ilya Arnoldovich Fainzilberg, 1897–1937, and Evgeny Petrovich Kataev, 1903–1942), a team of satirical writers and journalists from Odessa who met in Moscow in 1925. They gained fame as the authors of the hugely successful *Twelve Chairs*, an adventure novel published in 1928.

Ilinsky, Igor Vladimirovich (1901–1987). Comic actor who worked with Meyerhold on and off from 1920 to 1935.

Ivan IV, or Ivan the Terrible (1533–1584). He was the first ruler to assume the title of Tsar of Russia.

Ivan Franko Ukrainian Dramatic Theatre. Established in 1920, it became one of the leading dramatic theatres in Ukraine. The theatre is named after the Ukranian writer and dramatist, Ivan Franko.

Ivanov, Vyacheslav Ivanovich (1866–1949). Poet, critic, and scholar, Ivanov became one of the leaders of the Symbolist movement and it's principal theorist. Following his emigration in 1924, he settled in Italy where he continued his activities as a poet and scholar until his death.

Jaques-Dalcroze, Émile (1865–1950). Swiss educator and composer, inventor of a system of musical training called Eurhythmics which translated sound into physical movement.

Jasieński, Bruno (Viktor Yakovlevich Ziskind; 1901–1941). Polish writer, poet, and playwright, from 1921 until his death he lived in the Soviet Union.

    The Ball of the Mannequins (*Bal manekenov*, 1931).

Jelagin, Juri (Yuri Borisovich Elagin; 1910–1987). Russian musician, in the 1930s he played violin in the Vakhtangov Theatre orchestra. After moving to the United States in 1947, he joined the Houston Symphony Orchestra. From 1965 until his death, Jelagin worked as an editor and writer for the United States Information Agency.

    The Taming of the Arts (*Ukroshchenie iskusstv*; in English, 1951, in Russian, 1952).

Dark Genius (*Temnyi Genii* [*Vsevolod Meierkhol'd*], 1955).

Jessner, Leopold (1878–1945). German director, a leading figure in the Expressionist movement in Berlin; head of the Berlin State Theatre (1919–1930). He emigrated in 1933.

Kabuki. Popular drama of Japan which evolved from the older No theatre. Chiefly developed in the 17th century, it is characterized by elaborate costumes, stylized acting, music, and dance, with all roles, male and female, performed by males.

Kachalov (pseud. of Shverubovich), Vasily Ivanovich (1875–1948). Russian-Soviet actor, a leading member of the Moscow Art Theatre.

Kamerny Theatre. Moscow Theatre founded by Aleksandr Tairov in 1914. In 1950 it became the Pushkin Dramatic Theatre.

Karamzin, Nikolai Mikhailovich (1766–1826). Russian writer and historian. *"Poor Liza"* (*Bednaya Liza*, 1792).

Karatygin, Vasily Andreevich (1802–1853). Russian dramatic actor. Following the opening of the Alexandrinsky Theatre in 1832, he became the leading interpreter of tragic roles at that theatre.

Kataev, Valentin (1897–1986). Russian-Soviet prose writer, journalist, and playwright; best known for his play, *Squaring the Circle.*
I Am A Son of the Working People (*Ya syn trudovogo naroda*, 1937).

Kazan Cathedral (*Kazanskii Sobor*). More precisely, the Cathedral of our Lady of Kazan. Located on Nevsky Prospect in St. Petersburg, it was erected between 1801 and 1811.

Keaton, Buster (1895–1966). American comic actor who wrote, directed, and starred in silent film classics. His films were very popular in Russia in the 1920s.

Kellermann, Bernard (1879–1951). German novelist and war correspondent during World War I; author of the hugely popular novel, *The Tunnel*, glorifying scientific-technical developments in the twentieth century.
The Tunnel (1913).

Kerzhentsev, Platon Mikhailovich (1881–1940). Soviet Communist Party activist, historian and journalist. Head of the Committee on Artistic Affairs (1936–1938). The attack in *Pravda* (December 17, 1937) on Meyerhold and his theatre in his article, *"An Alien Theatre"* (*Chuzhoi teatr*) signaled the closing of the Meyerhold Theatre on January 8, 1938.

Kherson. City on the Dnepr River near its mouth on the Black Sea, founded by Grigori Potemkin in 1778. By the beginning of this century it had become an important port city and export center.

Khlebnikov, Velimir Vladimirovich (real given name: Viktor, 1885–1922). Russian poet and poetic theorist, one of the leaders of the Russian Cubo-Futurist movement.

Khmelev, Nikolai Pavlovich (1901–1945). Russian-Soviet actor best known for the psychological depth of his roles at the Moscow Art Theatre. In 1932 he organized a theatre studio in Moscow; in 1937 it was merged with the Ermolova Theatre-Studio to become the Ermolova Theatre which he headed from 1937–1945.

Kiligin, Sergei Aleksandrovich (1900–1967). Russian-Soviet dramatic actor at the Meyerhold Theatre in the 1930s.

KIM (*Kommunisticheskii Internatsional Molodyozhi*). Communist Youth International (1919–1943).

Kiprensky, Orest Adamovich (1782–1836). One of the most prominent portrait painters of the early nineteenth century in Russia and a leading figure of the Romantic movement in Russian art.

Kirsanov, Semen Isaakovich (1906–1972). Russian-Soviet poet.

Klyuchevsky, Vasily Osipovich (1841–1911). Russian historian noted for his scrupulous research and documentation.

Knipper-Chekhova, Olga Leonardovna (1868–1959). A graduate of the Moscow Philharmonic Drama School and founding member of the Moscow Art Theatre where she remained for the rest of her acting career; wife of Anton Chekhov.

Kock, Charles Paul de (1794–1871). French author of popular risqué, sentimental novels.

Koltsov, Mikhail Efimovich (1898–1940). Russian-Soviet writer and prominent journalist famous for his reportage from Spain during the Civil War. Hemingway portrayed him as Karpov in his *For Whom the Bell Tolls*. He was arrested in 1938 and executed two years later.

Komissarzhevskaya, Vera Fedorovna (1864–1910). One of the great Russian actresses, called by many "The Russian Duse". In 1904, she formed her own theatre in St. Petersburg.

Konchalovsky, Pyotr Petrovich (1876–1956). Russian-Soviet theatre artist and portrait painter.

Koran. The sacred text of Islam.

Korsh Theatre. Founded in 1885 by the Russian impresario, Fyodor Adamovich Korsh (1852–1923). In 1887 the first production of Chekhov's *Ivanov* opened there.

Kosheverov, Aleksandr Sergeevich (1874–1921). Co-founder in 1902 with Meyerhold of "A troupe of Russian dramatic actors" in Kherson.

Krupskaya, Nadezhda Konstantinovna (1869–1939). A Soviet official and wife of Lenin, she became a member and later vice-commissar of Narkompros. Assigned to the role of Lenin's widow under Stalin, she was no longer able to take an active part in Party affairs.

Krylov, Ivan Andreevich (1769–1844). Russian journalist, playwright, and fabulist.

Kugel, Aleksandr Rafailovich (pseud. Homo Novus, 1864–1928). Russian literary and theatre critic, publicist, playwright, and director. From 1897 to 1918, he was editor of the influential theatre journal, *Theatre and Art* (*Teatr i iskusstvo*).

Kukolnik, Nestor Vasilevich (1809–1868). Russian playwright and poet, best known for his patriotic plays on historical themes.

Labiche, Eugène (1815–1888). French playwright, author of more than 170 light comedies and farces, the best known of which is *The Italian Straw Hat* (1851).

Lang, Fritz (1890–1976). German film director, best known for his 1926 film, *Metropolis*. Following his emigration in 1933, he worked in the United States.

Lazarenko, Vitaly Efimovich (1890–1939). Russian-Soviet circus artist who combined topical satirical sketches and verse monologs with circus tricks. Following the Revolution he took part in a variety of theatre productions, pantomimes, and skits.

Leconte de Lisle, Charles Marie (1818–1894). French poet.

LEF. The Left Front of Art (*Levyi front iskusstva*). A literary group formed in 1922, made up largely of former members of the Futurist movement and formalist critics.

Léger, Fernand (1881–1955). French artist who incorporated industrial and mechanical images into his work.

Leistikov, Ivan Ivanovich (1892–1963). Russian artist and scenic designer.

Lenin (pseud. of Ulyanov), Vladimir Ilyich (1870–1924). Russian revolutionary, founder of Bolshevism, leader of the 1917 Russian Revolution, and first head of the U.S.S.R.
> *What is to be Done?* (*Shto delat'?*, 1902). The title was inspired by the novel of the same name written in 1862 by Nikolai Chernyshevsky (1828–1889).

Lenin Komsomol Theatre. Located on Chekhov Street in the center of Moscow, it was established in 1927 as the Young Worker's Theatre (TRAM). It was renamed in 1937.

Lensky (pseud. of Vervitsiotti), Aleksandr Pavlovich (1847–1908). Russian actor, director, and teacher.

Leonidov (pseud. of Volfenzon), Leonid Mironovich (1873–1941). Russian-Soviet actor, director, and teacher. He joined the Moscow Art Theatre in 1903, remaining there as actor, director, and teacher until his death.

León, María Teresa (1905–). Spanish theatre director, novelist, and poet, wife of the lyric poet and playwright, Rafael Alberti.

Lermontov, Mikhail Yurevich (1814–1841). Russian poet, novelist, and playwright.

The Demon (*Demon*, 1829–1839).

Masquerade (*Maskarad*, 1835–1836).

Two Brothers (*Dva brata*, 1836).

A Hero of Our Time (*Geroi nashego vremeni*, 1837–1840).

The Lesgaft State Institute of Physical Education. Founded in 1919, it was named after Pyotr Lesgaft, the father of physical education in Russia, whose pioneering courses in physical education became the basis of the Institute's curriculum.

Levidov, Mikhail Yulevich (1892–1942). Russian-Soviet journalist and critic.

Lezginka. A Caucasian dance usually danced by a man – straight as an arrow, yet light as a feather.

Liszt, Franz (1811–1886). Hungarian composer and piano virtuoso.

Litovsky, Osaf Semyonovich (1892–1971). Russian-Soviet playwright and drama critic. Chairman of the Main Repertory Committee (*Glavrepertkom*) from 1930 to 1937.

Livanov, Boris Nikolaevich (1904–1972). Russian-Soviet actor, he joined the Moscow Art Theatre in 1924 and spent the rest of his career there.

Lokshina, Khesya Aleksandrovna (1902–1982). Assistant director and bit player at Meyerhold's theatre until 1929 when she left to work in film as a director; wife of Erast Garin.

Lozinsky, Mikhail Leonidovich (1886–1955). Russian-Soviet poet and translator. He translated Shakespeare's *Hamlet* in 1933.

Lubyanka Prison. Located on Dzerzhinsky Square near the Kremlin, it is the best known of the NKVD (later KGB) prisons.

Lunacharsky, Anatoly Vasilievich (1875–1933). Soviet literary critic, publicist, and playwright. He became the first People's Commissar for Enlightment (1917–1929).

Maeterlinck, Maurice (1862–1949). Belgian Symbolist poet and dramatist.

The Intruder (1890).

Pelléas and Mélisande (1893).

The Death of Tintagiles (1894).

Malevich, Kazimir Severionovich (1878–1935). Russian artist of Polish parentage, he came to the forefront of the Moscow avant garde in December 1915 when he launched Suprematism, a radical non-objective style of painting which stressed the spiritual values of abstract art.

Malkin, Boris Fyodorovich (?). Soviet cultural worker.

Malraux, André (1901–1976). French writer and statesman.

Man's Fate (*La Condition humaine*, 1933).

Maly Opera Theatre. Organized in 1918 in the building of the former Mikhailovsky Theatre as a filial of the Mariinsky Theatre, in 1926 it became the Leningrad State Maly Opera Theatre; in 1964 it was renamed the Leningrad Maly Theatre of Opera and Ballet.

Maly Theatre. The oldest Russian dramatic theatre, it opened in Moscow in 1824.

Mandelshtam, Osip Emilievich (1891–1938). Russian-Soviet poet and essayist. His failure to conform to Soviet literary and ideological standards led to his arrest and exile in 1934. He was rearrested in May 1938 and executed shortly afterwards.

Manet, Edouard (1832–1883). French painter, considered the father of modern painting.

Mariinsky Theatre. St. Petersburg opera theatre built in 1859; it was named after Tsar Alexander II's wife, Maria. Following the Revolution it became the Leningrad State Kirov Theatre of Opera and Ballet.

Marinetti, Filippo Tommaso (1876–1944). Italian poet and novelist, founder of Italian Futurism.

The Mark of Zorro. A 1920 silent film directed by Fred Nibo and starring Douglas Fairbanks Sr. as a Robin Hood of Spanish California.

Markov, Pavel Aleksandrovich (1897–1980). Russian-Soviet theatre critic and historian. From 1925 to 1949, he was head of the literary department at the Moscow Art Theatre.

Martinet, Marcel (1887–1944). French writer and playwright.
    La Nuit (1921)

Martinson, Sergei Aleksandrovich (1899–1984). Russian-Soviet actor at the Meyerhold Theatre.

Mass, Vladimir Zakharovich (1896–1979) Russian-Soviet playwright and poet best known for his buffonades on topical issues, including *Good Treatment for Horses* (1921). In 1934 he co-authored with Nikolai Erdman the film scenario for *Jolly Fellows.*

Matskin, Aleksandr Petrovich (1906–1996). Russian-Soviet critic and theatre historian.

Mayakovsky, Vladimir Vladimirovich (1893–1930). Russian-Soviet poet and playwright.
    Mystery-Bouffe (*Misteriya-Buff,* 1918).
    How are Verses Made? (*Kak delat' stikhi?* 1926).
    "Very Good" (*Khorosho,* 1927).
    The Bedbug (*Klop,* 1928).
    The Bathhouse (*Banya,* 1930).

Médrano Circus. Founded in 1873 in the Montmartre district of Paris, it was named after a Spanish circus performer nicknamed "Boum! Boum!", who for a time headed it.

Mei Lan-fang (1894–1961). Chinese actor. He performed in Moscow in 1935.

Memling or Memlinc, Hans (c. 1430–1494). Flemish religious and portrait painter.

Mérimée, Prosper (1803–1870). French writer of romantic stories and novels. *Carmen* (1846), novella on which Bizet's opera is based.

Metalnikov. See: Talnikov, David Lazarevich.

Meyerholditis. A code word originally used by the Soviet cultural authorities in the 1930s to attack Meyerhold, it quickly became a weapon to condemn all modernistic affectations and formal experimentation not possessing great ideas.

Meyerhold (née Hess), Alvina Danilovna (–1905). Vsevolod Meyerhold's mother.

Meyerhold (Meyergold), Emil Fedorovich (1833?–1892). Vsevolod Meyerhold's father.

Meyerhold, Tatyana Vsevolodovna (1902–1983?). Vsevolod Meyerhold's daughter.

Meyerhold, Teodor Emilevich (1875–1916). One of Meyerhold's brothers; he was one year older than Vsevolod Emilevich.

Meyerhold (née Munt), Olga Mikhailovna (1874–1940). Meyerhold's first wife.

Meyerhold State Theatre School (*Gosudarstvennoe teatral'noe uchilishche imeni Vs. Meierkhol'da*). It existed from 1934, when it replaced GEKTETIM, until 1938 when the Meyerhold State Theatre was closed.

Meyerhold Theatre. See: TIM.

Michurin, Gennady Mikhailovich (1897–1939). Russian-Soviet actor. Formerly at the Bolshoi Dramatic Theatre in Leningrad, he joined the Meyerhold Theatre in 1931, remaining there until 1938.

Mikhoels (pseud. of Vovsi), Solomon (1890–1948). Jewish actor, a leading member of GOSET, which he headed from 1927 until his death. He is most famous for the title role in *King Lear* (1935).

Mochalov, Pavel Stepanovich (1800–1848). Russian dramatic actor.

Moissi, Alexander (Sandro, 1880–1935). German dramatic actor of Albanian nationality. He toured the Soviet Union in 1924 and 1925.

Moliére, Jean-Baptiste Poquelin (1622–1673). French playwright. *Dom Juan* (1665).

Mologin (pseud. of Mochulsky), Nikolai Konstantinovich (1892–1951). Dramatic actor in Meyerhold's Theatre.

Molotov (pseud. of Scriabin), Vyacheslav Mikhailovich (1890–1986). Leading Soviet politician, member of the Politburo from 1926 to 1957; chairman of the Council of People's Commissars, 1930–1941.

Moscow Art Theatre. Founded in 1898 by Konstantin Stanislavsky and Vladimir Nemirovich-Danchenko, it opened its doors on October 27, 1898 with the première of Aleksei K. Tolstoy's *Tsar Fyodor Ivanovich*. By order of Lenin, in 1920 the Art Theatre was designated one of the academic theatres and became MXAT (Moscow Academic Art Theatre). By the end of the 1920s, MXAT had become Stalin's favorite dramatic theatre. It was placed directly under the control of the state and in the 1930s it became the model for all dramatic theatres in the Soviet Union. Following the death of Maksim Gorky in 1936, MXAT was designated the Gorky Moscow Academic Art Theatre (MXAT im. Gorky).

Moscow Dramatic Theatre. There have been many Moscow Dramatic Theatres, but the one where Ilinsky worked was located on Bolshaia Dmitrovka (now Pushkin Street) from 1921 to 1922.

Moskvin, Ivan Mikhailovich (1874–1946). Russian-Soviet actor; he spent his entire career at the Moscow Art Theatre.

Moussinac, Léon (1890–1964). French writer, literary critic, director, theatre and film historian. In 1934 he staged *The Millionaire, the Dentist, and the Poor Man*, based on Labiche's *30 Million Gladiators* at GOSET in Moscow.

Mozart, Wolfgang Amadeus (1756–1791). Austrian composer.
   Don Giovanni (1787)

Munt, Olga. See Meyerhold, Olga.

Mussorgsky (Moussorgsky), Modest Petrovich (1839–1881). Russian composer, he was among the first to promote a nationalist style.

Muzil, Nikolai Ignatevich (1839–1906). Russian actor. He joined the Maly Theatre in 1866 and worked there until the end of his life.

NARKOMPROS (*Narodnyi komissariat prosveshcheniya*), 1917–1946. Acronym for the Peoples Commissariat of Enlightenment. From 1917 to 1929 it was headed by Anatoly Lunacharsky.

Neigauz, Genrikh Gustavovich (1888–1964). Russian-Soviet pianist, teacher and writer, he made his debut at the age of nine. During his lifetime he toured extensively both in his own country and abroad gaining renown for his interpretations of works ranging from Beethoven and Brahms to Scriabin and Prokofiev.

Neigauz, Zinaida Nikolaevna (1894–1966). Second wife of Boris Pasternak.

Nemirovich-Danchenko, Vladimir Ivanovich (1858–1943). Russian-Soviet director, writer, and playwright. Co-founder with Konstantin Stanislavsky of the Moscow Art Theatre.
   In Dreams (*V mechtakh*, 1901).

NEP (New Economic Policy). Economic policy introduced by Lenin in 1921 allowing for limited free enterprise. While it continued after Lenin's death in 1924, it was met by growing opposition from the left of the party and the public. Stalin effectively killed it in 1927 with his speeches at the 15th Party Congress.

The New LEF (NOVYI LEF). A revival of the journal *LEF* in 1927 under Mayakovsky's editorship. In all, twenty-four issues were published before the journal ceased publication at the end of 1928.

NKVD (People's Commissariat for Internal Affairs). The forerunner of the NKGB (1943–1946), in 1934 it replaced the OPGU as the principal organ of state security.

North, Christopher (pseud. of John Wilson, 1785–1854). Scottish author. Pushkin translated a scene from North's dramatic poem, *The City of the Plague*, as the basis for his *A Feast During the Plague*.

Oborin, Lev Nikolaevich (1907–1974). Russian-Soviet pianist, a graduate of the Moscow Conservatory where he later taught, he was noted for his simple, clear, expressive playing.

Okhlopkov, Nikolai Pavlovich (1900–1967). Russian-Soviet actor and director. Actor in the Meyerhold Workshop and subsequently at the Meyerhold Theatre. In 1930, he left to create the Realistic Theatre which he headed until 1939.

Okhranka. Department for "the protection of public security and order" set up to strengthen the national gendarmerie following the assassination of Tsar Alexander II in 1881. Elements of the Okhranka continued to work for various White governments up to 1920.

Olesha, Yuri Karlovich (1899–1960). Russian-Soviet novelist and playwright.
> *Envy (Zavist', 1927)*
> *A List of Benefits (Spisok blagodeyanii, 1931).*

On the Theatre (O teatre). Collection of articles by Vsevolod Meyerhold published in St. Petersburg in 1913.

Orlenev (pseud. of Orlov), Pavel Nikolaevich (1869–1932). Russian actor trained at the Maly Theatre Actors School. He played in the provinces and at the Korsh Theatre.

Ostrovsky, Aleksandr Nikolaevich (1823–1886). Leading nineteenth-century Russian dramatist and theatre reformer.
> *A Lucrative Post (Dokhodnoe mesto, 1857).*
> *The Storm (Groza, 1859).*
> *Vasilisa Melenteva (Vasilisa Melenteva, 1867).*
> *A Fervent Heart (Goryachee serdtse, 1868–1869).*
> *The Forest (Les, 1871).*

Ostrovsky, Nikolai Alekseivich (1904–1936). Soviet novelist. Author of *How the Steel was Tempered (Kak zakalyalas' stal', 1932–34)*.

Ostuzhev (pseud. of Pozharov) Aleksandr Alekseevich (1874–1953). A well-known actor with the Maly Theatre, he managed to continue a successful theatrical career after becoming totally deaf in 1910.

Ozerov, Vladislav Aleksandrovich (1769–1816). Russian playwright.

Pabst, Georg Wilhelm (1885–1967). German film director. *Don Quixote* (1933).

Parnakh (pseud. of Parnok), Valentin Yakovlevich (1891–1951). Russian-Soviet poet, translator, and dancer. In the 1920s he danced in the production *D.E.* at GosTIM.

Parny, Évaroste-Désiré de Forges, Vicomte de (1753–1814). French poet.

Pasternak, Boris Leonidovich (1890–1960). Russian-Soviet poet, prose writer, and translator; winner of the Nobel Prize for Literature in 1958.

Pavlov, Ivan Petrovich (1849–1936). Russian-Soviet physiologist and experimental psychologist best known for his discovery of the conditioned reflex.

Pechkovsky, Nikolai Konstantinovich (1896–1966). Russian-Soviet lyrico-dramatic tenor.

Penza. Provincial city on the Sura River in south central European Russia. It was occupied by Stenka Razin in 1670 and by Pugachev in 1774. Before the Bolshevik revolution it was an important agricultural trading center.

Persimfans. Acronym for "The First Symphonic Ensemble" (*Pervyi simfonicheskii ansambl'*). Symphony orchestra without a conductor, organized in 1922 on the initiative of a Moscow Conservatory professor, Lev Moiseevich Tseitlin (1881–1952).

Petrovsky, Andrei Pavlovich (1869–1933). Russian-Soviet dramatic actor, director, and teacher.

Petrov-Vodkin, Kuzma Sergeevich (1878–1939). Russian-Soviet painter, designer, and theatre artist; from 1910 to 1922, member of the "World of Art" group.

Philharmonic Drama School. More precisely, the Musical-Drama School of the Moscow Philharmonic Society (*Muzykal'no-dramaticheskoe uchilishche moskovskogo filarmonicheskogo obshchstva*). Organized in 1883, its alumni included many famous musicians and actors. In 1898, the graduates of the dramatic department together with the participants in the productions of the Society of Art and Literature became the basis for the Moscow Art Theatre. In 1918, the Muscial-Drama School was renamed the Musical Dramatic Institute; in 1919, the State Insititute of Musical Drama; and in 1922, the State Institute of Theatrical Art (GITIS).

Phrynichus (c. 512–476 B.C.). Athenian tragedian, considered by some ancients to be the founder of tragedy.

Picasso, Pablo (1881–1973). Spanish painter, sculptor, graphic artist, and ceramist who worked in France. One of the most prolific and influential artists of this century.

Pirandello, Luigi (1867–1936). Italian playwright, actor, novelist, and critic famous for his dramas dealing with the absurdities of human existence.

Piscator, Erwin Friedrich Max (1893–1966). German director who played a major role in the development of epic theatre. He left Germany in 1933, spending the years 1938–1951 in the United States before returning to direct at the Freie Volksbühne in Berlin.

Plekhanov, Georgi Valentinovich (1857–1918). Russian revolutionary and social philosopher. Instrumental in introducing Marxist theory to Russia, he has been called "The Father of Russian Marxism."

Podgaetsky, Mikhail Grigorevich (?). Russian-Soviet playwright and critic, best known for his stage adaptation, *D.E.* (*Give us Europe!*).
> *D.E.* (*Give us Europe!* [*Daesh Evropu!*], 1924).
> *D.S.E.* (*Give us Soviet Europe* [*dash Sovetskuyu Evropu*], 1930).

Poincaré, Raymond (1860–1934). Conservative French statesman, president of France from 1913 to 1920.

Polevoi (journalistic pseud. of Kampov), Nikolai Alekseevich (1796–1846). Journalist, critic, dramatist, and historian.

Polivanov, Lev Ivanovich (1838–1899). Russian teacher and literary specialist; author of works on Pushkin, Tolstoy, and others; founder of the Polivanov Gymnasium in Moscow, which he headed until his death.

Poltava. Ukrainian commercial center on the Vorskla River, a tributary of the Volga.

Popov, Aleksei Dmitrievich (1892–1961). Russian-Soviet director and teacher. After working at the Moscow Art Theatre, he moved on to direct at various other theatres, including the Vakhtangov, the Theatre of the Revolution, and the Central Theatre of the Soviet Army.

Popov, Gavriil Nikolaevich (1904–1972). Russian-Soviet composer.

Popova, Lyubov (1889–1924). Russian painter and designer. Famous for her linear Constructivist paintings, her set for Meyerhold's 1922 production of *The Magnanimous Cuckold* was hailed as a masterpiece of Theatrical Constructivism.

Presnya District. Western section of Moscow named after the stream that flowed through it. It was the site of bitter street fighting during the December 1905 uprising. In 1918 it was renamed the Krasnaya Presnya District.

Prokofiev, Sergei Sergeevich (1891–1953). Russian-Soviet composer and pianist.
> *Love for Three Oranges* (*Lyubov' k trem apel'sinam*, 1919).
> *Semyon Kotko* (*Semen Kotko*, 1939).

Protazanov, Yakov Aleksandrovich (1881–1945). A pioneer Russian-Soviet film director. In 1920, he emigrated to Europe, returning in 1923 to take an active part in Soviet film making.

    The White Eagle (*Belyi oryol*, 1928).

Przybyszewski, Stanisław (1868–1927). Neoromantic Polish novelist, essayist, and playwright.

    Snow (1903).

Pushkin, Aleksandr Sergeevich (1799–1837). Russian poet and writer. The central figure of the Golden Age of Russian literature, he has justifiably been called Russia's National Poet. He is also credited with creating the modern Russian literary language.

    Eugene Onegin (*Evgenii Onegin*, 1823–1831).

    Boris Godunov (*Boris Godunov*, 1825).

    The Little Tragedies (*Malen'kie tragedii*, 1832–1839):

      The Covetous Knight (*Skupoi rytsar'*);

      Mozart and Salieri (*Motsart i Sal'eri*);

      The Stone Guest (*Kamennyi gost'*);

      A Feast During the Plague (*Pir vo vremya chumy*).

    Rusalka (*Rusalka*, dramatic romance begun in 1832 and left unfinished).

    The Queen of Spades (*Pikovaya dama*, 1833). This short story served as the basis for the libretto of Tchaikovsky's opera of the same name.

Pushkino. A village about fifty miles northeast of Moscow on the Yaroslavl line.

Pushkin Theatre of Drama. The former Alexandrinsky Theatre, it received this name in 1937 on the one-hundredth anniversary of Pushkin's death.

Pyast (pseud. of Pestovsky), Vladimir Alekseevich (1886–1940). Russian-Soviet poet and translator.

Raccourci. An art term borrowed from the French meaning "foreshortening." Meyerhold used it to mean an instantaneous, expressive moment, a point of break between two movements. It is related to the *mie* of the Japanese theatre.

Radlov, Sergei Ernestovich (1892–1958). Versatile and innovative Russian-Soviet theatre director, organizer of the Theatre of Popular Comedy (1919–1922) and other experimental studios in Leningrad. He is best known for his 1935 production of *King Lear* at the Moscow GOSET (State Jewish Theatre) with Solomon Mikhoels in the title role.

Radlova (née Darmolatova), Anna Dmitrievna (1891–1949). Russian-Soviet poet and translator, wife of Sergei Radlov. She translated *Hamlet* in 1937.

Raikh, Zinaida Nikolaevna (1894–1939). Meyerhold's second wife; an actress who played leading roles in many of Meyerhold's productions during the 1920s and 1930s. She was murdered shortly after Meyerhold's arrest in 1939.

RAPP. Russian Association of Proletarian Writers (*Rossiiskaya assotsiatsiya proletarskikh pisatelei*). The dominant literary organization from 1928 until the liquidation by the Party of all separate literary groups in 1932 and the decreeing of a single Union of Writers.

Ravenskikh, Boris Ivanovich (1914–1981). Director; from 1935 to 1937, he was an assistant director at the Meyerhold Theatre.

Realistic Theatre. A small theatre in the Krasnaya Presnya district of Moscow, it was originally one of the studios attached to the Moscow Art Theatre. In 1932, following its takeover by Nikolai Okhlopkov, it was transformed into an environmental theatre with movable acting platforms and interaction between the actors and the spectators. The theatre was closed in 1938.

The Red Poppy (*Krasnyi mak*, 1927). Soviet ballet with music by Reingol'd Glier with libretto by Vasily Tikhomirov and Lev Lashchilin.

Reflexology. A study of the laws governing human reflexive action and behavior developed by Vladimir Bekhterev. Drawing on Pavlov's studies of conditioned reflexes in animals, Bekhterev formulated his theory of "associated motor reflexes": all human behavior can be explained by the pattern of reflexes produced by the individual's nervous system.

Reinhardt, Max (Max Goldmann; 1873–1943). Austrian-German theatre director and manager famous for his large-scale, experimental productions.

Réjane (stage name of Gabrielle-Charlotte Réju, 1857–1920). Celebrated French actress.

Remizov, Aleksei Mikhailovich (1877–1957). Russian novelist, short-story writer, poet and dramatist. His ornamental writing style influenced many other Russian writers at the beginning of the century. He emigrated in 1921, spending his remaining years in Paris.

Remizova, Varvara Fedorovna (1882–1951). Dramatic actress at the Meyerhold Theatre.

Renoir, Pierre Auguste (1841–1919). French painter, considered one of the greatest of the French Impressionists.

Rimsky-Korsakov, Nikolai Andreevich (1844–1908). Russian composer and conductor.

Rivera, Diego (1886–1957). Mexican painter, one of the founders of the Mexican mural renaissance.

Rodchenko, Aleksandr Mikhailovich (1891–1956). Russian-Soviet artist, graphic designer, and photographer. After 1922, he rejected fine art to concentrate on utilitarian work designing textiles, posters, and photomontage.

Rolland, Romain (1866–1944). French novelist, playwright, musicologist, and biographer. Rolland visited the Soviet Union in 1935 where he met Gorky and other members of the intelligentsia, including Meyerhold.

Rossi, Ernesto (1827–1896). Italian actor; he toured Russia numerous times from 1877 to 1896.

Rossov (pseud. of Pashutin), Nikolai Petrovich (1864–1945). Russian-Soviet actor specializing in the classical repertory. He became famous as "the Hamlet of Penza".

ROSTA posters (also called ROSTA windows). Colorful poster-size comic strips designed by Mayakovsky and other artists, and produced and distributed by ROSTA, the Russian Telegraph Agency (*Rossiiskoe telegrafnoe agentsvo*) as a substitute for newspapers following the Russian Revolution.

RSFSR Theatre No. 1 (*Teatr RSFSR 1-i* [The First Theatre of the Russian Soviet Federative Socialist Republic]). Russian-Soviet theatre headed by Vsevolod Meyerhold. It opened on November 7, 1920 with his production of *The Dawns*, and was closed down in September 1921.

Rubenstein, Anton Grigorevich (1829–1894). Russian pianist, composer, and teacher. He founded the St. Petersburg Conservatory in 1862.

    The Demon (*Demon*, 1871). Opera based on Lermontov's *The Demon*.

Rubinstein, Ida (1885–1960). Russian ballet dancer. She danced with Diaghilev's Ballet Russe from 1909 to 1915.

Rudnitsky, Konstantin Lazarevich (1920–1988). Soviet-Russian theatre historian and critic, author of the first major biography of Meyerhold following the director's rehabilitation in 1955.

Sadovsky, Mikhail Provovich (1847–1910). Russian actor, member of the famous Sadovsky family of actors at the Maly Theatre.

Sadovskaya (née Lazarevna), Olga Osipovna (1849–1919). Russian actress, wife of Mikhail Provovich. She made her debut at the Maly Theatre in 1879 where she continued performing for the rest of her life.

St. Basil's. More precisely, the Cathedral of St. Basil the Blessed (*Khram Vassilya Blazhennogo*). Located at the south end of Red Square, it was built (1554–1560) in the reign of Ivan IV to commemorate the conquest of Kazan.

Saint-Exupéry, Antoine de (1900–1944). French novelist whose writings are inextricably linked to his experiences as a pilot.

Sakhnovsky, Vasily Grigorevich (1886–1945). Russian-Soviet director, critic, and teacher. He began his directing career at the

Komissarzhevskaya Theatre; in 1926 he was invited to join the Moscow Art Theatre where he remained for the rest of his life.

Salvini, Tommaso (1829–1915). Italian actor famous all over Europe and North and South America. Between 1880 and 1901, he toured Russia several times. He retired from the stage in 1903.

Samoilov, Evgeny Valerianovich (1912–). Russian-Soviet actor. A graduate of the Leningrad Artistic Polytechnikum, in 1934 he joined the Meyerhold Theatre where he performed until the theatre was closed in 1938. In 1940 he joined the Theatre of the Revolution (later the Mayakovsky Theatre); since 1968 he has been at the Maly Theatre.

Sanin (pseud. of Schönberg), Aleksandr Akimovich (1869–1956). Russian actor and director at the Moscow Art Theatre and Alexandrinsky Theatre. In 1908, he directed Chaliapin in the Paris production of *Boris Godunov*. He emigrated in 1922.

Savina, Maria Gavrilovna (1854–1915). Russian dramatic actress who began her acting career in the provinces. She joined the Alexandrinsky Theatre in 1874, performing there until the end of her life.

Schiller, (Johann Christoph) Friedrich von (1759–1805). German playwright and poet, best known for his historical plays and long, didactic poems.

> *Kabale und Liebe* (1784).

Scriabin, Aleksandr Nikolaevich (1871–1915). Russian composer and pianist who experimented with incorporating visual arts into some of his compositions, including *Prometheus: A Poem of Fire* (1909–1910), whose performance called for an organ that produced a play of lights upon a screen.

Seifullina, Lidiya Nikolaevna (1889–1954). Soviet writer and playwright.

> *Natasha (Natasha,* 1937).

Selvinsky, Ilya (real name, Karl) Lvovich (1899–1968). Russian-Soviet playwright and poet.

> *The Second Army Commander (Komandarm* 2, 1928).

Serov, Valentin Aleksandrovich (1865–1911). Russian artist, member of Mamontov's Abramtsevo artist colony.

Sery, Nikolai Pavlovich (1912–). A star gymnast at the Lesgaft Institute, from 1936 to 1967 he directed the Leningrad program for the annual All-Union Day of Physical Training held each July in Red Square.

Shakespeare, William (1564–1616). English playwright and poet.

> *Romeo and Juliet* (1594–5).
>
> *The Merchant of Venice* (1596).
>
> *Hamlet* (1600–1).
>
> *Othello* (1604–5).
>
> *Anthony and Cleopatra* (1606–7).

Shakhovskoi, Aleksandr Aleksandrovich (1777–1846). Russian writer, playwright, director, and teacher.

Shaw, George Bernard (1856–1950). Irish-born British playwright.
Heartbreak House (1913/1919).

Shestakov, Viktor Alekseevich (1898–1957). Scenic artist, he designed several productions for Meyerhold at his own theatre and at the Theatre of the Revolution.

Shchepkin, Mikhail Semenovich (1788–1863). Born a serf, he became the most famous nineteenth-century Russian actor. After first performing in a serf theatre, in 1805 he became a professional actor. In 1822, he received his freedom.

Shchukin, Boris Vasilevich (1894–1939). Russian-Soviet actor most famous for his interpretation of Vladimir Lenin on the stage and in film.

Shebalin, Vissarion Yakovlevich (1902–1963). Russian-Soviet composer.

Sheller (pseud. of Mikhailov), Aleksandr Konstantinovich (1838–1900). Russian writer.

Shishkin, Ivan Ivanovich (1832–1898). Russian landscape painter who painted mainly forest scenes.

Shklovsky, Viktor Borisovich (1893–1984). Russian-Soviet literary scholar, essayist, and novelist. An exponent of the formalist movement, he later turned to more approved forms of literary scholarship.

Shostakovich, Dmitry Dmitrievich (1906–1975). Russian-Soviet composer.
Lady Macbeth of the Mtsensk District (*Ledi Makbet Mtsenskogo uezda*, 1932), later revised as *Katerina Izmailova* (*Katerina Izmailova*, 1963).
Bright Stream (*Svetlyi ruchei*, 1934).
A Hero of Our Time (*Geroi nashego vremeni*, unfinished).

Shtraukh, Maksim Maksimovich (1900–1974). Russian-Soviet actor. He performed at the Meyerhold Theatre from 1929 to 1931.

Sinclair, Upton (1878–1968). American writer, reformer, and dedicated socialist, best known for his novels exposing social evils.

Smyshlyaev, Valentin Sergeevich (1891–1936). Russian-Soviet actor, director, teacher, and critic, he spent the years 1915–21 at the First Studio of MXAT and the years 1924–1931 MXAT-2.

Sofronitsky, Vladimir Vladimirovich (1901–1961). Russian Soviet pianist, best known for his interpretations of the Scriabin, Rakhmaninov, Chopin and Schumann. Beginning in 1921, he gave concerts mainly in Moscow and Leningrad; in 1928–1929 he toured Poland and France. From 1936 to 1942 he taught at the Leningrad Conservatory, and from 1942 until his death at the Moscow Conservatory.

Sokolova (pseud. of Alekseeva), Zinaida Sergeevna (1865–1950). Russian-Soviet director and teacher; Stanislavsky's sister and his closest assistant at the Stanislavsky Opera Studio.

Solovyeva, Vera Grigorevna (1896–). Singer in the Stanislavsky Opera Studio; in the post-war years she taught voice in Leningrad.

Solovyev, Vladimir Nikolaevich (1887–1941). Director, theatre critic, teacher, and member of the editorial board of the journal *Love for Three Oranges*; he also took an active part in the activities of Meyerhold's Studio on Borodinskaya.

Sophocles (496?–406 B.C.). Greek dramatist.
   Oedipus Rex (c. 430/426 B.C.).

Soviet Art (*Sovetskoe iskusstvo*). Newspaper published from 1931 to 1940 dedicated to the arts. It was the principal mouthpiece of NARKOM-PROS, and beginning in 1936, of its successor, the Committee for Arts Affairs (*Komitet po delam iskusstv*) under SOVNARKOM USSR.

SOVNARKOM. Acronym for the "Council of People's Commissars" (*Soviet narodnikh kommissarov*). All-Bolshevik body elected by the second All-Russian Congress of Soviets in October 1917. With Lenin as its chairman, in November 1917 it served as the main governing body of the country. In 1946 it became the Council of Ministers.

"The Spark" (*Iskra*). Socialist newspaper founded in 1900 by Georgi Plekhanov and Vladimir Lenin.

Spielhagen, Friedrich (1829–1911). German novelist on social and political themes. Also author of theoretical works on drama, the novel, and the epic.

Stalin (pseud. of Dzhugashvili), Joseph Vissarionovich (1879–1953). Soviet Communist leader; secretary-general of the Communist Party from 1922 to 1953 and general secretary of the USSR from 1941 to 1953.

Stanislavsky (pseud. of Alekseev), Konstantin Sergeevich (1863–1938). Russian actor and director, co-founder in 1898 of the Moscow Art Theatre. He developed a revolutionary system of actor training which has become world famous.

Stanislavsky Opera Theatre. Organized in 1928 from the former Stanislavsky Opera-Studio Theatre, it was an effort to realize Stanislavsky's acting principles in the opera theatre.

Starkovsky, Pyotr Ivanovich (1884–1964). Russian-Soviet dramatic actor, he worked at the Meyerhold theatre from 1924 until its closing in 1938.

Stendhal (pseud. of Henri Beyle, 1783–1842). French novelist.

Stepanova, Varvara Fedorovna (1894–1958). The wife of artist Aleksandr Rodchenko; a leading member of the Russian avant-garde, she applied her talent to a wide range of design projects, from textiles to sets and costumes for the theatre.

Stiedry, Fritz (1883–1968). Austrian conductor. Forced to leave his position as principal conductor at the Städtische Oper in Berlin in March

1933, he went to Russia where he conducted concerts and operas in Leningrad and Moscow. In 1937, he emigrated to the United States.

Strasberg, Lee (1901–1982). American director and teacher; a leading proponent of Stanislavsky-influenced Method acting in the West. Co-founder of the Group Theatre in 1931; head of the Actors' Studio from 1950 until his death.

Strauss, Richard (1864–1949). German composer best known for his symphonic poems and operas.

> *Electra* (1909). See: Hugo von Hofmannsthal.

Stravinsky, Igor Fedorovich (1882–1971). Russian-born composer. He became a French citizen in 1934; three years later he moved to the United States, where he became a citizen in 1945. Considered by many the greatest composer of the twentieth century.

> *The Rite of Spring* (*Vesna Svyashchennaya*, 1913).

Studio on Borodinskaya (*Studiya na Borodinskoi*). Meyerhold's first permanent theatre studio. Organized in September 1913, it was initially located at 18 Troitskaya Street. A year later the Studio moved to a small concert hall belonging to the Petersburg Municipal Transport Engineers located at 6 Borodinskaya Street.

Studio on Povarskaya. See: Theatre-Studio on Povarskaya.

Sudakov, Ilya Yakovlevich (1890–1969). Russian-Soviet director, actor, and teacher. From 1916 to 1924, he was an actor and director at the Second Moscow Art Theatre Studio, and from 1924 to 1933 at the Moscow Art Theatre. In 1937 he was appointed chief director of the Maly Theatre.

Sukhovo-Kobylin, Aleksandr Vasilievich (1817–1903). Russian playwright whose trilogy – *Krechinsky's Wedding, The Case, and The Death of Tarelkin* – is considered a masterpiece of nineteenth-century Russian drama.

> *Krechinsky's Wedding* (*Svad'ba Krechinskogo*, 1852–1854).
> *The Death of Tarelkin* (*Smert' Tarelkina*, 1857–1869).

Sumbatov-Yuzhin. See: Yuzhin, Aleksandr Ivanovich.

Sverdlin, Lev Naumovich (1901–1969). Russian-Soviet actor. A student of Meyerhold's, he joined the Meyerhold Theatre in 1926, remaining there until the theatre was closed in 1938.

Tairov, Aleksandr Yakovlevich (1885–1950). Russian-Soviet director. Originally an actor, in 1914, he founded the Kamerny Theatre, which he headed until it was closed in 1950.

Talleyrand-Périgord, Charles Maurice de (1754–1838). French politician and diplomat known for his capacity to survive political change.

Talnikov (pseud. of Shpitalnikov, David Lazarevich; 1882–1961). Conservative Russian-Soviet literary and theatre critic, author of a critical book on Meyerhold's production of *The Inspector General: A New Revision of "The Inspector General"* (*Novaya revisiya "Revizora"*), Moscow–Leningrad, 1927.

Tarabukhin, Nikolai Mikhailovich (1899–1956). Russian-Soviet art critic and historian. Author of a monograph on Mikhail Vrubel.

Taylorism. System of scientific management developed by the American industrial engineer Frederick Winslow Taylor at the turn of the century. It became widely known throughout Europe in the early 1900s, including Russia.

Tchaikovsky, Pyotr Ilich (1840–1893). Russian composer.
   Eugene Onegin (*Evgenii Onegin*, 1879).
   The Queen of Spades (*Pikovaya dama*, 1890).

Telyakovsky, Vladimir Arkadevich (1861–1924). Theatre manager, director of the Imperial theatres from 1901 to 1917.

Temerin, Aleksei Alekseevich (1889–1977). Russian-Soviet actor at Meyerhold's Theatre, also an amateur photographer. Most of the photographs of Meyerhold's productions were taken by him.

Tenin, Boris Mikhailovich (1905–1990). Russian-Soviet theatre and film actor.

Tenishev Academy. Located on Mokhavaya Street in Petrograd (St. Petersburg), it is now a part of the Academy of Theatre Arts (from 1919 to 1994, the Leningrad State Institute of Art, Theatre, and Cinematography). The amphitheatre where Meyerhold staged Blok's *The Unknown Woman* looks much the same today as it did in 1914.

Tereshkovich, Maksim Abramovich (1897-1939). Russian-Soviet actor, director and teacher. After launching his acting career at the Komissarzhevsky Theatre in St. Petersburg, he moved to Moscow where he worked at both the Meyerhold Theatre and the Realistic Theatre before becoming artistic director of the Ermolova Theatre-Studio in 1933.

TEO. Theatre Department (*Teatral'nyi otdel*) of NARKOMPROS.

The Theatre Herald (*Vestnik Teatra*). Publication (1919–1921) of TEO. Meyerhold was the editor.

Theatre of the Soviet Army (The Central Red Army Theatre, later the Central Soviet Army Theatre). Founded in 1929, it boasts the largest theatre auditorium in the world.

Theatre-Studio on Povarskaya Street (*Teatr-Studiya na Povarskoi*). Cofounded by Stanislavsky and Meyerhold in May 1905, it closed in October of that same year.

Theosophy. A blend of Eastern and Western religions that believes in a gradual evolution of all humanity toward spiritual evolution. It also refers to the beliefs of a religious sect, the Theosophical Society, founded by Madame Helena Blavatsky in New York in 1875, incorporating aspects of Buddhism and Brahmanism.

Thirty-Three Swoons (*33 Obmoroka*). Name of Meyerhold's 1935 production of three of Chekhov's one-act plays: *The Anniversary*, *The Bear*, and *The Proposal*.

TIM. The Meyerhold Theatre (*Teatr imeni Meierkhol'da*). Established in 1923, in 1926 it became GosTIM.

Tolstoy, Aleksei Konstantinovich (1817–1875). Poet, playwright, novelist, and satirist; author of *Prince Serebryany* (1875), a novel dealing with the times of Ivan the Terrible; and a dramatic trilogy: *The Death of Ivan the Terrible, Tsar Fyodor Ivanovich*, and *Tsar Boris*.
> *Prince Serebryany* (*Knyaz' Serebryanyi*, 1861).
> *The Death of Ivan the Terrible* (*Smert' Ioanna Groznogo*, 1866).
> *Tsar Fyodor Ivanovich* (*Tsar' Fyodor Ioannovich*, 1868).
> *Tsar Boris* (*Tsar' Boris*, 1870).

Tolstoy, Aleksei Nikolaevich (1882–1945). Russian-Soviet writer and dramatist. A distant relative of Leo Tolstoy, he was initially opposed to the Bolsheviks and emigrated after they came into power. He returned in 1922 and became one of the régime's favorite authors. He is best known for his historical novels.

Tolstoy (or Tolstoi), Count Leo or Lev Nikolaevich (1828–1910). Russian writer and philosopher, considered one of the world's greatest writers.
> *Hadji-Murad* (*Khadzhi-Murat*, 1896–1904).

Trenev, Konstantin Andreevich (1876–1945). Russian-Soviet writer and playwright.
> *Lyubov Yarovaya* (*Lyubov' Yarovaya*, 1926).

Tretyakov, Sergei Mikhailovich (1892–1939). Soviet playwright, writer, and literary theorist. He was a keen supporter of utilitarian art and the "literature of fact". In the 1920s and 1930s, he collaborated closely with Sergei Eisenstein and Meyerhold.
> *Roar China!* (*Rychi, Kitai!*, 1926).
> *I Want a Child* (*Khochu rebenka*, 1927).

Trotsky, Leo (real name Lev Davidovich Bronstein), (1879–1940). Russian revolutionary theoretician and a leader of the 1917 Bolshevik Revolution, in 1927 he was banished for his opposition to Stalin's policies. Exiled in 1929, he spent his remaining years in Mexico where he was murdered by Ramón Mercader in 1940.

Tsarev, Mikhail Ivanovich (1903–1987). Russian-Soviet actor. From 1933–1937, he performed at the Meyerhold Theatre. After its closing, he joined the Maly Theatre.

Tsvetaeva, Marina (1892–1941). Russian poet, essayist, and critic.

Tyapkina, Elena Alekseevna (1897–1986). Russian-Soviet dramatic actress. A graduate of the Satire Studio and GVYRM, she worked at the Meyerhold Theatre from 1923–1927.

Vakhtangov, Evgeny Bagrationovich (1883–1922). Russian director and actor. One of Stanislavsky's first pupils, in 1912 he became a member of the Moscow Art Theatre First Studio where he acted and directed. Beginning in 1913, he also headed the Student Drama Studio, later the Vakhtangov Studio; and after 1921, the Third Studio of the Moscow Art Theatre.

Vakhtangov, Sergei Evgenevich (1907–). Architect, son of Evgeny Vakhtangov.

Vakhtangov Theatre. One of the first Soviet theatres; the date of its founding is considered to be 1921 when the Vakhtangov Studio was designated the Third Studio of the Moscow Art Theatre. In 1926 the Studio received the name Vakhtangov Theatre in honor of its founder.

Valentei (née Voroveva), Maria Alekseevna (1924–). Daughter of Tatyana Vsevolodovna Meyerhold, granddaughter of Vsevolod Emilevich. More than anyone else, she is responsible for the rehabilitation of her grandfather in 1955 and the establishment of a museum in Meyerhold's former apartment on Bryusov Lane. A school teacher by profession, in 1992 Maria Alekseevna was named director of the Meyerhold Apartment-Museum, a branch of the Bakhrushin Theatre Museum.

Varlamov, Konstantin Aleksandrovich (1848–1915). Russian actor, known as the "King of Russian laughter". He began his career in the provincial theatres. In 1875, he joined the Alexandrinsky Theatre in St. Petersburg.

Vasari, Giorgio (1511–1574). Italian architect, painter, and art historian.

Verdi, Giuseppe (Fortunino Francesco, 1813–1901). Italian composer of operas.
> *Rigoletto* (1851).

Verhaeren, Émile (1855–1916). Belgian poet and dramatist.
> *The Dawns* (1898).

Vishnevsky, Vsevolod Vitalievich (1900–1951). Russian-Soviet playwright and prose writer.
> *The First Cavalry Army* (*Pervaya konnaya*, 1929).
> *Battle in the West* (*Germany*) (*Na zapade boi* [*Germaniya*], 1931).
> *The Last, Decisive* (*Poslednii reshitel'nyi*, 1931).
> *An Optimistic Tragedy* (*Optimisticheskaya tragediya*, 1933).
> *We Are from Kronstadt* (*My iz Kronshtadta*, film scenario, 1933).

Vivien, Leonid Sergeevich (1887–1966). Russian-Soviet actor and director. In 1913, he joined the Alexandrinsky Theatre (later, the Pushkin Theatre of Drama) where he spent the rest of his career. In 1938, Vivien was appointed chief director of the theatre.

VOKS. All-Union Society for Cultural Relations with Foreign Countries (*Vsesoyuznoe obshchestvo kul'turnoi svyazi s zagranitsei*). The organization responsible for all arrangements for foreign visitors coming to the Soviet Union (1925–1958).

Volkov, Nikolai Dmitrievich (1894–1965). Russian-Soviet theatre critic and playwright. Author of *Meyerhold* (*Meierkhol'd*), a two-volume biography of Meyerhold published in 1929.

Vrubel, Mikhail Aleksandrovich (1856–1910). Russian painter, theatre artist, and sculptor. He was one of the most active participants in Mamontov's artistic colony at Abramtsevo.

Vyshinsky, Andrei Yanuarevich (1883–1954). Stalin's prosecutor in the purge trials beginning in 1929. After briefly serving as the Deputy Chairman of the Soviet People's Commissariat in 1939, he moved on to diplomatic service. In 1947, he succeeded Vyacheslav Molotov as foreign minister.

Wagner, Richard (1813–1883). German composer best known for his romantic operas.

   Rienzi (1842).

   Tristan and Isolde (1865).

Wallenstein, Albrecht Eusebius Wenzel von, Duke of Friedland (1583–1634). Austrian military leader who fought in the Thirty Years War. He is the central figure in the trilogy of the same name by Friedrich Schiller.

Whitman, Walt (1819–1892). American poet, author of *Leaves of Grass*, a seminal volume of poetry in this history of American literature.

Wilde, Oscar (Oscar Fingal O'Flahertie Wills Wilde, 1854–1900). Irish author and wit.

Wilson, John: see North, Christopher.

Woe to Wit (*Gore umu*). The title Meyerhold gave to his 1927 production of Griboedov's play, *Woe from Wit*.

Wrangel, Baron Pyotr Nikolaevich (1878–1928). Russian general who in late 1917 joined the anti-Bolshevik army in southern Russia. In April 1920, he took over the White Army only to be driven out of the Crimea by the Bolsheviks in November of that year.

Yakulov, Georgy Bogdanovich (1884–1928). Russian-Soviet painter and theatre artist.

Yurev, Yuri Mikhailovich (1872–1948). Russian-Soviet actor who spent virtually his entire career at the Alexandrinsky (later the Pushkin

Theatre of Drama). He is best known for playing Arbenin in Meyerhold's 1917 production of *Masquerade* as well as in all of the subsequent revivals of it.

Yutkevich, Sergei Iosifovich (1904–1985). One of the giants of Soviet cinema, he began his career as a set designer and experimental theatre director. Best known at home for a series of films about Lenin, he won international renown when in 1956 he won the best-director award at Cannes for his film *Othello*.

Yuzhin (pseud. of Sumbatov), Aleksandr Ivanovich (1857–1927). Russian actor, dramatist, and theatre activist.

Yuzovsky, Iosif Ilich (pseud. of Yuri Yuzovsky, 1902–1964). Soviet theatre and literary critic best known for his writings on Gorky's dramaturgy.

Zakhava, Boris Evgenevich (1896–1976). Russian-Soviet director, actor, and teacher. He spent his entire career at the Vakhtangov Theatre, first as an actor and then as a director. From 1923 to 1935 he also acted in several productions at the Meyerhold Theatre.

Zaichikov, Vasily Fedorovich (1888–1947). Russian-Soviet actor in the dramatic theatre and film. A pupil in the Meyerhold Workshop, he continued acting at the Meyerhold Theatre until it was closed in 1938.

Zlobin, Zosima Pavlovich (1901-1965). Dramatic actor and choreographer, a student at GVRM-GVTM, he quickly won a place in Meyerhold's actor training program as a teacher of Biomechanics.

Zola, Émile (1840–1902). French writer and critic, leading proponent of naturalism in fiction.

Zon, Boris Vulfovich (1898–1966). Russian-Soviet director who spent most of his career at the Leningrad Theatre of Young Spectators. He also staged productions at other Leningrad theatres, and beginning in 1940, was a professor at the Leningrad Theatre Institute (later, the Leningrad State Institute of Theatre, Music and Cinematography [LGITMiK]).

Zon Theatre (I. S. Zon Operetta Theatre). Named after its founder, Ignaty Sergeevich Zon, it was located at 20 Bolshaya sadovaya on Triumphal (now Mayakovsky) Square, at the intersection of Tverskaya Street and the Garden Ring (*Sadovoye Kol'tso*), in 1921 it became the home of the Meyerhold Theatre. In 1931 the Zon Theatre was torn down so that construction on the new Meyerhold Theatre could begin. Work on the new theatre came to a halt in 1938 with the closing of the Meyerhold Theatre, then located at 15 Tversky Arcade (presently Tverskaya Street, now the home of the Ermolova Theatre). After World War II began, the plans for the new theatre were extensively modified, and in 1940 it opened as the Tchaikovsky Concert Hall.

Zoshchenko, Mikhail Mikhailovich (1895-1958). Russian-Soviet satirical writer and one of the most popular Soviet writers in the 1920s and 1930s, he fell victim to the 1946 literary purge; he was expelled from the Union of Writers and his works were banned.

Zweig, Stefan (1881–1942). Austrian writer of poetry, fiction, and biography.

INDEX

Printed in the United Kingdom
by Lightning Source UK Ltd.
105330UKS00002B/73